GENDER, THEATRE, AND THE ORIGINS OF CRITICISM

In *Gender, Theatre and the Origins of Criticism*, Marcie Frank explores the theoretical and literary legacy of John Dryden to a number of prominent women writers of the time. Frank examines the pre-eminence of gender, sexuality and the theatre in Dryden's critical texts that are predominantly rewritings of the work of his own literary precursors – Ben Jonson, Shakespeare and Milton. She proposes that Dryden develops a native literary tradition that is passed on as an inheritance to his heirs – Aphra Behn, Catharine Trotter, and Delarivier Manley – as well as their male contemporaries. Frank describes the development of criticism in the transition from a court-sponsored theatrical culture to one oriented towards a consuming public, with very different attitudes to gender and sexuality. This study also sets out to trace the historical origins of certain aspects of current criticism – the practices of paraphrase, critical self-consciousness and performativity.

MARCIE FRANK is Associate Professor of English at Concordia University in Montreal. She has published essays on David Cronenberg, Susan Sontag and Horace Walpole.

GENDER, THEATRE, AND THE ORIGINS OF CRITICISM

From Dryden to Manley

MARCIE FRANK

CAMBRIDGE UNIVERSITY PRESS

PUBLISHED BY THE PRESS SYNDICATE OF THE UNIVERSITY OF CAMBRIDGE
The Pitt Building, Trumpington Street, Cambridge, CB2 1RP, United Kingdom

CAMBRIDGE UNIVERSITY PRESS
The Edinburgh Building, Cambridge, CB2 2RU, UK
40 West 20th Street, New York, NY 10011-4211, USA
477 Williamstown Road, Port Melbourne, VIC 3207, Australia
Ruiz de Alarcón 13, 28014 Madrid, Spain
Dock House, The Waterfront, Cape Town 8001, South Africa

http://www.cambridge.org

© Marcie Frank 2003

This book is in copyright. Subject to statutory exception
and to the provisions of relevant collective licensing agreements,
no reproduction of any part may take place without
the written permission of Cambridge University Press.

First published 2003

Printed in the United Kingdom at the University Press, Cambridge

Typeface Baskerville Monotype 11/12.5 pt   *System* LATEX 2$_\varepsilon$ [TB]

A catalogue record for this book is available from the British Library

Library of Congress Cataloguing in Publication data
Frank, Marcie.
Gender, theatre, and the origins of criticism from Dryden to Manley /
by Marcie Frank.
p.   cm.
Includes bibliographical references and index.
ISBN 0 521 81810 9
1. Criticism – Great Britain – History – 18th century.   2. Manley, Mrs. (Mary de la
Rivière), 1663–1724 – Knowledge – Literature.   3. English literature –
History and criticism – Theory, etc.   4. Criticism – Great Britain – History –
17th century.   5. Dryden, John, 1631–1700 – Knowledge – Literature.   6. English
drama – History and criticism – Theory, etc.   7. Dryden, John, 1631–1700 – Influence.
8. Sex role in literature.   9. Sex in literature.   I. Title.
PR63.F73   2002
801'.95'094109033 – dc21   2002067365

ISBN 0 521 81810 9 hardback

This book is for my family: Kevin, Emma and Violet Pask

Contents

Acknowledgments		*page* viii
	Introduction. The critical stage	1
1.	"Equal to ourselves": John Dryden's national literary history	15
2.	Staging criticism, staging Milton: John Dryden's *The State of Innocence*	42
3.	Imitating Shakespeare: gender and criticism	64
4.	The female playwright and the city lady	91
5.	Scandals of a female nature	116
Notes		140
Bibliography		163
Index		173

Acknowledgments

This book began as a dissertation written for the English Department at the Johns Hopkins University. It has incurred many debts to friends and colleagues over the course of its multiple transformations, and it is a pleasure to acknowledge them here. John Guillory and Jonathan Goldberg were generous supervisors who graciously helped me find my way. Susan Bernstein, Stephen Campbell, Alexandra Halaszc, Elizabeth Hansen, Beth Pittenger, Karen Sanchez-Eppler and Bill Walker made friendly and supportive ears and eyes available at early stages of this project's development. Judith Walkowitz asked a key question at my dissertation defense. Bonnie Honig has been a wonderful interlocutor throughout.

Michael McKeon's acute reading of much of the manuscript let me see the larger implications of my arguments. My debts to his work are evident throughout. A generous and thoughtful reading of the manuscript by an anonymous reader for Cambridge University Press helped me to produce a more integrated and coherent book.

Supportive colleagues and friends at Concordia University have frequently transformed going to work into something more pleasant. Terry Byrnes, Jason Camlot, Judith Herz, Catherine Mavrikakis, Chantal Nadeau, Ed Pechter, Eve Sanders, David Sheps and Kate Sterns have shared interests and laughs. Two exemplary graduate students, Danielle Bobker and Ciricia Proulx, each made me rethink aspects of my argument about Behn. Nicola Nixon – the ideal colleague and friend – has been unstinting with her time, steadfast with her support, and generous with her ideas.

The research for this project was supported by graduate fellowships from the Social Science and Humanities Research Council of Canada and the Johns Hopkins University, Faculty Research and Development funds from Concordia University, and a three-year award in the category of "Nouveaux Chercheurs" from the Fonds pour la Formation de

Chercheurs et l'Aide à la Recherche (FCAR) of Quebec. An earlier version of a portion of Chapter 3 appeared in *Eighteenth-Century: Theory and Interpretation* (1993); a substantially different version of part of Chapter 4 appeared in *Queering the Renaissance*, edited by Jonathan Goldberg.

A project with as long a gestation period as this one incurs another, precious, kind of debt – one in which it is hard to distinguish intellectual offerings from other gifts of love. Two special friendships – with Michael Moon and Jonathan Goldberg – have been confidence-sustaining for many years now. My parents, Esther and Harold Frank, and my siblings, Jill Frank and Adam Frank, have nurtured and supported me in all ways from the beginning. And Kevin Pask has been the ideal partner: he has willingly put his time, intelligence and emotional resources at my disposal.

Introduction. The critical stage

Gender, Theatre, and the Origins of Criticism from Dryden to Manley provides a historical account of criticism's emergence between 1660 and 1714 by looking at the critical writings of John Dryden and those of the women of the following generation whose writings his example shaped. Aphra Behn, Catharine Trotter and Delarivier Manley are not the usual figures through whom the history of criticism has been charted; but Dryden himself, while often mentioned, is equally often relegated to the margins in those histories that have taken the periodical essays of Joseph Addison and Richard Steele as criticism's point of discursive origin.[1] The first part of this book examines the critical enterprise as Dryden undertakes it when he rewrites his Jacobean precursors, in order to argue that, in Dryden's hands, criticism is historical in orientation; this historicism serves in his production – itself an intensely theatrical affair – of a national literary tradition that is transmitted as a lineal inheritance in the vocabulary of poetic genealogy. The second part then looks at the writings of Behn, Trotter and Manley as they claim access through Dryden to this native literary tradition and to the critical discourse whose subsequent histories have written them out. I would thus reconfigure our sense of who contributes to the early development of criticism, and, by redefining the conditions of its emergence, make accessible to observation hitherto overlooked aspects of criticism's legacy.

I call this introduction "The critical stage" to signal the main arguments of this book: the historical sense of the term "stage" as "moment" or "age" indicates that this book delineates a crucial stage in the advent of criticism; the theatrical sense points to the constitutive importance that dramatic writing had for criticism. By elaborating the connections among three assumptions – that criticism arose in the period between 1660 and 1714, that it was historical in orientation from its inception, and that its production was conditioned by its proximity to the stage – *Gender, Theatre and the Origins of Criticism* makes the case that the modern enterprise of criticism is articulated in the writings of Dryden, Behn, Trotter and Manley, and that gender and sexuality are key terms in this articulation.

The theatre was the site of the critical discourse of the period between 1660 and 1714 in multiple senses: theatrical texts were frequently the subject of criticism, offering analytical pretexts in the form of prologues, epilogues, letters of dedication and prefatory essays. While the materials appended to seventeenth-century plays were most often directed at an audience of social superiors, at potential or actual patrons, criticism itself became a platform for public discourse, its very proximity to the stage marking the critic's social position between the court and the theatre, between an older model of literary production dominated by court-sponsorship and patronage and one increasingly oriented towards a consuming public. Because of the textual location of criticism and the social position of the critic, theatricality thoroughly infused Restoration and early eighteenth-century criticism. Such theatricality shaped the national vernacular canon that Dryden developed and his followers took up. By figuring its transmission as a patrimony, he drew the lines of access to a native literary tradition for subsequent writers and critics. As my readings of Dryden, Behn, Trotter and Manley demonstrate, by restoring the role of the theatre to the story of criticism's emergence, we can come to acknowledge the performativity of criticism, both in the sense of what it accomplishes – the establishment of a native tradition coded as filiation – and in the appreciation of the means by which it does so.

The perception that English criticism emerges in proximity to the stage is not new, even though recent histories of criticism have chosen to ignore what I call the critical stage. This book is not, however, a study of the theatre itself; rather, it is an analysis of the theatricality that shapes criticism. A glance at the rehearsal play, a popular type of drama in the later seventeenth and eighteenth centuries, gives in broad outline the trajectory of the arguments I make in this book. *The Rehearsal* (1671), by the Duke of Buckingham and others, stages a satire of a heroic play in rehearsal to an audience of two critics – Smith and Johnson, gentlemen from the country and the town, respectively – and Bayes, the playwright, a caricature of Dryden. Although there were only 10 recorded performances before 1700, the play was performed 273 times in London between 1700 and 1800.[2] Bayes's play begins with the usurpation of the brother Kings of Brentford by their attendants, the Gentleman Usher and the Physician, and this doubling of the monarch and his problems satirically acknowledges the foreseeable difficulties with James

Stuart's status as the only legitimate heir to his brother, Charles II. The Glorious Revolution of 1688, in which James was deposed, remained of central interest to eighteenth-century audiences, and the doubled figure of the monarch is given a significant twist by Thomas Durfey in his 1721 rewriting of *The Rehearsal*. Durfey's *The Two Queens of Brentford: or Bayes no Poetaster*, subtitled "A Musical Farce, or Comical Opera. Being a Sequel of the Famous Rehearsal," as its title indicates, changes the gender of Buckingham's brother Kings. A 1753 rewriting of *The Rehearsal* by Catherine Clive, *The Rehearsal, or Bayes in Petticoats* (1753), picks up the change in gender to mount a satire on female authorship. These rehearsal plays draw insistent links between problematic monarchical succession as a theatrical subject, gender and criticism; in these plays, much of the dialogue is criticism directed towards the play being rehearsed. This persistent intersection, fueled, in part, by a general discussion of female readers and writers in the eighteenth century, evident in even so brief a survey, suggests that to properly situate criticism in relation to the theatre necessitates attention both to politics and to matters of gender, which I provide in my readings of Dryden and his female followers. Richard Brinsley Sheridan's *The Critic, or A Tragedy Rehearsed* (1777), itself a late rewriting of *The Rehearsal*, marks, perhaps, a decisive point of divagation for critic and dramatist. The vitality of the theatre itself as a site of criticism diminishes as criticism comes to be more fully associated with the free-standing prose essay, but I propose ways to understand its influence in critical practice long after the novel and the periodicals pick up the momentum relinquished by the theatre as venues for literary innovation.

Criticism arises in response to the seventeenth-century series of crises in aristocratic culture, and its historical orientation marks its contributions to the modern separation of literature as autonomous from political, legal and historical discourses. However, this historicism, expressed in the vocabulary of poetic inheritance or genealogy, also establishes continuities with the aristocratic culture whose decline is a primary condition of its emergence. I argue that criticism is not predicated, at least not initially, on the separation of criticism from "literature" itself; together, both literary and critical discourses seek to distinguish themselves from the body of discourses that share a deep investment in the institution of genealogical inheritance as an authorizing and legitimating activity even as they also rely upon them. Late seventeenth- and early eighteenth-century criticism is inseparable from the drama of the period, an understanding of which reshapes criticism's history and suggests some ways it informs the current stage of the critical enterprise. For example, literary criticism finds itself "in crisis" with a regularity that could almost be called soothing. I would suggest, however, that the rhetoric of crisis masks the fact that the question of legitimacy has haunted literary criticism from its late seventeenth-century beginnings. When criticism has not remained blind to its own history, its histories have situated its emergence out of crisis, but they have unselfconsciously recapitulated criticism's theatrical origins in their attachment to the drama of crisis.[3]

By attending to the theatrical-historical nature of criticism from its beginnings and tracking this aspect of its history through Dryden, Behn, Trotter and Manley, this book highlights the strategies by which literary criticism was inaugurated, that both enabled the development of "polite" criticism and were submerged as literature came to be seen as autonomous. By treating Dryden, Behn, Trotter and Manley on a continuum, I redescribe the history of literary criticism as a history of the critical gestures – some of them scandalous – by which critics accrue cultural authority for their practices, which accounts of criticism segregated by gender cannot acknowledge. By reading later seventeenth- and early eighteenth-century critical texts in their material and theatrical contexts, by reading criticism as a pre-eminently social discourse, and by integrating the critical writing by Dryden's female followers into the history of criticism, I propose a framework for our current struggle to understand the place of literary criticism.

The texts that I analyze are primarily appended to rewritings of previous texts, and it is no accident, in my view, that rewriting provides the occasion for the development of criticism. Much of Restoration writing was rewriting, but my argument, that criticism is historical in its orientation from the beginning, has guided my selection of rewritings. I have chosen texts that display a sustained critical interest in the means by which the literature of the past can be transmitted into the present. Dryden rewrites a number of Shakespeare's plays, including *The Tempest* (with Sir William Davenant), *Antony and Cleopatra* and *Troilus and Cressida*, and Sophocles' *Oedipus Rex* (with Nathaniel Lee), as well as Milton's *Paradise Lost* as the unstaged opera *The State of Innocence*; Catharine Trotter adapts Aphra Behn's short novel, *Agnes de Castro*, for the stage; and Delarivier Manley rewrites Trotter's romance, *Olinda's Adventures*, in order to satirize its author in *The New Atalantis*, and retools the heroic play, a genre associated with Dryden, to provide a female hero in *The Royal Mischief*. On all of these occasions, rewriting necessitates critical attention to the texts under revision. This attention is historical in nature and it elicits the revisor's comments. While rewriting is, perhaps, the Restoration practice that seems most archaic to us, I would argue such acts of revision continue to inform critical practice even after it sloughs off its dependence on the theatre. Even when criticism stops being found in dramatic form or in paratextual relation to drama, and criticism no longer comes "adapted for the stage," its practice continues to be paraphrase. Moreover, criticism that rises above the level of plot-summary succeeds because it rewrites its textual objects in ways that enact those texts' powers, dramatizing them, albeit most often in nondramatic prose, to make them amenable to critical description, appreciation and argument. By providing a new history of criticism as intertwined with the theatre, then, I want to highlight the persistent residues of its underacknowledged dramatic inception. By reading drama, prologues, epilogues, appended letters of dedication and defenses as the sites of critical practice, I capitalize on the ambiguous relations between texts written to be performed and texts written to be read in order both to bring out the historical distance between our critical assumption that texts are to be read and the vital theatrical culture out of which criticism emerges, and to illustrate the continuities that exist between historical and current critical practice. These have not been perceived, I suggest, because of the negative valences associated with theatricality.

Indeed, as Michael Fried, David Marshall and others have shown, theatricality was a central term of eighteenth-century philosophical, aesthetic and literary discourses.[4] However, theatricality is put under suspicion both in Fried's privileging of "absorption" over "theatricality," and in Marshall's understanding that the "theatrical position" alternately posed "the threat of appearing as a spectacle before spectators," or expressed "the dream of an act of sympathy" (2) that required the transcendence of theatrical distance. In contrast, Jean-Christophe Agnew's brilliant treatment of the parallel and divergent histories of the theatre and the market, which allows them to come to appear worlds apart, makes it impossible to consider the one without the other.[5] Agnew's work, moreover, provides a most productive framework in which to situate the emergence of criticism out of its dependence on the theatre into the new-found literary marketplace. This framework, which accommodates literary concerns in the very terms of its analysis, is thus hospitable to a social understanding of literary history; furthermore it offers a broader historical spectrum (in its focus on the years between 1550 and 1750), and a more flexible and nuanced vocabulary for describing what Jürgen Habermas calls the emergence of the bourgeois public sphere.

Habermas sees the development of literary criticism in England at the end of the seventeenth century as a key symptom of and contribution to the "bourgeois public sphere."[6] However, to situate the rise of critical discourse properly in its transitional context is to see that while criticism heralds some aspects of public sphere modes of representation, it contradicts others. Although recent accounts of the formation of the English canon use Pierre Bourdieu's notion of cultural capital to modify Habermas, and to describe the processes through which literature attains a status autonomous from religion and politics, they nevertheless retain a commitment to a cleaner break between court and public cultures than I would argue is warranted.[7] As a result, they give short shrift to the residual aspects of aristocratic ideology that continued to permeate the discourses of taste and connoisseurship in the eighteenth-century cultural marketplace and beyond. They also share the view that the canon formed in the later eighteenth century marks the autonomy of literary culture. Whereas they rightly emphasize the reorientation of critical discourse from providing models of how to write in a court-dominated rhetorical culture to describing how to read in a public-oriented consumer culture, in their focus on reading as *the* form of literary consumption, they ignore the theatre as a key venue for literary production and consumption, the site which, I argue, mediates criticism's emergence.[8]

Douglas Lane Patey, Trevor Ross and Jonathan Brody Kramnick demonstrate that the canon is produced alongside new kinds of literary history, whose production in the service of forging and maintaining that canon comes to constitute the vocation of the literary critic.[9] A closer examination of Restoration critical practices, however, corrects the assumption that true literary history is produced only in the eighteenth century. When Kramnick asserts, for example, that John Dryden's and Joseph Addison's narratives of literary improvement show that "the pastness of the author, the text, or the period at large was an issue insofar as it had to be overcome" (1089), he ignores the fact that Dryden's two court appointments, as poet laureate and royal historiographer, attested to the proximity of poetic and historiographic writing in the period. Indeed, rather than overcoming or negating the past, Dryden's "improvements," illustrated most fully in his rewriting of his Jacobean and other literary precursors, but also evident in his critical narratives, exhibit the historical awareness that comes to constitute the historicism of the later eighteenth-century criticism that Kramnick so eloquently analyzes.[10] Locating Dryden's critical rewriting in the context of the crisis in the aristocratic authority of inheritance makes legible his sense of the differentiation of the past from the present. The critical practice of "improvement" becomes Dryden's guarantee that a literary inheritance will be transmitted in a present otherwise cut off from the past; indeed, it mediates relations between the present and the past and testifies to the pastness of the past.

Samuel Johnson, who figures prominently in the narratives of the English canon, is perhaps the eighteenth-century figure most readily associated with the full-blown articulation of critical practice, yet he recognized Dryden as the "father" of criticism in English, using the terms of genealogy developed by Dryden to do so. Those terms still dominate our understanding of the literary tradition even as that most traditional of categories has been revised. Neither its renomination as "the canon," however, nor its expansion to include other genealogies – of women writers, African-American writers, and others of "minority" status – have called into question what is preserved in the lineations, the familiality, of genealogy. When Dryden proposes that the relations between current poets and their predecessors are lineal and familial, which he does at various points in his career, he retools and appropriates an aristocratic notion of inheritance for the dissemination of literary culture. Perhaps the most pressing question for Dryden is whether cultural continuity can be forged and sustained in an era remarkable for political upheaval. In response, he invests a national literary patrimony with a prestige designed to ensure that the present generation of writers will inherit greatness, despite the threat that their (literary and nonliterary) forefathers may have squandered the estate, even as he announces that the present writers can improve that estate. Criticism provides the means both to guarantee the transmission of a literary legacy and to augment that inheritance.

The imbrication of inheritance, transmission and improvement with criticism itself is most visible in Dryden's epilogue to the *Conquest of Granada, Part II*, in which he criticizes his Jacobean forebears for failing to transmit "their fame" to their literary heirs. By pointing out that they have "kept [their fame] by being dead," however, Dryden establishes critical discourse as the vehicle through which literary fame is transmitted. He goes on to explain his criticism of Shakespeare, Fletcher and Jonson:

> Think not it envy, that these truths are told,
> Our poet's not malicious, though he's bold.
> 'Tis not to brand 'em that their faults are shown,
> But, by their errours, to excuse his own.
> If Love and Honour now are higher rais'd,
> 'Tis not the Poet but the Age is prais'd.[11]

Indeed, for Dryden, criticism restores literary inheritance.

Dryden's defense of this act of criticism in "Defense of the Epilogue" (1673) elaborates the concept of "the age." Explicitly a tool of periodization, and thus of literary historiography, this concept permits Dryden to explore the discontinuities between his contemporaries and the poets of a previous generation, all the while establishing the continuities between them. "The age" is thus a metonymy of criticism itself insofar as it is criticism that allows current poetic production to distinguish itself, even though it also might dim the appreciation that Dryden would seek for his singularity as a poet. The poetic genealogies that he articulates in subsequent writings carry forward a critical practice that is thus historical from its inception. While readers of Dryden have long recognized that his critical writing is historical, they have not agreed on how to characterize his views of history; moreover, they are so caught up in exploring the changing attitudes towards history he expressed at various points that they neglect to establish the significance of his thinking in terms other than those of his career.[12] I look at the epilogue and its defense in greater detail in the first chapter of this book, which provides an overview of Dryden's critical practice insofar as its historical orientation and theatrical articulation produce a vernacular literary tradition that is transmissible as an inheritance.

In some crucial ways, Johnson sets the tone in his treatment of Dryden for the latter's reception. Johnson's discomfort with the degree to which Dryden's criticism is socially embedded, and his horror at the venom and bitterness of seventeenth-century critical debate, support arguments for the development of the autonomy of literary culture; they measure the degree to which criticism had emerged, by the 1760s, as a "polite" discourse, as a paradigmatic instance of "reasoned debate" in a "public sphere" in which the merits of an argument count more than the status of the man. A brief look, however, at the terms in which Johnson assesses Dryden's vituperative battles with his contemporaries in the "Life of Dryden" suggests that Johnson's discomfort is telling in other ways as well, ways that complicate his narrative and invite a closer examination of the scene he repudiates.

For example, Johnson sees fit to indulge the curiosity he has provoked in his readers about Dryden's unseemly battles by providing them with large amounts of Dryden's *Remarks on [Elkanah Settle's] The Empress of Morocco* and Settle's reply. He justifies this reproduction with the claim that the pamphlets in question had not been widely circulated.[13] Summarizing their battle from a characteristically neutral-seeming moral vantage point, Johnson comments,

Such was the criticism to which the genius of Dryden could be reduced, between rage and terrour; rage with little provocation and terrour with little danger. To see the highest minds thus levelled with the meanest may produce some solace to the consciousness of weakness, and some mortification to the pride of wisdom. But let it be remembered that minds are not levelled in their powers but when they are first levelled in their desires. Dryden and Settle had both placed their happiness in the claps of the multitudes. (346)

Johnson's sneer at the desires of the Restoration playwrights to please their audience attests to his understanding of the poetic vocation as removed from the social arena, which, significantly, he describes as a theatrical space in which success is measured by applause. He nevertheless cultivates a certain degree of popular accessibility himself by supplying his readers with unavailable texts. All the more curious, then, is his metaphorical use of "levelling," a term that evokes the threatening radicalism of the Civil War. For Johnson, "levelling" is the worst consequence of Dryden and Settle's battle, particularly disturbing because the abstract qualities of Dryden's mental powers are evidently so superior. In its figurative application to the battle between poets, Johnson uses the historically loaded vocabulary of the Civil War to assert the real discrepancy between Dryden's and Settle's literary talents, from which he draws the modern implication, which he applies to these poets of the past, that literary vocation should have permitted them to rise above social concerns. It is noteworthy that, despite his modern separation of the poet's concerns from those of the social and political world, Johnson nevertheless to a certain extent here recapitulates the association of Dryden's higher literary talent with his court-affiliated social status. It is ironic that the modern separation is marked by Johnson's historically inflected diction because that separation is inaugurated, as I argue in Chapter 2, by Dryden, in his rewriting of Milton's *Paradise Lost* as the opera, *The State of Innocence*. In the preface to that text, "The Author's Apology," Dryden reinforces this separation by introducing what I call critical identification to ground proper criticism. Dryden's critical identification, enabled by his dramatization of *Paradise Lost*, separates Milton's poetic achievement from his more problematic political or theological commitments. One might say that Johnson disavows Dryden's theatrical precedent and augments the separation he had initiated by dismissing the clapping multitudes. Dryden's separation can also be seen as contributing to the discourse of literary biography which Johnson's *Lives* so famously exemplify. Johnson's condescension towards the Restoration playwrights' desire to please their audience bespeaks the crucial difference between the reading public of his own day and the theatre-going public of theirs, a difference elided in the histories of criticism which ignore its theatrical nature.

Although accounts of the formation of the English canon have not fully acknowledged the role genealogy has played, this term has received attention from another direction – the psychoanalytically inspired literary history of Harold Bloom, whose understanding of the tropic elasticity of inheritance and the family romance is, at times, breathtaking. Bloom's account, however, detaches literary production from its historical contexts, insisting that it be understood instead as the expression of transhistorical psychic processes.[14] Bloom's telling omission of the Augustans in his accounts of English poetic production reveals the limits of his transhistorical method. Only by restoring Dryden and his contemporaries' preoccupation with inheritance in their descriptions of literary relations to its specific socio-historical context can we come to understand both the terms of Samuel Johnson's appreciation of Dryden as the "father of criticism in English," and the long-term function of inheritance and genealogy in criticism.[15] The genealogical vocabulary that describes and guarantees literary transmission may indeed betray anxieties, but I would understand these anxieties as more than psychological, as responses to both the long-term crisis in aristocratic notions of inheritance and the seventeenth-century upheavals in the domain of monarchical succession.

By the time Johnson applies the genealogical model of literary transmission to Dryden, that model had been well established by Addison and Pope, following Dryden's lead in classifying past literary production according to "poetic schools" or "ages."[16] Dryden's male heirs predictably abstract the transmission of a literary inheritance from a reproductive dynamic, charting clear lines of filiation from fathers to sons in a way that makes one wonder why Bloom ignored them. Interestingly enough, Dryden makes no such gendered distinction. In "To Congreve" he revises the process by which Congreve inherits Shakespeare's mantle by emphasizing his own intervention as critic, mediator and maternal figure. Such an expansion of genealogical models to include women clearly had its effect, for Dryden had a host of female followers, whose filiation cannot be described adequately by such feminist Bloomians as Sandra Gilbert and Susan Gubar, or Dale Spender, who seek to redress the lack of attention to female writers by proposing a counter-tradition of strictly female genealogy.[17]

Scant attention has been paid to female-authored criticism; the few essays analyzing women's critical writing have nonetheless retained and reinforced the traditional assumption that criticism is a male genre.[18] The recent, groundbreaking anthology, *Women Critics*, provides a salutary corrective to the standard genealogy of criticism.[19] Its editors make the important observation that "Early women's critical writings invite us to expand the generic boundaries with which criticism has been traditionally identified and to explore the relationship between critical content and critical form" (xv). However, they also attest to the resilience of the assumption that critical writing is somehow inherently a male genre when they register their surprise that so much female-authored material takes conventional critical form (xv). I call into question this link between gender and genre in order to analyze the crucial role that gender difference plays in criticism's emergence – whether it is authored by men or women. For Dryden's theatrical criticism, the role of gender in it, and the theatrical criticism of his female followers show that in the later seventeenth and early eighteenth centuries, criticism was not a male genre. Johnson's dismissal of the clapping multitudes would seem to suggest, moreover, that elevation of the critic above the populace by disengaging him from the theatre might contribute to the alignment of criticism with male writing, which is, in any case, a later phenomenon.

Dryden was a key figure for Aphra Behn, Catharine Trotter, Delarivier Manley and others, providing them not only with a model for critical discourse but also with access to the classical texts, of which he was a major translator. Not only were these female critics participants in the field almost from the very beginnings of criticism in English, but their presence was enabled by Dryden's criticism. Moreover, the particular cultural conjuncture that gave rise to literary criticism is the one Michael McKeon identifies when he describes the advent of "modern patriarchy." According to McKeon, the separation of the category of gender from biological sex involves the distinction not only of "socialized behavior from natural fact but also [of] masculinity from femininity"; these distinctions facilitate the emergence of bourgeois masculinity and the "public sphere" culture it enshrines.[20] Modern patriarchy thus inflects the later critical enterprise as it is practiced by its more familiar male exponents. Addison, Steele, Pope and Johnson tend to insist on the separation of social, political and literary discourses, a process of distinction to which Dryden's criticism contributes, even though varying social and political agendas, no doubt, also inform their literary projects; like Dryden, these later male writers often use gender and sexuality as levers to achieve this separation, although they do so in a less open-ended, more rigid way than he does.[21]

As Ros Ballaster has observed, the postures of impartiality Richard Steele and Joseph Addison used to empower their literary judgments in the *Tatler* and the *Spectator* rely on Isaac Bickerstaff's and Mr. Spectator's identifications with women, who were, by definition, non-participants in party politics. By appropriating the stereotypically female activities of "tattling" and "spectating" to a male sphere, she argues, Addison and Steele functionally revalue impartiality as male.[22] The assumption that impartiality is gendered masculine continues to inform histories of criticism, but the critical writings of Dryden, Behn, Trotter and Manley expose the field in which this revaluation occurs.

Dryden establishes his impartiality as a critic in the preface to *All for Love* on the basis of an act of self-criticism when he points to the flaw in his play as his introduction of the figure of Octavia and his representation of the competition between Octavia and Cleopatra for the title of Antony's legitimate wife. As I argue in Chapter 3, this competition is one of the ways in which Dryden figures his literary competition with Shakespeare, and, as a result, the impartiality he would claim as a critic relies on his representation of male rivalry as a fight between women over domestic legitimation. Dryden's rewritings of Shakespeare make legible the reliance of what come to be some of the commonplaces of criticism, such as "impartiality" and the appeal of such judgments to "all reasonable men," on a sentimentalization of Shakespeare in *All for Love* and on the production of Shakespeare's "universal mind" through a disembodying process of abstraction, underwritten by a complicated application of such gendered terms of literary evaluation as "feminine" and "masculine" in "The Grounds of Criticism in Tragedy," the preface to his revision of *Troilus and Cressida*. The women writing in Dryden's wake claim access to criticism through his feminization of literary judgment and his representation of a literary patrimony that includes Shakespeare. To account fully for the contributions that Dryden, Behn, Trotter and Manley make to the shape of criticism by situating them in relation to the advent of modern patriarchy is thus also to revise the history of literary criticism, and to invite ways of rereading the contributions of those men through whom the history of criticism is usually charted, for whom Dryden was, as Johnson claims, also exemplary.

As I suggest in Chapters 4 and 5, Behn and Manley, like Dryden, use gender and sexuality to exploit the intersections of political and literary discourses, thereby borrowing the residual aristocratic prestige associated with libertinism for their criticism, although neither can lay unproblematic claim to aristocratic status. Their legacy as "loose" writers, moreover, points to the grounds of the discursive separation and the *embourgeoisement* of criticism. Trotter, by contrast, insists on the political efficacy of her writings as a woman, using gender to separate feminine from masculine and effeminate literary styles, and she does so out of the bourgeois position of the "City Lady." Trotter's criticism thus instances the shift Thomas Laqueur describes from an older, hierarchical one-sex model of gender difference, which understands women to be inferior versions of men, to a newer, incommensurate, two-sex model, which understands men and women to be members of opposite sexes.[23] By reading Dryden's strategies for forging a social position for the critic in conjunction with those of the women who elaborate them, we can come to understand both the processes through which literary, social and political discourses ultimately come to be separated, and what is at stake in their separation.

My analysis, however, does not seek to fix an alignment between gender and social space, or gender and literary genre. Because criticism arises in conjuction with theatre and attests to its theatricality at every turn, it is, from its inception, a performative mode that invites us to interrogate gender encodings of, say, the public as male or even criticism as the purview of men – despite the historical evidence to the contrary. There is no question, as Laura Runge points out, that gender was an important evaluative term for Dryden, nor is there any doubt, as James Winn observes, that sexual passion was central to Dryden's creative process.[24] But my interest here is larger, for, as I suggest, gender is a crucial component in Dryden's entire critical enterprise, contributing to his conception of mutual critical and artistic practices and facilitating the adoption of such practices by women writers. As Laqueur and others have persuasively shown, the terms in which gender difference and sexuality were understood in the later seventeenth century were in crisis.[25] However, in my analysis, neither "gender" nor "criticism" assume an unchanging status. Of necessity, as I move from considering Dryden's writing to considering that of his female heirs, "gender" shifts from being primarily a term of analysis used in the twenty-first century to historicize criticism, to being understood as itself a historical feature of literary criticism. Moreover, while I share Runge's and Winn's observations of the importance of gender to Dryden, I diverge from them in my treatment of the category of gender as inseparable from the category of sexuality, and thus in my assessment of what this importance means.[26] Indeed, gender difference and scenes of homoeroticism between women and between men offer Dryden and the women critics writing in his wake an effective vocabulary for negotiating complex attitudes towards aristocratic ideology and for establishing and maintaining the inheritance of a national literary tradition.

Gender, Theatre and the Origins of Criticism brings a broadly construed understanding of theatricality to an analysis of criticism's history in order to suggest that performativity has also contributed to this history. Rescuing it from the branch of ordinary language philosophy known as speech act theory, Judith Butler and Eve Kosofsky Sedgwick have recently recuperated the term "performative" for productive use in queer theory.[27] While the term may have only a (rather short) history in the discourse of philosophy, by understanding literary criticism to have emerged out of a dependence on the stage, and by treating the intersections of gender and sexuality with the early critical practices of Dryden, Behn, Trotter and Manley, I propose that it has a much longer-standing importance in criticism's history. By recovering its role in the history of criticism itself, we can appreciate the immediate and revitalizing impact its embrace has had on current literary studies as it opens itself, however unselfconsciously, to its own history.

The long-term processes by which criticism extricates itself from its proximity to the theatre lie beyond the scope of this project. However, we can find residual traces of this early dependency in critical gestures which can otherwise look quite faddish and new-fangled. In contemporary critical discourse, for example, critics frequently position themselves. Indeed, variations on the form, "as a white, middle-class, Jewish, married mother of two...," litter the landscape of contemporary literary criticism. This (self-)exposure of the investments and affiliations of the individual critic, which pays debts to identity politics on the one hand, and to post-identitarian theory on the other, would seem to be an idiosyncratic tic of current academic prose style. This history of criticism, however, makes it possible to propose that such routines of critical self-consciousness are neither mere stylistic tics nor reactions against the assumption of impartiality, enshrined most dramatically in the formalism that held sway in the discipline of literary studies for much of the twentieth century. The development of the criteria of impartiality and critical self-consciousness – both products of the late seventeenth- and early eighteenth-century literary critical discourse – shows that these hallmarks of aesthetic judgment emerge together rather than in dialectical opposition to one another, in the writings of John Dryden and his female followers.

CHAPTER I

"Equal to ourselves": John Dryden's national literary history

At the end of the seventeenth century, towards the end of his life, John Dryden wrote "The Secular Masque."[1] Janus, the mythological figure who faces in two directions, presides over a procession of Diana, Mars and Venus, who come on stage one at a time to describe the hunts, the battles and the loves that dominate the age each has ushered in. In certain respects, this is familiar territory, at least in terms of the critical reception of Dryden – he treats the "age," the *seculum*, as mediated through classical tropes and figures in a form associated with outmoded absolutist court entertainment that nevertheless promises amelioration of both the immediate and the ancient past. Chronos complains of being "Weary, weary" (line 7) of the weight of the globe on his back, and laughing Momus, a figure for ridicule, finally announces: "'Tis well an Old Age is out, / And time to begin a New" (lines 90–91). It would be easy to see "The Secular Masque" as representing a characteristic problem in Dryden's work – an inability to relinquish neo-classicism and an equal inability to endorse fully the "New."

Dryden's critical career has traditionally been viewed as the site of struggle between his adherence to a neo-classicism, which offers unhampered access to the achievements of the literary past, and a modernism, which insists on the ability of present writers to "improve" that past. Accounts of this struggle could thus be said to take the two-faced Janus as an emblem for Dryden's criticism. However, some have emphasized one profile at the expense of the other. Robert Hume and Edward Pechter, for example, explain the changing attitudes towards the neo-classical rules that Dryden expressed at various points in his career, and they are consequently less interested in the service to which Dryden puts his neo-classicism in his articulation of a national literary tradition.[2] Others have depicted Dryden, like his Janus, as stuck, looking simultaneously in two different directions. Both Ralph Cohen and Earl Miner have recognized that it is to Dryden that we owe "our idea of a literary period or age."[3] Cohen, however, goes on to minimize the continuities between Dryden's historicism and our own when he represents Dryden as treating Homer, Virgil and Ovid as "literary models that lived in his time," and Miner emphasizes that Dryden's treatments of past poets, especially in his translations, should be understood as "contemporizing."[4]

Yet the casting of Dryden, by Cohen and Miner, as a Janus with monocular vision, unable to bring into focus both the lines of filiation made available by the classical tradition and the availability of that tradition to vernacular, national description, fails to recognize the novel perspective of Dryden's secular historicism which aligns them, repeatedly offering strategies for their reconciliation. Such strategies are most evident in and mediated through Dryden's readings of his immediate literary precursors, namely Jonson, Milton and Shakespeare. Their works become, for Dryden, stages of reconciliation between the native and the classical that can be reiterated, critiqued and improved upon – especially in the cases in which he rewrites them. These reconciliations serve to consolidate a native literary tradition that is rooted in but is also an amelioration of the classical tradition – a native (national) classicism that forms a patrimony and a genealogy.

Dryden often describes the relations between past and present poets in lineal terms. In the "Preface to the Fables" (1700), he puts it this way: "*Milton* was the Poetical Son of *Spencer*, and Mr. *Waller* of *Fairfax*; for we poets have our Lineal Descents and Clans, as well as other Families; *Spencer* more than once insinuates, that the Soul of *Chaucer* was transfus'd into his Body; and that he was begotten by him Two Hundred years after his Decease."[5] Many readers have recognized Dryden's contribution to the articulation of a literary tradition as genealogical.[6] Yet, Dryden is not unaware that this patrimony risks resonating as aristocratic. Fending off the collapse of a patrimonial tradition, a crisis-ridden mode of succession associated with absolutism and an aristocratic drive to legitimation which is in decline, Dryden retools an aristocratic concept of genealogy in order to assess and disseminate literary culture, while laying the groundwork for a historicism that will ultimately describe a native literary tradition. Indeed, we might better recognize his reconciliations, which mediate between the classical and the vernacular, under their modern name: a national vernacular canon.[7]

In the letter of dedication to his version of *Troilus and Cressida* (1679) that prefaces his most rigorously classical emendation of Shakespeare, Dryden gives a brief description of what he does to improve the impoverished state of the English vernacular as a literary language – a description that provides the most concise view of his critical position as mediator of classical and vernacular languages. The way Dryden proposes to make the English language "worthy of English wit" is to translate English into Latin and back again:

> I am often put to a stand, in considering whether what I write be the Idiom of the Tongue, or false Grammar, and nonsence couch'd beneath that specious Name of Anglicisme; and have no way to clear my doubts, but by translating my English into Latine, and thereby trying what sence the words will bear in a more stable language.[8]

For Dryden, English requires the mediation of Latin to become literarily worthy; moreover, he is its mediator. Dryden's improvements, like his emendations of Shakespeare, can be seen as a means of establishing "a national print language" situated below Latin and above the spoken vernacular. Benedict Anderson understands the stabilization of written language to occur in response to the needs of print-capitalism, but Dryden's project to standardize written English by translation augments the technological process Anderson describes, and could even be said to articulate its ideological underpinnings.[9] Dryden's translation operates as a version of his emendatory and critical practices – in both, he mediates between classic and vernacular texts, with results, he claims, that are superior to each. In both practices, moreover, he is the source of all improvements, providing the texts that form, and the critical vocabulary that describes, a national classic literary tradition.

Despite Dryden's depiction of the sorry state of the literary potential of the English vernacular, however, he goes to great lengths to establish its superiority to the French vernacular, and he does so in terms that differentiate his native classicism and the literary tradition it consolidates from the tradition established by French neo-classicism. Addressing the uses to which Dryden put his neo-classicism, David Bruce Kramer has recently made an impressive case for an "imperial Dryden," whose neo-classicism derives from Corneille and Racine in ways Dryden cannot directly acknowledge. As Kramer sketches Dryden's career, however – from an early militant advocacy of a national English literary tradition on the basis of disavowed debts to the French to a later subdued subordination of English poetic achievement to the classics as he turns his hand, after 1688, to translation – he minimizes the coherence of Dryden's criticism as constitutive of a national vernacular literary tradition.[10] Granted, Dryden's brief account of his translation practice does not reveal the historicism of his criticism. But some of Dryden's most famous treatments of his immediate precursors – Jonson and Shakespeare – in the *Essay of Dramatick Poesy* (1668), and in the prologue to Dryden's *Troilus and Cressida*, bring his strategic reconciliations into focus, and thus provide a context that enables us to perceive the historical aspects of his national classicism.

Dryden's historicism had an immediate impact upon a range of subsequent writers, enabling them to conceive of their work in terms of a native tradition; but Dryden's critics nevertheless tend to ignore the efficacy of his strategies in the interest of delineating either Dryden's supposedly uneasy fluctuation between the classical and the modern, or his transcendance of this ambivalence, with much attention to its local contexts but little attention to its results. My interest here is to recuperate the emblem of the two-faced Janus for Dryden's critical work but to understand it as self-consciously deployed. I want to map out the ways in which Dryden highlights this fluctuation precisely so that he can arrive at a historicized vernacular. This new sense of Dryden's critical accomplishment not only recasts what his most famous followers, Addison, Steele, Swift and Pope, took from him but also allows us to see Aphra Behn, Catharine Trotter and Delarivier Manley as capitalizing on the access to a native literary tradition that Dryden supplied in the critical vocabulary he inaugurated.

"The Secular Masque" falls short of expressing the new age; it can only point towards it. The tension between the two terms of the title, however, can certainly attest to the inadequacy of the older allegories of absolutist court entertainments. The masque clearly depicts aristocratic court culture at its end: the "old age is out." Perhaps this is one reason why critics interested in the long-term history of literary criticism prefer to emphasize the achievements of writers like Addison and Steele, who were more clearly produced by and themselves exponents of public, as opposed to court, culture. Indeed, for René Wellek, "genuine literary history" did not exist in England in the seventeenth century; it coalesced, he argues, only when concepts of "individuality" and "development" became available.[11] Indeed, recent accounts of the development of the English canon agree with Wellek that literary history did not develop in England until the mid eighteenth century.[12] Yet, Samuel Johnson acknowledges Dryden as "the father of criticism in English," using Dryden's own critical vocabulary of filiation and poetic genealogy to do so.[13] The network of familial relations that lies at the heart of the English literary tradition as it was espoused by eighteenth-century literary critics, who, like Johnson, recognized Dryden as their progenitor, retains traces of a conception of genealogy whose residual aristocratic overtones are powerfully felt in Dryden's critical retooling.

Wellek, distinguishing the development of literary history from general historical scholarship, which "improve[s] beyond recognition" in the seventeenth century (English Literary History, 14), dismisses the "much discussed and overrated controversy between the Ancients and the Moderns" (43) as insignificant to the emergence of literary history. Joseph Levine's careful study of the battle between the Ancients and the Moderns echoes Wellek's distinction in its concern with developments in historiography *per se* and not with literary historiography.[14] Yet, this distinction makes it possible to overlook the contributions to literary history of earlier appropriations of aristocratic and courtly forms that access a national literary tradition.

Howard Weinbrot has recently demonstrated a strong current of nativism underlying the Augustan tradition's self-representation along neo-classical lines, a nativism that infuses Dryden's treatment of the Ancients versus the Moderns debate in the *Essay of Dramatick Poesy*, as well as the one between the French and English dramatists.[15] Noting Dryden's interest, in the *Essay* and elsewhere, in national character, Wellek delimits the contributions this interest might make to literary historical awareness because of the seventeenth-century attribution of such character to climate. This delimitation, however, distracts from a key feature of the *Essay*.

Most critics of the *Essay* focus – as Dryden himself seems to – on the two debates it renders in dramatic dialogue: the national (synchronic) championing of the English over the French drama and the modernist (diachronic) championing of the modern over the ancient dramatists. There is, however, another conflict underlying these more ostensible aims: the rivalry between Restoration and Jacobean dramatists. This rivalry condenses synchronic and diachronic, nationalist and modernist, questions; the generational conflict between the present literary achievement and that of the recent past is both historical and domestic, or internal (and in this sense, synchronic), in nature. Mediating both conflicts for the wits of Dryden's *Essay* is the figure of Ben Jonson, who enables both the victory of the Moderns over the Ancients and the triumph of the English over the French; Jonson thus represents the condensation and convergence of the two debates. Dryden's critical production of Jonson in the *Essay of Dramatick Poesy* turns him into a national classic. A consideration of Dryden's treatment of Jonson as he comes to articulate a native English literary tradition in familial terms opens up for discussion the ways Dryden adumbrates this tradition as a national and classical patrimony through his treatment of Shakespeare in the prologue to his rewriting of *Troilus and Cressida*. I turn to Dryden's *Oedipus* at the end of this chapter in order to explore his apparently paradoxical production of a national literary tradition when he claims access to a classical text unmediated through his Jacobean predecessors. However, a full appreciation of Dryden's mediations of the national and classical traditions becomes possible only after we account for the conjuncture in his criticism of his historicism and his descriptions of a literary genealogy in the term "the age." Since Ben Jonson is also crucially present in Dryden's earliest articulation of "the age" in his crystallization of critical practice in the epilogue to the second part of *The Conquest of Granada* and the appended essay which defends it (1672), I begin with these texts.

THE AGE

Dryden's contemporaries found his epilogue to the second part of *The Conquest of Granada* shrill; indeed, its disconcerting combination of bold assertion and deferential modesty have made it a difficult text to negotiate. "The Defense of the Epilogue" indicates that, for Dryden, at least, the epilogue required defense. Yet the attention in the poem and its "Defense" to the new status of the critic provides some leverage on the otherwise recalcitrant aspects of these texts. I cite the epilogue in full:

> They, who have best succeeded on the Stage,
> Have still conform'd their Genius to their Age.
> Thus Jonson did Mechanique humour show,
> When men were dull, and conversation low.
> Then, Comedy was faultless, but 'twas course:
> Cobbs Tankard was a jest, and Otter's horse.
> And, as their Comedy, their love was mean:
> Except, by chance, in some one labour'd Scene,
> Which must attone for an ill-written Play:
> They rose; but at their height could seldome stay.
> Fame then was cheap, and the first commer sped;
> And they have kept it since, by being dead.
> But were they now to write, when Critiques weigh
> Each Line, and ev'ry word, throughout a Play,
> None of them, no not Johnson in his height
> Could pass, without allowing grains for weight.

> Think not it envy, that these truths are told,
> Our Poet's not malicious, though he's bold.
> 'Tis not to brand 'em that their faults are shown,
> But, by their errours, to excuse his own.
> If Love and Honour now are higher rais'd,
> 'Tis not the Poet, but the Age is prais'd.
> Wit's now ariv'd to a more high degree;
> Our native Language more refin'd and free.
> Our Ladies and our men now speak more wit
> In conversation, than those poets writ.
> Then, one of these is, consequently, true;
> That what this Poet writes comes short of you,
> And imitates you ill, (which most he fears)
> Or else his writing is not worse than theirs.
> Yet, though you judge, (as sure the Critiques will)
> That some before him writ with greater skill,
> In this one praise he hath their fame surpast,
> To please an Age more gallant than the last.[16]

In this poem, Dryden argues that the status of a poet's achievement reflects "the age" in which he lives; in its "Defense," he elaborates this claim. It is clear that Dryden understands literary change to be a consequence of other (social and political) changes. When, however, he suggests that if past writers were to write now under critics' eyes, they would satisfy the critics no more than do contemporary writers, Dryden takes criticism to be the condition that differentiates writing in the past from writing in the present. Dryden depicts criticism constructing literary difference at the same time as he represents it as a consequence of the difference between the past and the present, a difference understood to be the result of Revolution and Restoration. Dryden sustains the ambiguity in which criticism is both a symptom and a cause of changing literary conditions partly in order to vindicate the critical enterprise, the nature of which emerges more clearly in the "Defense."

According to Dryden, however, the decline in the status of the poet is one of the consequences of the improvement that the current age makes on the past. Whereas before, the poet received the praise for his linguistic skills, now, complains Dryden, the age receives that praise. The historical concept, "the age," thus constructs a double bind for current poets: if poets now write better, their achievements go unrecognized because the age gets praised instead. The very concept which allows current poets to supersede those of the past also absorbs all the advantages that they would otherwise gain. Although the death of the fathers inaugurates the new age, the fact of their death is no protection from them: as Dryden puts it in the epilogue, "they have kept [their fame] since, by being dead" (line 12). Pointing to the absorptive capacity of "the age," Dryden seems to be anthropomorphizing it, giving it the characteristics of the vengeful forefathers whom he wants to criticize. In the epilogue, "the age" thus might be said to reenact the problem that it is meant to redress. Historical awareness of the greatness of past writers would seem to threaten the status of literary achievement in the present; however, the possibilities for improvement on the past offered by criticism, the hallmark of the new age, are compensatory because they secure a literary inheritance whose transmission had been in doubt.

Almost forty years before "The Secular Masque," which exhibits a resigned, almost melancholy, tone towards the passing of the age, Dryden had expressed anxiety about the transitions between ages in terms that inform the self-vindicating attitude he takes in the epilogue. In "Astrea Redux" (1663), reversing the Renaissance topos of the prodigal son, he worries that the fathers have been prodigal, leaving the current generation with nothing to inherit:

> Youth that with joys had unacquainted been
> Envy'd gray hairs that once good days had seen:
> We thought our Sires, not with their own content,
> Had ere we came to age our portion spent.
> (25–28)[17]

When Dryden explains that he is not motivated by envy or malice to criticize his forefathers, but by the imperatives of self-defense, he passes off his own errors as matter he has inherited. Showing the errors of the forefathers in order to excuse his own, he implies both that such an act of specification differentiates between the generations and that it guarantees that the sons inherit something, even if it is only error. The specification of error is the practice of the critic, the changed condition that defines the new age. The practice of criticism not only creates and marks historical difference but also holds out the possibility for correcting this error, for making "improvement[s]." Criticism thus performs a historical negotiation that opens up the possibility for establishing poetry as an alternative inheritance to the one squandered by the wasteful forefathers. Thus the double bind of "the age" – the condition that elicits criticism – offers its own justification: to correct, from the improved perspective of the present, the overinflated status of the poets of the past. Dryden proposes a way to understand the position of the current poet:

the poet's inability to exceed his own age leaves him with apparently two alternatives.

> Then, one of these is, consequently, true;
> That what this Poet writes comes short of you,
> And imitates you ill, (which most he fears)
> Or else his writing is not worse than theirs.
>
> (27–30)

Either he can imitate the witty lords and ladies of the court who are his models, or he can match or outstrip the writers of the past. It seems strange that Dryden presents as alternatives the possibilities he might argue are equivalent. When, however, Dryden says, "Then, one of these is, consequently, true," despite his suggestion of an "either/or," the two "consequences" are not mutually exclusive. By presenting them as such, Dryden forces his audience to make a selection that yokes the status of the poet with the status of his forefathers. If his audience tries to criticize the poet for falling short of imitating his times, Dryden's conditional wittily elicits a concession: his status is equal to that of his literary forefathers. Conversely, if his audience allows that he has imitated it successfully, then, by virtue of his conditional, the poet will also have superseded his literary forefathers. The threat of historicism is thus ironically replaced in Dryden's tongue-in-cheek logic, in which status equal or superior to the previous generation is secure precisely because Dryden represents the evaluation of present writers as impossible without their being compared with past writers. Reenforcing historical comparison, Dryden cleverly transforms his defensiveness into a complimentary deference to his audience by locating the current poet in a social context – a gallant new age – that compensates its poets because its gallantry rubs off on them.

The witty conversation of the new age also, as the "Defense" establishes, guarantees that a literary inheritance is transmitted, even if it is one that requires critical improvements. The critic can only secure this inheritance, however, in the delineated social space of the theatre, whose audience draws from the social groups Erich Auerbach calls "the court and the town."[18] In the "Defense," Dryden ultimately ascribes the literary improvements enabled by the gallantry of the age to the status of conversation under the influence of the king. However, in that essay's elaboration of the reasoning compressed in the epilogue's closing lines, the specific referent of this comparison between the present generation and the past is Ben Jonson – significantly, the only poet named in the epilogue.

As for Ben Jonson, I am loath to name him, because he is a most judicious Writer yet he very often falls into these errours. And I once more beg the readers' pardon, for accusing him or them. Onely let him consider that I live in an age where my least faults are severely censur'd: and that I have no way left to extenuate my failings but by my showing as great in those we admire. (XI: 207)

Elaborating the criteria that measure the improvement of the present, Dryden elucidates the task of criticism: "[To] show that the Language, Wit and Conversation of our Age are so improv'd and refin'd above the last: [since] then it will not be difficult, to inferr, that our Playes have receiv'd some part of those advantages" (XI: 204).

Since conversation registers the improvements of both language and wit, it serves to illustrate Dryden's claims in general for the "improvement" of "the age." In the following paragraph, we can see the relation "conversation," as a literary criterion, constructs between living in the past and living in the present, as well as the position Jonson occupies as representative poet of the past who stimulated criticism then as he does now:

And this leads me to the last and greatest advantage of our writing, which proceeds from conversation. In the Age, wherein those Poets liv'd, there was less of gallantry than in ours; neither did they keep the best company of theirs... I cannot find that any of them were conversant in Courts, except Ben. Jonson: and his genius lay not so much that way, as to make an improvement by it: greatness was not, then, so easy of access, nor conversation so free as now it is. I cannot, therefore, conceive it any insolence to affirm, that, by the knowledge, and pattern of their wit, who writ before us, and by the advantage of our own conversation, the discourse and Raillery of our Comedies excel what has been written by them: and this will be deny'd by none, but some few old fellows who value themselves on their acquaintance with the Black-friars: who, because they saw their Playes, would pretend a right to judge ours. The memory of these grave Gentlemen is their only Plea for being Wits: they can tell a story of Ben. Jonson, and perhaps have had fancy enough to give a supper in Apollo, that they might be call'd his Sons: and because they were drawn in to be laught at in those times, they think themselves now sufficiently intitled to laugh at ours. Learning I never saw in any of them, and wit no more than they could remember. In short, they were unlucky to have been bred in an unpolish'd Age, and more unlucky to live to a refin'd one. They have lasted beyond their own, and are cast behind ours: and not contented to have known little at the age of twenty, they boast of their ignorance at threescore. (XI: 216–17)

In this passage, Dryden pursues the goals, formulated at the outset of the "Defense," of an evenhanded and disinterested assessment of past and present: "to ascribe to dead Authors their just praises, in those things wherein they have excell'd us" and to "acknowledge our advantages to the Age and claim no victory from our wit" (xi: 203). The genial renunciation of any interest in victory, however, is belied by the ostentatious display of Dryden's own rhetoric in the elaborate and lethally satiric wit of the passage.

As the one with whom the would-be wits assert their familiarity and kinship, Jonson is here a figure of paradigmatic past possibilities no longer available in the present, a father whose loss necessitates criticism. Dryden transforms this loss into a gain, however, by presenting the access would-be critics had to Jonson as a liability and the social mobility of the present as deserved compensation, an out-and-out advantage. By proposing conversation as a determinant of value in poetry and as a criterion for literary evaluation, Dryden thus uses the social sphere to mediate the transmission of a literary inheritance from "Father" Ben.[19]

Dryden's critique of the ease with which the older wits, by buying a dinner at the Apollo, come to call themselves Jonson's sons, is overlaid by his representation of social demarcations. Disavowing that the same social constraints operate in the present, now that greatness is ostensibly of free and easy access, Dryden mobilizes terms loaded with status markers to portray the insufficiency of the past generation. The "grave Gentlemen" who consider themselves "intitled" to laugh at the present because they "value themselves on their acquaintance" reveal themselves as attached, in a visibly old-fashioned way, to a residual social order. But wit, the solvent of social hierarchies, enforces its own restrictions on the easy access to greatness, as becomes clear in his treatment of Jonson's wit.[20]

Jonson's example measures the improving effects that the increase in gallantry in the present has on poetry:

That the wit of this Age is much more courtly may be easily proven by viewing the Characters of gentlemen which were written in the last. First for Jonson, *True-Wit* in the *Silent Woman*, was his Master-piece, and True-Wit was a Scholar-like kind of man, a Gentleman with an allay of Pedantry: a man who seems mortifi'd to the world by much reading. The best of his discourse is drawn, not from the knowledge of the Town, but Books, and, in short, he would be a fine Gentleman in an University. (xi: 215)

Even though he was "conversant in the Courts," Truewit, Jonson's "masterpiece," comes across not as courtly but as pedantic.[21] Although Dryden would seem to be drawing a simple distinction between an "unpolish'd Age" and a "refin'd one," between the university and the court, he nevertheless gives the "Town" a greater weight. The possibilities for improvement offered by "conversation" are not absolute but relative to historical changes. For Dryden, "conversation" measures the arrival of "the Town" as polite society.[22] This is not immediately evident, however, as Dryden, at the end of the "Defense," moves to attribute the improvement of conversation to the king:

> Now, if they ask me, whence it is that our conversation is so much refin'd? I must freely, and without flattery, ascribe it to the Court: and, in it, particularly to the King; whose example gives law to it. His own mis-fortunes and the Nations, afforded him an opportunity, which is rarely allow'd to Sovereign Princes, I mean of travelling, and being conversant in the most polish'd courts of Europe. (XI: 216)

Dryden here describes Charles transforming a problematic inheritance into a boon, whose side-effect, improved conversation at court, contributes to the improved state of literature. The poet-critic, who recognizes this improvement and makes more direct use of it, would thus seem to be authorized by analogy with the restored monarch; his critical expertise allows him to displace Ben's would-be sons but he must, like Charles, transform a problematic inheritance into a boon for the nation.

In a curious passage in *An Account of the English Dramatick Poets*, Gerard Langbaine explicitly points to the epilogue and its defense as the source of his interest in exposing Dryden's "plagiarisms":

> [A]nd as if the proscription of his Contemporaries Reputations, were not sufficient to satiate his implacable thirst after Fame, endeavouring to demolish the Statues and Monuments of his Ancestors, the Works of those Illustrious Predecessors, Shakespeare, Fletcher and Johnson: I was resolv'd to endeavour the rescue and preservation of those excellent Trophies of Wit, by raising a *Posse-comitatus* upon this Poetick Almanzor, to put a stop to his Spoils upon his own Country-men.[23]

Representing Dryden as Almanzor, the outsized hero of *Conquest of Granada*, Langbaine takes him to task both for betraying his own country and for what would have seemed to him to be an aristocratic, heroic model of criticism. Langbaine's response makes it obvious that, by 1691, when he published his *Account*, national gain was no longer allied with a heroic identification with the monarch, as it had been for Dryden. Dryden's treatment of Jonson in monarchical language in the *Essay of Dramatick Poesy*, however, invites closer comparison between the status Dryden gives to Jonson and the monarch and each one's impingement on the question of inheritance.

In the *Essay of Dramatick Poesy*, Dryden compares Jonson to an absolutist monarch. In borrowing from past playwrights, Jonson "has done his Robberies so openly, that one may see he fears not to be taxed by any Law. He invades Authours like a Monarch; and what would be theft in other Poets, is onely victory in him."[24] Unlike Charles, whose example gives the law, Jonson offers an example that is above the law; unlike Charles, whose past is problematic and needs to be obscured, Jonson can freely access past playwrights. Jonson is a crucial figure in the *Essay of Dramatick Poesy*; yet, throughout the *Essay*, Jonson raises the specter of discontinuity between the Jacobean past and the Restoration present, between absolutist and restored monarchs. In the "Defense," the critic, like the restored monarch, is bound to both the advantages and disadvantages of "the age" – the social conditions of a problematic inheritance. The nature of "the age" and the vulnerabilities of inheriting a literary tradition so clearly articulated in the epilogue and its defense also inform the more magisterial and detached critical pronouncements of the *Essay*, an impression that derives in part from its form, the dramatic dialogue. Close attention to the theatrical and performative contexts of this text, however, reveals that it is equally concerned with such social issues, even though they are here ventriloquized.[25] The international conflict that frames both debates, set as they are against the backdrop of the Battle of Solebay, fails to contain fully, or neutralize, the domestic struggle between the present and the past. These contexts lay the ground for an assessment of Dryden's use of Jonson to theatricalize literary history and to produce a literary genealogy in the *Essay of Dramatick Poesy*.

THEATRICALIZED LITERARY HISTORY

Dryden's selection of the Battle of Solebay, one of the few unambiguous English victories of the Second Dutch War (1665–67), as the backdrop for his inaugural piece of critical writing reflects the importance of national victory to his critical enterprise, especially because events intervening between the writing and publication had so qualified English success.[26] The idea of commercial superiority, attained through competition over trade, thus sets the stage for Dryden's establishment of a national literary patrimony.[27]

From the beginning of the *Essay*, the question of literary judgment is vexed by the commercial contexts in which it repeatedly appears. The commercial battle is the source of the verse that the courtly wits feel called upon to judge in the first place, and Eugenius counters Crites's and Lisideius's casual critique of rhyme by referring to an unnamed poet who received such popular acclaim in 1660 that people's interest in him surpassed their interests in a bargain: "I have seen them reading it in the midst of Change time; nay, so vehement they were at it, that they lost their bargain by the Candles ends" (XVII: 12). The popular success of this poet prompts Eugenius to satirize new "mercantile" cultural forms when he raises what we might call the question of the canon. He wonders how to tell if "someone will be received among the great ones." This question leads him, as it does us, to examine the standards of evaluation from the perspective of national(ist) literary history: "If your quarrel to those who now write, be grounded onely on your reverence to Antiquity, there is no man more ready to adore those great *Greeks* and *Romans* than I am: but on the other side, I cannot think so contemptibly of the Age in which I live, or so dishonourable of my own Countrey" (XVII: 12). The question of how to judge one's contemporaries, a question that arises in the commercial arena because of a trade war, develops into the structures of opposition that form the debates.

Later in the *Essay*, when Neander wants to score points in his debate with Lisideius about the greater merits of the English over the French, the commercial context resurfaces. Neander claims, "We have borrowed nothing from them; our plays are weaved in English looms" (XVII: 53). The status of the English cloth industry provides the analogy for national literary self-sufficiency. Since the interests of the cloth industry were anti-Dutch, Neander's claim serves as a weapon in both commercial and aesthetic battles: just as the interests of the English cloth industry compete with the Dutch and emerge victorious, so English plays, in their independence from French rules, outstrip French plays.[28]

Curiously, commercial victory over the Dutch, however provisional, permits the assertion of English aesthetic predominance – over the French.[29] As Dryden puts it in the note, "To the Reader," that prefaces the *Essay*: "The drift of the ensuing discourse was chiefly to vindicate the honour of our English writers from the censure of those who unjustly prefer the French before them" (XVII: 7). Dryden's theatricalization of conflict – in the debates themselves, in their being staged against the backdrop of battle and, as we shall see, in their deployment of a set of tropes of historical understanding – permits the generalization of victory across nations in which commercial victory is tantamount to aesthetic superiority. Oddly enough, international struggle is the context in which intergenerational competition – the problematic relation between literary past and present – can be redressed through the articulation of criticism as the means of differentiating between the past and the present.

In the debate over the greater merits of English or French dramatists, Ben Jonson supplies Dryden with crucial support for the English claim to surpass French literary achievement. Jonson's plays elucidate the degree to which composition should accord with or deviate from the rules. Jonson allows the English to achieve aesthetic victory over the French both because he has followed the rules more closely than any other English poet, and because he has shown how much can be achieved by defying the rules. He is therefore the perfect counterexample to the French, since he can be made to speak their language even as he outdoes them at it. The passage I cited earlier, in which Jonson is described as "invad[ing] Authours like a Monarch," continues with Neander's assertion of English aesthetic ascendancy over the French: if Jonson were translated into French, "I believe the controversy would soon be decided betwixt the two nations, even making them the judges" (XVII: 63). The simile comparing Jonson to a monarch, probably because it recalls the trauma of the regicide, prompts Neander to redescribe the role of adjudication and regulation in critical debates:

But we need not call our Hero's to our ayde; Be it spoken to the honour of the *English*, our Nation can never want in any Age such who are able to dispute the Empire of Wit with any people in the Universe. And though the fury of a Civil War, and Power, for twenty years together, abandon'd to a barbarous race of men, Enemies of all good Learning, had buried the Muses under the ruines of Monarchy; yet with the restoration of our happiness, we see Poesie lifting up its head, and already shaking off the rubbish which lay so heavy on it. (XVII: 63)

The speed with which the English have recovered from the Civil War is testimony to their superiority, as is their feature of never having lacked the ability to dispute. Neander, Dryden's spokesman, claims that to call upon the heroes of the literary past, such as Jonson, may needlessly expose weakness. The fear of exposure, however, is prompted less by a concern that English writers will appear weak to the French than that Restoration writers will suffer in their own self-image. Jonson opens up the wound that the Civil War has created, the gap between the plenitude of past great plays and the dearth of new ones. Therefore, Neander completes the panegyrical description of the Restoration by stating, "We have seen since His Majesties return, many Dramatick Poems which yield not to those of any forein Nation, and which deserve all Laurels but the English" (XVII: 63). Contemporary English plays deserve victory in any international contest, but they do not deserve their own laurels. What is implied by this double standard is that the English are harsher judges of their own products than the French are of theirs because they can refer to the great achievement of their literary inheritance. Criticism is thus presented as a national strength. As Neander puts it, " [I]f we, I say, can be equal to ourselves, I ask no favour from the French" (XVII: 64). As important as victory in the international arena may be, as much as it can supply Dryden and the wits he ventriloquizes with a position of power out of which to evaluate literature, the problem is still to overcome, or even to match, what the previous generation has achieved.[30] Indeed, international victory may mollify historical anxieties about domestic matters, but once the specter of past achievement is raised, critical measures must be taken.

Crites, who defends the achievement of the Ancients over that of the Moderns in the first debate of the *Essay*, expresses the converse of this manner of historical critical thinking in that context. Crites's formulation allows us to see how Dryden's criticism dramatizes Jonson as a national classic:

[T]he greatest man of the last age [Ben Jonson] was willing to give place to [the Ancients] in all things: he was not only a professed imitator of Horace, but a learned plagiary of all the others; you track him everywhere in their snow... you will pardon me, therefore, if I presume he loved their fashion when he wore their clothes. But since I have otherwise a great veneration for him, and you, Eugenius, prefer him above all other Poets, I will use no further arguments than his example: I will produce before you father Ben. dress'd in all the ornaments and colours of the Ancients. (XVII: 21)

By assigning to Eugenius, his interlocutor, a preference for Jonson, Crites bolsters his argument to produce Jonson instead of "further argument." And yet this sleight of hand is also a theatricalizing trope of historical thinking: it stages the past. Whereas Neander's formulation imagines Jonson as his contemporary at the expense of his literary achievement (he could never equal himself were he to rise and write again), Crites makes even recent events recede into the past: Ben Jonson, dressed in the garb, is an Ancient. For Crites, Jonson exemplifies a historical awareness; he has assimilated the techniques of the Ancients, but, as a modern English writer, he is a national classic.

By ascribing a love of fashion to Ben Jonson, Crites makes him resemble the famous dandy, the fop of the Restoration stage. Even as he historicizes Jonson by noticing his imitation of the Ancients, he theatricalizes him by making that imitation into a costume donned by Jonson. For Dryden, Jonson can be an Ancient because he is also a Restoration actor playing that part. Dryden uses Crites's point of view to effect an ironic reversal that further complicates the theatrical as a critical strategy:

Crites's Jonson is a manifestation of a theatrical production even though Crites's namesake is the poet and masque-writing figure in Jonson's play, *Cynthia's Revels* (1601).[31] Dryden thereby reverses the history of the theatre when he has Crites "produce" Jonson rather than the other way around. By this reversal, Dryden turns Jonson's criticism of the theatrical in *Cynthia's Revels* into dramatic criticism; he capitalizes on and reverses Jonson's antitheatrical presentation of his plays in order to dramatize criticism.[32] He also turns the theatre into a subject of history and a subject of criticism.

Crites would access through Jonson a cultural inheritance from the ancient past; Neander, the new man who is the only non-aristocratic wit, would defend the achievement of the English dramatists over the French and the Moderns over the Ancients, and shares this view of Jonson as a national classic, but, for him, the historical awareness that enables this view is contingent upon being culturally disinherited. When Neander produces "Jonson" to defeat the claim that the French have a superior national literature, it becomes clear that the international battle is really an outward projection of an internally divided English national literature. At the end of the *Essay*, Neander calls Crites's attention to:

> the beginning of your discourse, where you told us we should never find the Audience so favourable to this kind of writing, till we could produce as good Plays in Rhyme as *Ben. Jonson, Fletcher* and *Shakespeare*, had writ out of it. But it is to raise envy to the living, to compare them with the dead. They are honour'd, and almost ador'd by us, as they deserve; neither do I know any so presumptuous of themselves as to contend with them. Yet give me leave to say thus much, without injury to their Ashes, that not onely we shall never equal them, but they could never equal themselves, were they to rise and write again. We acknowledge them our Fathers in wit, but they have ruin'd their estates themselves, before they came to their children's hands. (XVII: 73)

The analogy that the *Essay* sustains, between domestic and international relations, between England's literary achievement and its commercial victory over the Dutch, encourages us to see the argument of "the age" in an international context. The point of departure of Neander's perception is an implied similarity between past and present interests in English commercial ascendancy; indeed, the restored monarchy aimed to consolidate the expansion of overseas trade developed by Cromwell, even though their domestic policies differed.[33] Neander complains that, despite shared foreign policy, at the domestic level the Commonwealth squelched literary achievement, which allowed the literary fathers, who are thereby associated with the wasteful nobility Dryden had described in *Astrea Redux*, to squander their estates. This condition necessitates more aggressive international competition on the part of Dryden's generation, whose achievements in the international spheres of commerce forge a cultural space for the Restoration writers – a space in which their criticism of their forefathers ensures the valuation of their own literary achievements. However, the strategy of outweighing domestic losses by international gains cannot be sustained: Neander proclaims the impoverishment of the present and holds the previous generation responsible. According to his reasoning, fathers who squander the estate before the children come to inherit deserve to be retrospectively vilified. Whereas Jonson thus bolsters the status of English literary achievement in the international arena, once self-reflection on the achievement of the last age comes to the surface, criticism is required.

Significantly, Neander prefaces his *examen* of Jonson's *The Silent Woman* with a short discussion of Jonson's place among his Jacobean contemporaries, Fletcher and Shakespeare. In what is perhaps the most famous passage of the *Essay*, Neander describes Shakespeare as "The man who of all modern, and perhaps ancient poets, had the largest and most comprehensive soul." This preamble ends: "If I would compare [Jonson] with Shakespeare, I must acknowledge him the more correct poet, but Shakespeare the greater wit. Shakespeare was the Homer, or father of our dramatic poets; Jonson was the Virgil, the pattern of elaborate writing; I admire him but I love Shakespeare." The terms which exempt Shakespeare from the stringencies of criticism to which Jonson is subject in the *Essay of Dramatick Poesy* – the greatness of his love-inspiring soul – are audacious: an authentic classical lineage is more available through Shakespeare than through Jonson. In his classicizing of Shakespeare's *Troilus and Cressida*, Dryden explores the ways in which he can access a vernacular classical tradition through Shakespeare. In a counterpart text in which he Englishes Sophocles *Oedipus*, Dryden reveals that the classical and the native are not simply reciprocal; although he establishes the native tradition by linking it to the classical one, he finally authenticates the native only by insisting on its separability from the classic.

CLASSICIZING THE NATIVE LITERARY TRADITION

Dryden's prologue to his version of *Troilus and Cressida* stages the problem of transmitting a native literary tradition through the figure of Shakespeare by negotiating the relations between classic and vernacular languages. This prologue is spoken by Shakespeare's ghost, who, in an extension of the trope of theatricalized literary history that Dryden developed in the *Essay of Dramatick Poesy* when he had Crites "produce" Ben Jonson, describes the troubled transmission of English literary achievement in the present day. The specter of this insufficiently classical writer who composed in the vernacular also raises questions about the possibility of literary nationalism. By having Shakespeare's ghost vindicate the corrections he has made to *Troilus and Cressida*, Dryden proposes himself (as a poet and, more importantly for our purposes, as a critic) as the guarantor of Shakespeare's transmission, as Virgil to Shakespeare's Homer.

Shakespeare's ghost begins by addressing fellow Britons and by identifying himself as one of them: "See, my lov'd Britons, see your Shakespear rise" (line 1). A few lines on, his genius is made English:

> Untaught, unpractis'd, in a barbarous Age,
> I found not, but created the first Stage.
> And, if I drain'd no Greek or Latin store,
> 'Twas, that my own abundance gave me more.
> On foreign trade I needed not rely,
> Like fruitful Britain, rich without supply.
>
> (XIII: 249)

"Shakespear's" greatness is augmented by his not having taken anything from classical sources; in this respect, Shakespeare is like his nation. Dryden here overstates the pure self-sufficiency of both Shakespeare's literary achievement and British trade in order to draw attention instead to the feebleness of the current age. Where can Shakespeare's ghost find worthy successors?

> Now, where are the Successours to my name?
> What bring they to fill out a Poets fame?
> Weak, short-liv'd issues of a feeble Age;
> Scarce living to be Christen'd on the Stage!
>
> (XIII: 249)

Dryden has Shakespeare's ghost propose a mythic genealogy that recuperates the greatness of the English tradition and secures the otherwise dubious transmission of his literary inheritance. At the conclusion of the prologue to *Troilus and Cressida*, "Shakespear" overcomes the difficulties in transmitting the literary patrimony and vindicates Dryden's rewriting of Shakespeare as an instance of such transmission by the mythic device of depicting the British as descendants of the Trojans through Brutus.[34] The prologue ends:

> But I forget that still 'Tis understood
> Bad Plays are best descry'd by showing good:
> Sit silent then, that my pleas'd Soul may see
> A Judging Audience once, and worthy me:
> My faithful Scene from true records shall tell
> How Trojan valour did the Greek excell;
> Your great forefathers shall their fame regain,
> And Homer's angry ghost repine in vain.
>
> (XIII: 250)

Whereas in the *Essay of Dramatick Poesy*, Shakespeare was aligned with Homer and Jonson with Virgil, in these remarkable lines Dryden aligns Shakespeare with Troy as against Homer's Greece. Promising that English ancestors "shall their fame regain," "Shakespear" gestures backwards towards a lineage that descends to the English nation from Aeneas to Brutus to Shakespeare. Dryden has Shakespeare claim that the "faithful Scene" is from "true records," by which he presumably means those of Geoffrey of Monmouth, whose *Historia Regum Britanniae* (1136) articulates a view continuous with Dryden's national classicism.[35] However, this lineage passes through Shakespeare only as he is rewritten by Dryden. Dryden goes over Shakespeare's head to classicize him, thereby providing him with the "Greek or Latin store," the knowledge he lacked of his "Roman" origins.

Dryden's willingness to bypass much of what we consider "classic" in his valorization of the Trojans over the Greeks is noteworthy. Even more so is his self-inscription, as a critic and emender of Shakespeare, at the point of reception of a double inheritance from Shakespeare and the classics. Exploding the opposition between classic and vernacular languages inherited from English Renaissance Humanism, Dryden exploits his position as the beneficiary of a classically empowered native line.[36]

Perhaps even more remarkable in these lines is the way Shakespeare's ghost uses pronouns: he refers directly to the play's audience, enjoining them to be silent, judging and worthy of him, even though the play they are about to see is Dryden's. Thus when he says, "my faithful Scene," he refers to a scene in Dryden's play, in which Dryden, altering Shakespeare's drama, makes Cressida faithful to Troilus. Dryden thus has Shakespeare's ghost assert the faithfulness of Dryden's plays, both to "true records," and to Shakespeare. Indeed, Dryden is faithful to Shakespeare *because* of the alterations he has made to his play. Using Shakespeare's voice, Dryden here claims that criticism, and the emendatory dramatic practices it accompanies and informs, is the vehicle through which a national vernacular literary tradition is transmitted as an inheritance.

At the end of the prologue, Homer's "angry ghost repine[s] in vain" when Dryden's audience sees how Trojan valor exceeds that of the Greeks. Trojans triumph over Greeks and Shakespeare is elevated above Homer – both national achievements made possible by means of Dryden's rewriting. Vernacular literature triumphs over classical literature, and the ancestral lineage of Shakespeare and the English nation through Brutus continues into the present – it runs on via Dryden, through his classicizing of Shakespeare. Ventriloquizing Shakespeare's ghost to establish the authority for the changes he has made, Dryden announces that, as the one who criticizes, emends and revises Shakespeare, he is his successor. The prologue thus documents Dryden's self-inscription within the literary genealogy. His own "faithfulness" to Shakespeare, which depends on Cressida's faithfulness to Troilus, thus has the payoff of a literary inheritance.

The means by which Dryden accesses a national-classical literary tradition, as he does in the prologue to *Troilus and Cressida*, where Homer's ghost languishes before the "improved" Shakespeare's, are in evidence throughout the preface to that play, "The Grounds of Criticism in Tragedy." Modeled on Aristotle's account of tragedy in *Poetics*, the preface echoes Aristotle – many of the examples are taken from Sophocles – except that for every mention of Sophocles' *Oedipus Rex*, Dryden offers his own version of *Oedipus*. In his emendation of Sophocles, in which his access to the classics is not mediated through the English literary tradition, Dryden puts forward a paradigm of succession that consolidates and complements the transmission of a native literary inheritance enabled by his criticism.

Dryden and Lee's collaborative *Oedipus* (1679) was one of the most popular successes of its day.[37] In the epilogue and preface that Dryden contributed,[38] we can see the ways Dryden's classical nativism reshapes the inheritance of a national literary tradition he described in the *Essay of Dramatick Poesy*. In a pattern that should be familiar from the prologue to *Troilus and Cressida*, the epilogue to *Oedipus* establishes the ancient authority of Sophocles' play in the very same terms that justify Dryden and Lee's alterations.

The epilogue begins by modestly depicting the need for a joint effort on Dryden and Lee's part if they are to match Sophocles' grandeur:

> What Sophocles could undertake alone,
> Our Poets found the work of more than one;
> And therefore two lay tugging at the piece,
> With all their force, to draw the ponderous Mass from Greece,
> A weight bent ev'n Seneca's strong Muse,
> And which Corneille's Shoulders did refuse.
> So hard it is th'Athenian Harp to string!
> So much two Consuls yield to just one King.
> Terrour and pity this whole Poem sway;
> The mightiest machines that can mount a Play;
> How heavy will those Vulgar Souls be found
> Whom two such Engines cannot move from Ground!
>
> (XIII: 214)

Dryden emphasizes his and Lee's fidelity to Sophocles, which exceeds both Seneca's and Corneille's. "[T]wo such engines" as "[t]errour and pity" should move even the vulgar English, and in the ambiguity that allows the phrase "two such engines" to refer also to Dryden and Lee, Dryden insists on their success despite the difficulties. Dryden's reference to the challenge of rewriting Sophocles, "So hard it is th'Athenian Harp to string," echoes a similar strategic self-representation as weak, only to claim superiority, when he describes rewriting Shakespeare in the preface to *All for Love* as "string[ing] the Bowe of Ulysses." Representing rewriting Shakespeare as equivalent to the Herculean task of rewriting Sophocles, Dryden augments Shakespeare's classic status. As we saw in the prologue to *Troilus and Cressida*, however, it is Dryden's Shakespeare who becomes the classic.

This strategic self-inscription is also visible in the other terms the epilogue proposes for appreciating Sophocles' achievement: "So much two Consuls yield to just one King." While this phrase proclaims Sophocles' superiority, it also prompts the question: how much is "so much"? Dryden's "just" is both admiring and dismissive, an ambiguity inviting us to pay further attention to the line. Dryden aligns Sophocles with Oedipus the king, setting him against two Roman consuls, Dryden and Lee, whose republican virtues offer an alternative to tyranny. At the same time, the two consuls are invested with an authority more ancient than Sophocles' in the chiasmus that describes Dryden and Lee as Roman and represents Sophocles' authority in terms more applicable to a modern sovereign. The convolutions Dryden requires to capitalize on classic authority are evident in the equivalence he proposes between Dryden and Lee and Sophocles that offsets the imbalance in which it takes two English writers to match a single classical one. The strain registers in the grotesque image of Dryden and Lee's Herculean poetic labor: the "two lay tugging at the piece, / ... to draw the ponderous Mass from Greece."

But can the single authority of one king be said to be endorsed in a play about tyranny? Significantly, in Dryden and Lee's play, Oedipus is a monarch threatened by usurpation by a deformed Creon, whom contemporary audiences would have recognized as a Tory version of Shaftesbury. The threat to Oedipus' reign tends to legitimate it; for Dryden and Lee, Oedipus' tragedy comes from his blind enactment of his fate, and not from obtaining the throne by the most illegitimate of means: patricide and incest. The two consuls yield to the king in the political domain, but Dryden's epilogue shows ambivalence about such yielding in the literary domain; there, Dryden yields with a rhetorical flourish that establishes his own gain.

Of all the changes Dryden and Lee make to Sophocles, most remarkable is the ending to their play, in which all of the main characters die. Jocasta murders the offspring of her incestuous union with Oedipus, and then kills herself; and after pulling out his own eyes, Oedipus throws himself off a high tower.[39] Although Dryden expresses interest in ensuring that the English stage be perceived as inheriting a classical tradition from Sophocles, the ending of the play would appear to short-circuit the classical legacy by cutting off the possibility for the Theban play cycle: neither *Oedipus at Colonus* nor *Antigone* is possible if Oedipus, Creon and Antigone are all dead!

Indeed, this bizarre catastrophe is highlighted in the commentary of an anonymous gentleman who attended the play and singled out the ending as an "extraordinary Incident in this English Tragedy":

Oedipus appears at the Window, as having his Eyes put out, and then, as from a Tribunal, he makes a beautiful Harangue, which he concludes comically, by throwing himself out of the Window, and killing himself by that extravagant Fall: nevertheless, it is not the Actor that represents Oedipus, who throws himself out of the Window; but a Man of Past-board, made like him, which is thrown down: For had it been the Actor, he would really have killed himself. The People usually laugh very heartily, at so bold and heedless a Leap: Thus ends that fine Tragedy, whose Catastrophe evidently shews, what kind of Brain the Author had. (XIII: 495)

Rather than make us reflect on the "kind of brain[s] the Author[s] had," the audience's defamiliarizing laughter might prompt us instead to examine more closely the ending of Dryden and Lee's English tragedy. Oedipus' suicide is, in Dryden's presentation of it, an improvement of Sophocles' "most celebrated piece of all antiquity" (XIII: 115). Although it appears that only a truncated transmission of the classical literary inheritance would be possible if everyone in the play dies, it is precisely by staging this curtailment as an improvement that Dryden and Lee establish the classic status of the English literary tradition.

In the preface Dryden wrote for the play, he takes pains to distinguish his and Lee's English Sophocles from Corneille's, and, in so doing, he measures the superiority of English national classicism to French neo-classicism by its distance from absolutism. His comments there, read in conjunction with his comparison of the French and English vernaculars in "The Grounds of Criticism in Tragedy," allow us to see that Oedipus' suicide enables a native literary tradition to be transmitted as a classical national inheritance because it figures the dead end of an absolutist model of succession. This model undergoes one of the last in a series of death-throe convulsions during the Exclusion Crisis of the late 1670s.

Dryden and Lee borrow a romance plot from Corneille's *Oedipe*, but they replace Thesée, the lover of Oedipus' sister, Dircé, by Adrastus, Prince of Argos. Dryden explains this replacement: Corneille confuses his audience by introducing another hero who will overshadow Oedipus. The logic of Corneille's choice, however, is dictated by Sophocles' *Oedipus at Colonus*, in which Theseus inherits Oedipus' legacy as ruler of Athens.[40] Dropping Theseus from their play thus serves to highlight Dryden and Lee's terminal interest in Oedipus. The main problem with Corneille's play is that the character of his Oedipus is a "miserabl[e] fail[ure]": "If he desir'd that Oedipus should be pitied, he shou'd have made him a better man. He forgot that Sophocles had taken care to shew him in his first entrance, a just, a merciful, a successful, a Religious Prince, and in short, a Father of his Country" (XIII: 115). Dryden's attack on Corneille obscures the French origins of his own neo-Aristotelianism and enables Dryden to lay direct English claim to the classical tradition – one, moreover, which he has improved. The terms Dryden uses to deride French neo-classicism echo those he uses in "The Grounds of Criticism in Tragedy," when he discusses the need for the "Manners" of a character to "be [both] suitable to the Age, Quality, Country, Dignity etc.," and natural (XIII: 240–46). That discussion suggests that the problem with the French vernacular is also a problem with French absolutism: "The present French Poets are generally accus'd, that wheresoever they lay the Scene, or in whatsoever Age, the manners of their Heroes are wholly French: Racine's Bajazet is bred at Constantinople; but his civilities are convey'd to him by some secret passage, from Versailles into the Seraglio" (XIII: 238). For Dryden, the French vernacular is too French. More specifically, the

French spoken on the stage is too exclusively modeled on the court to be truly decorous or natural.[41] Significantly, Dryden's example of perfectly natural manners in a dramatic character is provided by Shakespeare's Henry IV: "But our Shakespear, having ascrib'd to Henry the Fourth the character of a King, and of a Father, gives him the perfect manners of each Relation, when he either transacts with his Son or with his Subjects" (XIII: 238). In addition to Henry's diversified relations, what makes him a perfectly natural character is that he speaks English in populist accents, using a vernacular that is more socially diversified and more perfectible than French. Dryden refers again to Henry IV a few pages later, when he singles out a description of Richard II after he is deposed and led in triumph by Bolingbroke through the streets of London to exemplify Shakespeare's "divinity" as a poet, and thereby to offset his critique of the excesses of the player's speech in *Hamlet* (XIII: 246). Dryden here implies that the English vernacular is superior to the French because of its social diversification, a feature whose roots he locates in the Jacobean past. Reaching back to legitimate the superior diversification of the English vernacular, however, only highlights the series of crises English absolutism undergoes over the course of the seventeenth century – including the Revolution, the Restoration and the Exclusion Crisis. As an elaboration of Dryden's earlier representation, in "Defense of the Epilogue," of the conversation at the court of Charles II, where greatness is ostensibly of easy access, as the source of linguistic improvement, Dryden's claims here recall the basis of this improvement in Charles's exile in France during the Interregnum.

Dryden thus takes pains to establish that the social elasticity of the English vernacular, which the latinate French lacks, stems from its non-classical roots. When Dryden discusses the "disadvantage" of English's "being founded on Dutch [stock]" (XIII: 223), he uses the vocabulary of trade to transform the poverty of English, to which he also alludes in the letter of dedication when he describes his translation practice (which I discussed earlier), into a potential abundance and richness: "'Tis true that to supply our poverty, we have traffiqu'd with our Neighbour Nations; by which means we abound as much in words, as Amsterdam does in Religions; but to order them, and make them useful after their admission is the difficulty" (XIII: 223). Indeed, the criteria for the successful improvement of English, which Dryden specifies a few lines later, are "speak[ing] and writ[ing] a language, worthy of the English wit, and which foreigners may not disdain to learn" – an improvement to which his practice of translating English into Latin and back again – contributes.

When the international arena of trade is taken as the field in which national worth is measured, as it is both here and in the *Essay of Dramatick Poesy*, English is better equipped than French for success.

When Dryden uses the epithet, "Father of his Country" to describe the superiority of the English Oedipus in the preface to his *Oedipus*, he proposes that his suicidal king has more natural manners than either his Greek or French precedents. The phrase, which is also the subtitle of another Exclusion Crisis play, Nathaniel Lee's *Lucius Junius Brutus* (1681), signals in a highly compressed fashion the widespread crisis in the authority of inheritance.[42] In Lee's play about the founding of the Roman republic, Lucius Junius Brutus becomes "father of his country" by killing his own sons.

At first glance, Brutus' "sacrifice" of his sons looks like the opposite of Oedipus' murder of his father. Indeed, the immediate political valences of the two Exclusion Crisis plays pull in opposite directions: *Lucius Junius Brutus* was banned for its endorsement of the Whiggish critique of monarchical tyranny, while *Oedipus* defended the monarchy, condemning Shaftesbury in the representation of Creon as a deformed usurper.[43] Both texts, however, dramatize the same apparent contradiction: family bloodlines must be terminated if national patrimony, understood, nevertheless, in familial terms, is to be established. These texts manipulate the vocabulary of patriarchal absolutism to dramatize what we might recognize as a moment of Hegelian *Aufhebung*: the ruling family is literally cancelled out and familial, domestic bonds are reinstituted at a national level. For Lee and Dryden, then, like Lucius Junius Brutus, Oedipus is a "Father of his Country" who bequeaths nothing to his sons in order to establish and preserve his country. The models of succession explored in these Exclusion Crisis texts register the shift Michael McKeon describes as the movement from patriarchalist to patriarchal culture, a discussion I pursue in greater detail in Chapter 3, when I take up the gendered but universal Shakespeare Dryden produces by means of his sentimental rewritings of *Antony and Cleopatra* and *Troilus and Cressida*.

More relevant for us, at this point, is that these plays resolve anxieties about the continuities of literary authority by presenting a structure that guarantees a literary inheritance – one in which a tradition is established by means of terminating its foreign foundations, relocating them in a domestic, national field, and using melodramatic violence to mystify the relocation. Terminating Oedipus makes the story into a terminal – a transmission site through which the texts of the classical, as well as the Elizabethan and Jacobean, pasts pass into the present.

This key strategy both establishes the ascendancy of a classicized vernacular, and consolidates a native literary tradition. Other readers of Dryden have been preoccupied with establishing how neo-classical he is, for purposes of either affirmation or critique, and have not observed the uses to which Dryden has put his neo-classicism. Although Dryden and Lee's *Oedipus* has been forgotten, its contributions to the shape of English critical practice remain. As an examination of the gendered terms of evaluation by means of which Dryden establishes Shakespeare's universality will attest, Dryden installs a domestic and familial model of literary succession, in which nationalist authority is genealogically derived. This domestic and familial model comes to replace the initially enabling foreign and public model of the *Essay of Dramatick Poesy*, in which English literary achievement is established in an arena of international competition. As we have seen, this achievement is compromised by the complications of being Ben Jonson's son, but it is ultimately consolidated as Dryden discovers the means for transmitting a native literary tradition through a historically oriented practice of criticism.

CHAPTER 2

Staging criticism, staging Milton: John Dryden's The State of Innocence

In 1677 John Dryden published *The State of Innocence and the Fall of Man*, an operatic rewriting of John Milton's *Paradise Lost* that he had probably completed four years earlier.[1] In his preface, "The Author's Apology for Heroic Poetry and Poetic Licence," Dryden indicates that criticism depends on the critic's identification with the writer he is examining. Milton, however, provides a particularly recalcitrant site for such an assumption: the only acceptable condition under which Dryden could identify with him would be if Milton's poem were no longer regarded as a vindication of revolution or regicide. Consequently, Dryden must produce a literary transformation of Milton, one that masks the political differences between them.

Dryden's *The State of Innocence* accomplishes this goal, rewriting Milton in ways that explicitly contradict Milton's understanding of heroic poetry. By translating Milton's blank verse into rhyme and his epic narrative into dramatic form, Dryden separates both the man and his authoritative stylistic choices from the poem he wrote. Because Milton's choices make manifest his theological-political-literary authority, Dryden's revision of them necessarily reconstitutes that authority. He thereby makes discursively available Milton's work, divorced from his political beliefs, recasting it as a literary contribution to a native tradition. In "The Author's Apology," and in Dryden's subsequent writings about Milton, he develops a set of critical terms that sustain the separation of Milton's poetic achievement from his politics. In this chapter, I examine Dryden's revisions in order to trace the means by which he achieves this separation and its consequences for his (and future) criticism.

When Dryden overrides Milton's "authorial intentions," he transforms his opposition to them into a source of his own critical authority. Stunningly, Dryden invents a notion of "literary" authority in the very process of discarding aspects of Milton's; Milton's writing then becomes an example that, according to Dryden's prefatory essay, puts English literary achievement in the same league as Homer, Virgil and Tasso. But the classic status that Dryden wants to claim for Milton in "The Apology for Heroic Poetry and Poetic Licence" and elsewhere, is compromised not only by Milton's politics, but also by his contemporaneity with Dryden. If, as I have already suggested, Dryden develops a strategic historical perspective, in which literary achievements of the "last age" can be represented as national classics, he is forced into specific maneuvers around the conferral of classic status on Milton. The problems Milton poses for such a conferral – his contemporaneity and his radical politics – necessitate, I want to argue here, nothing less than Dryden's rewriting of *Paradise Lost*.

Rewriting, the Restoration literary practice that seems most archaic to us, gives rise, in Dryden's revision of Milton, to a critical vocabulary of wit, taste and talent in its preface – terms of literary evaluation that constitute the currency of eighteenth-century criticism and that continue to be in use. The comparison of Dryden and Milton entailed by a consideration of Dryden's revision thus allows us to specify the modernity of his critical enterprise as an early instance of the attempt to pry aesthetic matters away from their imbrication in political and theological discourses. A number of critics and theorists have proposed a variety of approaches and contexts to account for the entry of these terms into what comes to be called, by the end of the eighteenth century, aesthetic discourse.[2] Such terms, I want to suggest, are derived directly from Dryden, specifically from his dramatization of Milton's epic, and from his implicit reliance, in its preface, on the world of Restoration theatre. By doing so, I am not proposing that all subsequent uses of this critical vocabulary find a singular source in Dryden's *The State of Innocence*. Rather, by describing the theatrical dynamics of these components of criticism at the moment of its emergence, I underscore the ways they point to a specific social space – between the court and the theatre, between a mode of literary production sponsored by aristocratic culture and one increasingly oriented towards a consuming public – whose traces we continue to find in criticism, even after it leaves behind its discursive dependence on the theatre.

Yet Dryden's treatment of Milton's poem as an autonomous aesthetic artifact cannot succeed in fully separating the literary from the political and the theological. The changes that Dryden makes to *Paradise Lost* do split the literary off from the political and theological, but Dryden's revision – and the critical vocabulary to which it gives rise – nevertheless continues to register social and political matters. His revision of

Milton's poem strips it of Milton's radicalism and updates, or makes more relevant, the political scene it allegorizes. It is important to note that the emergent separability of the aesthetic from the political also informs Milton's own writing, although his strategies for dealing with the divergence of theological and political power from something more strictly literary are different than Dryden's.[3] Dryden's theatricalization of the epic, and the critical terms it permits him to generate, relegate political and theological questions to the contingent realm of change, rather than leaving them, where Milton would have them, in the permanent realm of truth. Dryden's critical terms, enmeshed as they are in their own historical moment, subordinate the theological and political to questions of aesthetic judgment. Despite the specific political pressures that inform Dryden's treatment of Milton, recent critical understandings of Milton still depend on the terms Dryden generates out of his theatricalization of *Paradise Lost*. Indeed, the hostility with which *The State of Innocence* has been greeted exhibits current critics' outright anti-theatricality more so than it does their rejection of Dryden's terms.

STAGING MILTON

Dryden's rewriting of *Paradise Lost* is not the usual act of rewriting: unlike most such Restoration revisions, it is not derived from a Jacobean text, nor is Dryden rewriting a play; finally, *The State of Innocence* was never performed.[4] Differentiating it even more fundamentally is the fact that Milton was probably still alive when Dryden started to rework his epic.[5] It is therefore strange that by rewriting *Paradise Lost*, Dryden treats his contemporary, Milton, as if he were a writer who belonged to the past of Shakespeare. Stranger still is the attitude towards Milton which Dryden expresses in the short poem that appeared on the frontispiece for the fourth edition of *Paradise Lost* (1688):

> Three Poets in three distant Ages born,
> Greece, Italy and England did adorn.
> The first in loftiness of thought surpass'd
> The next in Majesty: in both the Last.
> The force of Nature cou'd no farther goe:
> To make a Third she joynd the former two.[6]

Dryden puts Milton in the company of Homer and Virgil, but he places him so far back in the past that, somehow, he belongs to a distant age that is beyond Nature: "The force of Nature cou'd no farther goe." Dryden's construction of Milton is echoed by later critics, and is even noticeable in our own times: Milton is depicted as a classical poet, the height of English poetic achievement, and a "natural force" allied with the sublime. Moreover, as most university syllabi will attest, Milton more often gets taught as a Renaissance poet, than as a figure belonging to the Restoration.

Particularly remarkable in Dryden's initial portrait, however, is the entirely manufactured aspect of the projection backwards – Milton only died in 1674, the same year Dryden finished *The State of Innocence*! Ironically, the poem's strange backward projection reveals the feature that makes Milton's text available for rewriting: despite its grandeur, it is old-fashioned and therefore can be "improved" by "translation." Although when he rewrites Shakespeare, Dryden also treats him as if he were old-fashioned, when he rewrites Milton, he reproduces Milton's *self*-presentation as old-fashioned.[7]

Abbe Blum has compared Milton's self-presentation as an author to Ben Jonson's. The comparison is useful for gauging Dryden's response to Milton since despite the similarities between Milton and Jonson, Dryden's attitude towards each differs. Blum observes:

> Jonson's obsession with his 1616 *Workes* as printed autonomous text; his self-conscious ordering of his pieces; and even his general, "'textual' certification of his name (Jonson, not Johnson)" make him a striking precursor for Milton. Milton's practical attention to his works can certainly be demonstrated. He carefully arranged the order of the poems within and the general appearance of the 1645 *Poems* which came out the year after *Areopagitica*; this volume, like *Areopagitica* but unlike any of the other tracts of domestic liberty is advertised as the product "of Mr. John Milton." Both works function as exercises in self-documentation.[8]

Although Milton and Jonson both participated in the publication of their own works, Dryden finds that the differences between each as a model of authority ultimately outweigh the similarities. Unlike Jonson, Milton does not become a professional poet, and his authority as an author is not modeled on the substitution of his own body by the body of the book, as Jonson's is; instead Milton's authority is constituted by the extension of his voice through a text.[9] His text is authorized by his inspiration or vision, which is then projected away from his body; it remains attached to him nonetheless, as his property. The bardic tradition to which Milton aspires makes the dispersal or distribution of his authority (in textual form) dependent on the effectiveness of the voice. A call, it elicits a response that, like the scattered limbs of truth of *Areopagitica* that need to be collected and pieced back together, comes to be coherent only in a projected future; the text is authorized at the moment it converts its reader to Milton's own position and beliefs.[10] We have seen that when Dryden dramatizes Jonson as a national classic, he capitalizes on and reverses Jonson's anti-theatricality to produce dramatic criticism that takes the theatre as its subject. The project of *Essay of Dramatick Poesy*, however, did not involve rewriting Jonson. Dryden also claims national classic status for Milton, now put forward in a heroic register. In order to do so, he must negotiate not only Milton's contemporaneity, but also, what is even more problematic, a conception of heroic poetry altogether at variance with his own. Rewriting *Paradise Lost* in dramatic form enables him to do so.

The changes Dryden makes to Milton's poem record Dryden's reactions to Milton's self-presentation. Briefly, the generic translation from epic to opera entails a compression of focus which Dryden obtains by concentrating primarily on Books 2, 4, 8 and 9 of the epic. He captures the highlights of *Paradise Lost* by dramatizing the scenes of the council in Hell, Satan's first view of Eden, Raphael's visit, the temptation and the fall. Indeed, all of Dryden's choices ensue from the basic decision to *dramatize* Milton's epic. Despite the implicit claim that he will improve Milton, Dryden does not invent much substantial new action for his opera; he takes what Milton has provided in *Paradise Lost* and modifies it. However, both the major formal changes and the minor substantive ones measure the political differences between the two poets, between their respective senses of their times.

Although opera, along with other musical entertainments of the period (such as semi-opera), would seem to have had strong royalist overtones deriving from the tradition of the courtly masque, Dryden's generic choice to dramatize Milton's epic can seem, to today's readers of *The State of Innocence*, at once entirely "literary" and a literary failure, in part because of Dryden's critical achievement.[11] Modern critics almost uniformly describe *The State of Innocence* in literary terms, but they see it as travesty; they thus further the project Dryden initiates in his rewriting of Milton – the project of separating politics from literature – but they derogate what they see as Dryden's fundamentally wrong evaluation of Milton's literary intentions and merits. They cannot get beyond the "outrageousness" of Dryden's idea of dramatizing Milton's epic in the first place, representing such a choice as in itself a "poetic" loss.[12] James Winn, Dryden's biographer, rescues Dryden from the blame of modern critics by claiming that it is *Dryden* who gives classic status to *Paradise Lost*.[13] The means by which he achieves this claim reveal much about his critical procedures, foremost among which is his response to a crucial feature of Milton's self-presentation: his ambivalence towards the theatre.

Disclosing both the depth of Milton's investments in theatrical forms and his ambivalence to them, Steven Zwicker reads *Paradise Regained* as Milton's response to Dryden's achievement in the heroic drama. Reversing the critical expectation to see Dryden as operating anxiously in Milton's shadow, Zwicker portrays Milton as the one made nervous. Notwithstanding his recognition of Dryden's dramatic accomplishments, along with what he characterizes as his intention to diminish Milton, Zwicker echoes the contemporary critical consensus when he finds *The State of Innocence* to be a "ridiculous" text that cannot sustain critical examination.[14]

Perhaps a more familiar instance of Milton's attitude towards the theatre, however, is his paradoxical presentation of *Samson Agonistes* as *A Dramatic Poem* "never intended" for the stage. Early plans for *Paradise Lost* show that Milton first conceived it as a play; as an epic, it still retains signs of his conflicted attitude towards dramatic forms and effects.[15] Book 4, in particular, is full of examples of Milton denying that he deploys theatrical effects even as he does so. Our first view of Eden is Satan's, and it is Satan's status as a spectator that allows Milton to use a theatrical perspective. Satan sees "a woody Theatre / Of stateliest view" (*PL*, 4: 141–42) in which innocence can first be staged, before Milton castigates the audience's perspective. This solves Milton's problem: since he has to theatricalize innocence in order to depict it at all, he can stage it before he chastises the viewer, implicitly affiliating this perspective with Satan. On stage in the "woody Theatre," Adam and Eve seem to Satan "Imparadis't in one another's arms" (*PL*, 4: 506), and, much as this sight pains him, his "fallen" point of view enables *our* witnessing of innocence.

Our sharing of Satan's perspective is, of course, problematic for Milton, but, as if to address this dilemma, he reforms the problem of spectatorship somewhat by presenting Adam's response to Eve's question about the stars. Eve asks Adam,

> "[W]herefore all night long shine these, for whom
> This glorious sight, when sleep hath shut all eyes?"
> (*PL*, 4: 658–59)

Adam gives two answers. The first is functional: the stars enlighten and warm all things at night so that they remain capable of receiving the daytime sunlight. The second is aesthetic, turning the question of visibility and beholding into one that is explicitly about theatricality: the stars are "Heav'n['s] spectators":

> These then, though unbeheld in deep of night,
> Shine not in vain, nor think, though men were none,
> That Heav'n would want spectators, God want praise.
> (*PL*, 4: 674–76)

Through the syntax of negation, Adam subordinates Eve's suggestion that the stars perform frivolously to their enduring purpose, to praise God. He offers, moreover, an implicit critique of such frivolousness to the reader, who can thereby be edified by Adam's caution. Even Satan, the paradigmatic spectator, has a purpose – to tempt Adam and Eve into disobedience. Eve is the one who questions the purpose of what she sees. She is also at the center of the events unfolding in Paradise. When Eve tells Adam about her initial pleasure in her own appearance (*PL*, 4: 440–90), her narcissism becomes the grounds upon which non-purposive spectatorship is castigated.

Milton chastises Eve, and, through her, theatricality, but then he rehabilitates her by assimilating her looks and looking to a (reproductive) purpose. He repeatedly shows her being instructed out of viewing without a purpose: first, God admonishes her to look for Adam instead of at her own reflection (*PL*, 4: 467–75), and, later, Adam teaches her the importance of purposiveness when he talks about the stars (*PL*, 4: 674–77). Eve embraces the position of actress, spectator or the two simultaneously only until she learns better. Absorbing *Paradise Lost*'s theatricality, and emptying it of its negative or cautionary gloss, Dryden capitalizes on its drama. It is therefore not surprising that Dryden's depiction of Eve is the source of the problem for critics of *The State of Innocence*.

Anne Ferry, for example, notes the outrageous aspects of Dryden's transformation of Milton's Eve into a Restoration coquette and the Edenic lovers into the witty couple of the Restoration stage.[16] Indeed, Dryden's Eve asserts that Adam "long should beg, I long deny" (XII: 112). To object to Dryden's Eve, however, is to object to his choice to dramatize the epic without acknowledging the drama in Milton's own text – to display, in other words, an unacknowledged anti-theatricality; it is also not to see Dryden grappling with the literary and political import of Milton's self-presentation. The dismissal of Dryden's opera thus ironically registers the process by which Dryden enables a "literary" Milton. The objection to Dryden's dramatization of Milton's potentially and finally anti-dramatic Eve obscures the fact that it is precisely by dramatizing her (and in doing so, flying in the face of Milton's discomfort with her theatricality) that Dryden finds the grounds on which to separate Milton's literary authority from his political and theological positions. Indeed, Dryden's theatricalization of Milton's Eve is symptomatic of his making the theatre central to his critical enterprise, which we have seen in operation in his production of Jonson as a national classic in the *Essay of Dramatick Poesy* and his ventriloquism of Shakespeare's ghost in the prologue to his version of *Troilus and Cressida*. The ways in which our literary Milton derives from Dryden's critical vocabulary measures the extent to which our practice has been shaped by his.

Nathaniel Lee, Dryden's sometime collaborator, wrote an unusual prefatory poem for *The State of Innocence* in which he praises Dryden for his treatment of Eve. Lee depicts Dryden turning Eve into a courtly lady of fashion, a view that is consonant with his presentation of the differences between Milton and Dryden as differences of fashion. Whereas Milton

> [f]irst beheld the beauteous rustic maid,
> And to a place of strength the prize convey'd:
> You took her thence; to court this virgin brought,
> Drest her in gems, new weaved her hard-spun thought,
> And softest language sweetest manners taught.[17]

Lee's poem treats Milton and Dryden as belonging to different locales – the rustic landscape and the fashionable court, respectively. The poem, which appeared in 1677, three years after Milton had died, also provides a temporal gloss for the spatial description of difference that contributes to the sense that the poets belong to different ages. Lee treats Dryden's use of ornament as an indication of the gap between poets by representing it as a matter of fashion as well as technology:

> To the dead bard your fame a little owes,
> For Milton did the wealthy mine disclose,
> And rudely cast what you could well dispose:
> He roughly drew, on an old-fashioned ground,
> A chaos; for no perfect world was found,
> Till through the heap your mighty genius shined:
> He was the golden ore which you refined. (v: 17)

According to Lee, the difference between Milton and Dryden is that Milton has found the raw material, but Dryden has refined it and thereby increased its value. Refining Milton's "golden ore," according to Lee, has given Dryden the means to ornament Milton's "rustic" Eve in courtly, indeed royalist, garb. Lee implies that, unlike Dryden, Milton has access to the processes neither of dressing up the rustic maid in gems, nor of refining ore into bullion. In the "Defense of the Epilogue," the appendix to *The Conquest of Granada* (1672), Dryden associates the technology of mining with the minting of currency, which he then presents as an analogy for the linguistic improvement of rhyme. In that essay, in order to assert that present poets improve the value of past poetry, he calls two current poetic activities, using rhyme and inventing new words, "refinement." Indeed, as we have seen in Dryden's "Defense of the Epilogue," "refinement" has as its social referent the conversation at the court of Charles II. Praising Dryden for "refining" Milton's ore, Lee applies a crucial term from Dryden's critical vocabulary to his poetry; he praises Dryden for grafting Milton onto a royalist context.[18]

Lee is not the only one who uses "fashion" to describe the differences between Dryden and Milton. While he might seem to be using an inadequately serious term to twentieth-century ears for discussing either political beliefs or literary authority, Andrew Marvell also uses "fashion" to distinguish between Milton and Dryden in his poem "On Mr. Milton's 'Paradise Lost'" that prefaces the 1674 edition. In that poem, Marvell describes Dryden's use of rhyme with the word "tag," a term that refers to the metal stays used for clothing. For Marvell, the difference between Dryden and Milton is the difference between the alluring town fashion-plate, or modish rhyming poet, and the substantive, transcendent, sublime Milton:

> Well mightst thou scorn thy Readers to allure
> With tinkling Rime, of thy own sense secure;
> While the Town-Bayes writes all the while and spells,
> And like a Pack-horse tires without his Bells:
> Their Fancies like our Bushy-points appear,
> The poets tag them, we for fashion wear.
> I too transported by the Mode offend,
> And while I meant to Praise thee must Commend.
> Thy Verse created like thy Theme sublime,
> In Number, Weight, and Measure, needs not Rime.[19]
>   (45–54)

Implying that political differences can be reduced to matters of fashion, Marvell nevertheless writes his own poem in rhyme – he himself is "too transported by the Mode." His self-inclusion in the camp of the fashion-conscious contributes to the sense that Milton is exceptional; in not "needing" rhyme, his poem stands beyond fashion in a sublime and timeless realm.[20] Lee and Marvell each depict political affiliation as the choice of articles of dress. "Fashion" thus supplies its own temporal scheme and thereby encodes the issues of evaluation and status within literary history. A sort of aesthetic Act of Oblivion, fashion neutralizes political differences by relocating them in a discussion of aesthetic concerns where preference (as one expression of affiliation) is justified by currency or the mode as opposed to, for example, priority or the tradition.

Fashion provides Restoration writers with a vocabulary that veils politics with aesthetics and posits both as subject to the forces of historical change. From this point of view, it is significant that in responding to Milton's imbrication of theology and politics with literary matters, Dryden takes his cues from Milton's self-presentation as old-fashioned. Some of the minor substantive changes Dryden makes to *Paradise Lost* attest to the pains he takes to update and correct Milton's politics, making evident the ways in which his separation of Milton's literary achievement from his theological and political commitments is nonetheless marked by Dryden's own, very different, political beliefs. Nevertheless, at the level of content, as well as that of form and genre, Dryden responds to Milton's self-presentation.

In Act I, Dryden shows the fallen devils in a council that is not a parliament but a cabal. Instead of Milton's parliamentarian Satan who asks for volunteers to investigate God's project on earth and decides to go himself only when he gets no response (*PL*, 2: 365–455), Dryden presents a more obviously tyrannical Satan (called Lucifer) who insists that he is the only one in a position to go anyway. By means of a rhetorical question, Milton's Satan simultaneously draws attention to the rewards he considers his due for the risk he takes and manages to sound momentarily modest:

> Wherefore do I assume
> These Royalties, and not refuse to Reign,
> Refusing to accept as great a share
> Of hazard as of honor due alike
> To him who Reigns, and so much to him due
> Of hazard more, as he above the rest
> High honor'd sits?   (*PL*, 2: 450–57)

Equating refusing the risk with refusing to rule, Satan accepts both, but his question makes his ascent to power sound like a generous offer: he would take the risk and refuse to rule, or so he implies, except for the fact that God already receives so much honor for so little hazard that Satan ought to provide an alternative model, ruling by risk as well as by honor. Juggling the relations between risks and power, Satan's rhetorical feints exploit an obscure link that is nevertheless crystal clear to all of the devils in Dryden's council. They compete for the glory, each eager to assume the power they all take as automatically accruing to heroic behavior:

> BELIAL: Some one (but who dares that task undertake?)
>   Of this new Creature must discovery make...
> MOLOCH: This Glorious Enterprize – – (*Rising up.*)
> LUCIF: Rash Angel, stay; (*Rising, and laying his Sceptre on Moloch's head*)
>   That Palm is mine, which none shall take away...
>   Why am I rank'd in State above the rest,
>   If, while I stand of Sovereign Pow'r possest,
>   Another dares, in danger, farther go?
>   Kings are not made for ease, and Pageant-show.
>   Who would be Conquerour, must venture all:
>   He merits not to rise who dares not fall.   (XII: 103–4)

The ease with which Dryden's Lucifer refers to "kings" as the paradigm of power contrasts sharply with Milton's Satan's indirect critical gesture towards God as "him who reigns." Dryden's royalism informs his revision of Milton's Satan and his acceptance of monarchy as the model for divine rule.

In the stage directions of the opera, Dryden pushes his recharacterization of the devils a little further; his description of the dance, reminiscent of the anti-masque, at the end of Act I depicts the disappointments of thwarted cavalier ambitions:

Betwixt the first Act and the second, while the Chiefs sit in the Palace, may be expressed the Sports of the Devils: as Flights and Dancing in Grotesque Figures: And a Song, expressing the change of their condition; what they enjoy'd before, and how they fell bravely in Battel, having deserv'd Victory by their Valour; and what they would have done if they had Conquer'd. (XII: 104)

Milton's satire of Parliament in his version of the council in Hell depicts individual self-interestedness giving rise to factionalism not only in the "Stygian Council" but also in the devils' activities after it dissolves (*PL*, 2:506–629). Dryden's devils bring this representation up to date when they perform a comic dance "while the Chiefs [who] sit in the Palace" depict the formation of the privileged elite group within Parliament known as the Cabal. Milton had himself, however, presented his political beliefs as old-fashioned when, on the eve of the Restoration, in "The Readie and Easie Way" (1660), he explicitly took up "the language of the good old cause."[21] Identifying his interests in preventing the restoration of the monarchy with an opportunity almost self-consciously perceived as already lost, Milton could be said to invite Dryden's modernization, even though their attitudes towards the Restoration – and, indeed, their political ideologies more generally – differ so profoundly.[22]

As paradoxical as it might seem, it is Milton who presents himself as though he belonged to a former age. He does not, however, neutralize the political impact of being outmoded; rather, he uses it to bolster his authority. Indeed, he goes a long way towards facilitating the response that he is old-fashioned. In the note from "The Printer to the Reader" which prefaces the 1674 edition of *Paradise Lost*, Milton affiliates himself with Homer and Virgil, thereby defending his use of blank verse and making overtly political what must have been implicitly so in the 1667 edition:

The measure is English Heroic Verse without Rime, as that of Homer in Greek, and of Virgil in Latin; Rime being no necessary Adjunct or true Ornament of Poem or good Verse in longer Works especially, but the Invention of a barbarous Age, to set off wretched matter and lame Meter... This neglect then of Rime so little is to be taken for a defect, though it may seem so perhaps to vulgar Readers, that it is rather to be esteem'd an example set, the first in English, of ancient liberty recover'd to Heroic Poem from the troublesome and modern bondage of Riming. (*PL*, 210)

Probably in response to the controversy over rhyme in the 1660s, Milton construes blank verse as a mode of literary authority with explicitly political affiliations.[23] Indeed, Christopher Kendrick reads this passage as an indication that Milton locates his political intent necessarily at the level of form rather than at the level of narrative.[24] The reader is encouraged to see the choice of blank verse as an affirmation of political liberty to be associated with classical republicanism. For Dryden and his contemporaries, the old-fashioned quality of Milton's versification can easily and conveniently be made to stand for his old-fashioned revolutionary politics.

Milton's monolithic self-presentation of authority in *Paradise Lost*, perhaps best exemplified in the invocations, might seem to make his availability for Restoration rewriting unlikely, but it is precisely this feature that makes it imperative for Dryden to devise strategies for rewriting him. Where Milton represents himself as a monolithic authority in *Paradise Lost*, Dryden finds the convergence of political and literary authorities, a convergence he wants to separate into discrete strands. Milton's self-professed antiquity supplies Dryden with the leverage he needs to place him in the past. Just as he capitalizes on Milton's anti-theatricality by rewriting *Paradise Lost* as an opera, Dryden capitalizes on Milton's self-presentation as old-fashioned to change his blank verse into rhymed couplets. It is by means of the latter change that Dryden intervenes most directly in the dissemination of Milton's authority.

Dryden replaces Milton's conception of the form of heroic poetry with his own; he thereby simultaneously reconstitutes Milton's authorial self-presentation. Describing Dryden's heroic couplet, Richard Kroll proposes that it is a "symbolic argument [which] substitutes the normal behaviour of language as such – its intrinsic atomism and linearity – for aesthetic and political theses."[25] For Kroll, Dryden's heroic couplet imposes method on the reader's appropriation of meaning; moreover, Kroll represents this imposition of method as a neo-classical gesture, in which linguistic, cognitive and spiritual behaviors serve as metaphors for one another. Kroll finds this neo-classical method to be most conspicuously deployed by Milton himself in *Paradise Lost*. Curiously, he does not juxtapose Dryden to Milton. However, by turning Milton's blank verse into rhyme, Dryden redirects attention from the representation of the voice in Milton's poem to a focus on the rhyme-sounds. Rhyme allows Dryden to dismantle the closure that Milton presents, intervening in Milton's projection of his inspired voice into his text by emphasizing the phonetic materiality of the signifiers upon which rhyme relies. He can thus retain the poetic or figural aspect of Milton's power and discard the theological and political accompaniments to his brand of subjectivity.

A number of Milton critics emphasize the dependence of Milton's authority on the projection of his voice.[26] In *Areopagitica*, Milton presents his authority in the form of a printed speech that extends and distributes his voice, depicting it as something that emanates from him but that also has an existence independent of him; the claim that *Paradise Lost* is inspired repeats this presentation in the prophetic register.[27] Dryden's revisions of *Paradise Lost* address Milton's presentation of his own authority by combatting it; by explicitly contravening Milton and his putative intentions in *The State of Innocence*, Dryden makes them visible. The changes he makes to Milton's text retroactively create a "literary" Milton whose aesthetic value is available separately from his political or theological commitments. By discarding Milton's self-presentation of his own authority, Dryden makes available the notion that the author's authority is "literary" rather than political or theological; in his criticism, this notion of "literary authority" is then used to efface the political basis for his own "literary" choices.

CRITICAL IDENTIFICATION

"The Author's Apology for Heroic Poetry and Poetic Licence" is more known as the place where Dryden offers his famous definition of wit, "the propriety of Thoughts and Words" (XII: 97), than it is treated as an important critical essay in its own right. Wit and taste come to constitute the currency of eighteenth-century critical discourse, and, in this essay, Dryden uses them to ground a distinction between acceptable and unacceptable critical practice. It would be an overstatement to claim that the purpose of this essay is to define criticism; he does so only incidentally and in a scattershot fashion. His elucidation of the characteristics of criticism, however, exhibits the same features as his rewriting of *Paradise Lost*: the use of theatrical forms to distinguish literary from political matters.

In "The Author's Apology," Dryden introduces a practice of critical identification, which he extends in his subsequent writings on Milton, that permits the figure of the poet to emerge independently from the problematic political or theological commitments of the person whom he criticizes. Dryden uses this mode of identification to ground "proper" critical practice. The notion that criticism depends upon an identification with the author whom one criticizes both promotes the fantasy of an autonomous aesthetic sphere whose boundaries are defined in the psychological or psychoanalytic vocabulary of intra-poetic relations and, at the same time, displays the specific social (and gendered) location of the critic. Dryden repeatedly takes note of Milton's status as a man, both as a biographical entity – in Dryden's hands, a poet rather than a political figure – and as an instance of masculinity. Critical identification, as I show, relies on the modes of dramatizing and disciplining masculine identification and homosocial desire found in the Restoration comedies of manners. Dryden's use of critical identification – informed as it is by the definitions of wit and taste – to usher the poet into critical discourse suggests that any aesthetic vocabulary will retain the imprint of social relations even after the aesthetic has come to be divorced from concerns with politics, religion or status.

In "The Author's Apology," Dryden offers a series of oppositions between "hypercritics," "false critics" and "laughers," on the one hand, and (implicitly) true critics and "all reasonable men," on the other, in order to establish the realm of acceptable critical practice, and, with it, acceptable heroic poetry, if only by defining and excluding the unacceptable. Dryden distinguishes the marks of the true critic, in large part, on the basis of the literary authority he both perceives in and establishes for Milton by having dramatized his epic. The exclusionary logic of definition with which he empowers wit and taste in the essay derives its force from the ethos of Restoration comedy, which is equally intent on drawing a magic circle around those who have wit and taste to exclude those who do not.

As Dryden makes clear in this essay, not everyone can be a critic. Moreover, many people do not understand the nature of criticism. Dryden undertakes "to tell them that they wholly mistake the Nature of Criticism who think its business is principally to find fault" (XII: 87) but the endorsement of what one likes seems to be more complicated. As we might expect from Dryden's other critical writings, his distinction between "hypercritics," or "laughers," and true critics is drawn as if its force lay in such cultural categories as nationalism and learnedness; indeed, such social criteria are an important aspect of Dryden's critical legacy. However, the language of this essay makes it evident that the fundamental power to distinguish between true and false critics derives from the desire for critical identification with the author one criticizes.

When he outlines the function of the true critic, he uses metaphors of food and consumption; "taste" is not yet a dead metaphor for Dryden. The metaphorics of food accompany Dryden's grounding of true criticism in "wit," at the same time as they raise the uncomfortable possibility that it may not be possible to reach consensus about either wit or taste.[28] As far as their opinion of heroic poetry goes, the "hypercritiques of English poetry" differ from the critics of antiquity, from the international neo-classicists of Italy and France, "indeed, from the general taste and approbation of all Ages" (XII: 88). Dryden directs his antagonism towards these Englishmen because their dislike for heroic models involves excluding English literature from the international arena and compromising English access to a classical tradition. "Hypercritiques" do not recognize that English literature has produced a heroic poem worthy of comparison with Homer, Virgil and Tasso – that is, Milton's *Paradise Lost*. This failure to adopt the standards shared by modern Italian and French critics and ancient Greek and Latin critics signals a failure of national awareness. In contrast, however, to the dictatorial hypercritic who (wrongly) hates heroic poetry, Dryden enjoins his reader not to increase his national pride but to cultivate his manners: to "let every man enjoy his taste... Let them please their appetite in eating what they like; but let them not force their dish on all at the Table" (XII: 89).

The distinction between "laughers" and critics is also sustained by metaphors of food. Dryden refines his understanding of what a critic does by examining an attack that "laughers" have made on his own text. He quotes the four lines of *The State of Innocence* that "have been sufficiently canvassed by my well-natured censors":

> Seraph and Cherub, careless of their charge,
> And wanton, in full ease now live at large:
> Unguarded leave the passes of the Sky;
> And all dissolv'd in Hallellujahs lye.

Then he proceeds: "I have heard (sayes one of them) of Anchove's dissolv'd in Sauce; but never of an Angel in Hallelujahs. A mighty Wittycism, (if you will pardon a new word!) but there is some difference between a Laugher and a Critique. He might have Burlesqu'd Virgil too, from whom I took the image" (XII: 95). What distinguishes the "laugher" from the critic is the former's ignorance – his failure to recognize the allusion to Virgil. Dryden offers to end the dispute over heroic poetry in a way that reveals the rationale behind his treatment of criticism as an almost literal issue of taste:

If our Critiques will joyn issue on this Definition, that we may *convenire in aliquo tertio*; if they will take it as a granted Principle, 'twill be easie to put an end to this dispute: No man will disagree from anothers judgement, concerning the dignity of Style, in Heroique Poetry: but all reasonable Men will conclude it necessary, that sublime Subjects ought to be adorn'd with the sublimest, and (consequently often) with the most figurative expressions. (XII: 97)[29]

The definition of wit that Dryden enjoins critics to agree on, "the propriety of Thoughts and Words" (XII: 97), is offered in pointed contrast to the new term, "Wittycism," a distinction often lost in modern English. Dryden offers the definition of true wit not only to consolidate the status of heroic poetry, but also to exemplify the practice of the true critic. What really makes the false critic false is not only his missing the reference to Virgil – he could, after all, pick it up and still make the joke about anchovies – but also his admiration for witticism rather than wit, the idea that he would want to make a joke of Virgil. In what comes to be criticism's paradigmatic mode of address, Dryden appeals to "all reasonable men" to agree to his definition of wit because this agreement would identify them as true critics. If, however, it would seem possible to recognize true wit as easily as one recognizes Virgil, it turns out that learnedness is, like nationalism, important but secondary to this process; the critic's homosocial desire to identify with the author he criticizes enables the recognition of true wit.

In her account of *The Country Wife*, a play whose author Dryden praises in "The Author's Apology,"[30] Eve Kosofsky Sedgwick defines wit in a manner that shows what underwrites Dryden's reliance on it when he establishes the boundaries of critical practice: "Wit [is] a seventeenth-century name for the circulable social solvent, the sign that both represented political power in the male-homosocial framework and could through sublimation (through shedding its relation to a material signified) come to be a supposedly classless commodity in its own right."[31] Sedgwick delineates the possibility that "a share of the prestige that belongs to the economic and political position [of Horner, Dorilant and Harcourt] can also be achieved by men [like Sparkish] who cultivate the signifier 'wit' even in the absence of its economic and political grounding" (63). Whereas the availability of prestige on the basis of wit works in Dryden's interest, he also wants to dissociate himself from the Sparkishes, or, as he calls them, the hypercritics – those overinvested in the forms of fashion. By distinguishing wit from witticism, and, on that basis, distinguishing good from bad criticism, Dryden gives critical and social grounding to what might otherwise be free-floating; he associates the prestige of wit with literary judgment and attempts to limit it to *good* literary judgment.

Adopting Dryden's distinctions among "laughers," "hypercritics" and true critics in 1693, John Dennis also adopted the dramatic dialogue as a form for criticism, in order to vindicate Dryden (and Shakespeare) from the too strict neo-classicism of Thomas Rymer. Interestingly, "The Impartial Critic" seeks to delimit the role of "wit" in critical discourse, condemning Rymer's "laughing" style and calling for a "Didactick Stile," "fit for instruction, [which] must be necessarily on that account, pure, perspicuous, succinct, unaffected and grave."[32] As such debates among Dryden, Rymer and Dennis attest, however, reason, or even definition, like matters of taste, does not produce consensus. The conclusion of "The Author's Apology" is belied by one of the examples ostensibly produced in its service: the subject upon which "all reasonable men" supposedly agree, that is, the appropriateness of sublime and figurative language to heroic poetry, is best illustrated, paradoxically, by the failure of agreement in the case of Dryden's dissolving angels.

As a result, when Dryden contrasts the "malicious and unmanly" snarlings of false critics to a Longinian tolerance for small errors in a sublime poem, he defines a stronger relation between the critic and the poet, one that displays the male-homosocial interactions Sedgwick argues are sublimated in wit in order to conjoin good judgment to critical expertise. Dryden paraphrases Longinus in order to make the claim that criticizing an author expresses the desire to be him:

> I could, sayes my Author, find out some blemishes in Homer: and am perhaps, as naturally inclin'd to be disgusted at a fault as another Man: But, after all, to speak impartially, his failings are such, as are only marks of humane frailty: they are little Mistakes, or rather Negligences, which have escap'd his pen in the fervor of his writing; the sublimity of his spirit carries it with me against his carelessness: And though Apollonius his Argonautes, and Theocritus his Eidullia, are more free from Errors, *there is not any Man of so false a judgment who would choose rather to have been Apollonius or Theocritus, than Homer*. (XII: 88, my emphasis)[33]

The ultimate critical authority in "The Author's Apology" comes from Dryden's desire *to be* the poet whom he criticizes. Although he finds it easier to express the desire to be Homer than to be Milton, we should see these acts of critical identification, in conjunction with his efforts to separate literary from political and theological matters in rewriting *Paradise Lost*, as constituting a set of critical terms that are recognizably "literary."

In his account of Dryden's later career, David Bywaters proposes that his dislocation from the centers of power after the Glorious Revolution, when his Catholicism and his loyalty to James marginalized him politically, did not prompt him to develop a poetics of retirement. Instead, Bywaters argues, Dryden finds new strategies for sustaining his cultural authority, to which his literary successes of the 1690s attest; the main one is his elevation of the literary over the political and theological. In both the poetry and various letters of dedication, Dryden suggests that shared literary judgment cements bonds between poet and patron, overcoming their political and religious differences. Bywaters proceeds to give a reading of Dryden's late works that is sensitively attuned to their sustained, though buried, political valences. However, more interesting for my purposes is his claim that Dryden bolsters his own position as poet by separating the poet from the man.[34] Whereas Bywaters persuasively establishes the increased importance of this separation to Dryden in his late works, I believe that the basis of this separation can be found earlier on in his career, particularly in such critical writings as the preface to *The State of Innocence*.

The implications of this understanding of criticism may help us to negotiate the complexities of Dryden's career, but, I would argue, they are even more far-reaching. Criticism understood to be based on a desire to identify with the writer in question conjures the category of the "author" into being; under the rubric of "reason" it specifies a voluntarism that is nevertheless prescribed in certain directions – who would not choose to be Homer? Such an appeal to "reason" may fail to produce consensus, but the pressures of a regulatory identification then suture the gaps within an emergent sphere of discourse – an increasingly autonomous aesthetic domain.[35] The regulatory imaginative identification is the signal rhetorical gesture for the critic as social arbiter, the direction in which Addison takes criticism in Dryden's wake.[36]

The consequences of critical identification for the constitutive role of masculinity within critical practice become more prominent in Dryden's later treatments of Milton. In 1693, in "The Discourse Concerning Satire," Dryden assesses Milton's use of blank verse:

Neither will I justify Milton for his blank verse ... for whatever causes he alleges for the abolishing of rhyme (which I have not now the leisure to examine), his own particular reason is plainly this, that rhyme was not his talent; he neither had the ease of doing it, nor the graces of it; which is manifest in his juvenilia, or verse written in his youth, where his rhyme is always constrained and forced, and hardly comes from him, at an age when the soul is most pliant, and the passion of love makes almost every man a rhymer, tho' not a poet.[37]

Dryden acknowledges Milton's poetic gifts grudgingly in this passage, focusing on the importance of rhyme even though it postdates his renunciation of rhymed couplets as his preferred dramatic form.[38] Significantly, instead of explaining why Milton does not rhyme by referring to the reasons he thinks Milton has himself supplied in the Printer's Note, Dryden presents Milton's not rhyming because he is unlike "almost every man." Replacing the Printer's Note, which also reflects Milton's political beliefs, by a statement about his exceptional status as a man, Dryden effaces political motive, replacing it with a critical evaluation that works as an explanation: Milton lacks "talent." Dryden attacks Milton's self-conscious self-presentation as a poet, especially in the juvenilia, and assumes that his critical view of Milton will be the privileged one.[39] Replacing the Milton of problematic theological and political commitments with a sketch of his literary development as a poet, Dryden turns the religious overtones of the term "talent," which Milton would have embraced, against him. Secularizing the term "talent," mobilizing only its aesthetic sense, Dryden reroutes Milton's authority, directing it, by means of his critical characterization of him, towards an increasingly autonomous aesthetic domain.

When Dryden describes Milton's exceptional status – he is unlike "almost every man" – he again modulates the homosocial desire for critical identification with a literary "author" rather than a political or theological agent. We can trace the development of this gesture in another of his rather infrequent treatments of Milton which occurs between "The Author's Apology" (1677) and "The Discourse Concerning Satire" (1693), in *The Preface to the Sylvae* (1685):

> Imitation is a nice point, and there are few poets who deserve to be models in all they write. Milton's *Paradise Lost* is admirable; but am I therefore bound to maintain that there are no flats amongst his elevations, when 'tis evident he creeps along sometimes for above an hundred lines together? Cannot I admire the height of his invention, and the strength of his expression, without defending his antiquated words and the perpetual harshness of their sound? 'Tis as much commendation as a man can bear to own him excellent; all beyond it is idolatry. (Watson, *Of Dramatic Poesy*, II: 32)

Here the literary criteria of excellence and worthiness of imitation are put in direct proportion to what a man can bear, but, significantly, it is Dryden's manly capacities that are represented as strained. The defensive naming of what is beyond a certain measure of commendation of Milton as "idolatry" is strangely appropriate to Dryden's project of divorcing a literary Milton from his theological and political beliefs. It is also noteworthy, however, that the vocabulary registering the stress of the efforts Dryden expends in maintaining the gap between the biographical entity (the man) and the poet (the author) is the gendered one of manliness.

I emphasize Dryden's repeated concern with the relation between the biographical entity – the man and his masculinity – and such literary activities as rhyming or commendation at the transitional point between the homosocial desire for critical identification of the "Author's Apology" and the construction of the category of aesthetic talent of 1693, in order to propose that Dryden's reliance on wit and taste to define the practice of the critic registers the sublimation of homosocial relations that Sedgwick describes in her discussion of "wit." The pervasive insistence in the Restoration comedies of manners on sketching a continuum of masculine behaviors ranging from the fops and foolish would-be wits to the accomplished witty rakes, using the terms of taste, fashion and talent to do so, provide, I would suggest, the best context in which to see Dryden's delimitation of a proper critical practice through his theatricalization of Milton.

If my suggestion that critical identification is homosocial, even though it evacuates the biographical man and replaces him with a literary author, seems counter-intuitive, this is because of the inextricability acquired by the-man-and-his-works in later eighteenth-century biographical criticism. In Dryden's hands, the desire to be the author one criticizes or rewrites involves substituting the attributes of the biographical entity, here Milton, by literary criteria of "talent" or "worth," substitutions enabled by his dramatic rewriting of Milton's poem, which separates his literary achievement from his amalgamated theological-political-literary authority. The repeated concern with Milton as a man demonstrates that Dryden manipulates the gender category to address the possibility that homosocial desire might be desublimated, containing it within an aesthetic discourse increasingly distinguished, but not ultimately separable, from politics. Dryden's use of gender categories to effect the firmer delimitation of a proper critical sphere becomes more prominent in his rewritings of Shakespeare; I explore the crucial implications his treatment of gender has for critical practice in the next chapter.

The series of revaluations of heroic poetry not only shapes Dryden's critical career but also influences the later reception of Milton, the "literary" lion of English letters. The clearest expression of the way literary concerns displace political motivations, taking them up instead as questions of genre, is fittingly also Dryden's last reference to Milton. In 1697, in the "Dedication of the Aeneis," Dryden sets the tone for the Romantic reception of Milton by taking the devil as the hero of *Paradise Lost*. In a discussion comparing classical and modern epics, Dryden notices:

Spenser has a better plea for [the inclusion of] his *Fairie Queen*, [in the list of great epics] had his action been finished, or had been one. And Milton, if the devil had not been his hero, instead of Adam; if the giant had not foiled the knight, and driven him out of his stronghold, to wander through the world with his lady errant; and if there had not been more machining persons than humans in his poem. (Watson, *Of Dramatic Poesy*, II: 233)

Dryden here distorts Milton with the aim of bringing *Paradise Lost* into a tradition of English poetry initiated by *The Fairie Queene*. Using the terms of romance to characterize the plot, the most striking of which is the description of Eve as "lady errant," can be seen as the residual effect of having conceived of *Paradise Lost* as a heroic play.

As Dryden defines it theoretically in "The Author's Apology" and practically in *The State of Innocence*, criticism is an identification in which one has to efface the historical individual in order to make an "author" – a figure with whom one can identify in order to be a critic. The text thus becomes a projection of an author and not a man, enabling the very rewritings that constitute criticism, the rewritings that place the text firmly in the realm of the literary by removing it and its author from any recognizable non-literary context. Realizing the instability of any appeal to wit or taste, Dryden supplements the discourse of "all reasonable men" by imaginative identifications that look voluntary but are regulatory in order to ground "true" criticism. As we will see in the following chapter, he thus introduces into critical practice a forceful evaluative vocabulary whose purpose is to guide those identifications, and does so by using the terms of political and gender ideologies.

The imaginary identification, the desire to be the writer whom one criticizes, is founded on an impulse to substitute oneself for that author, even if it means obliterating the historical man. Rewriting *Paradise Lost* counter to Milton's beliefs and aesthetic choices simultaneously accomplishes the substitution and makes separately available as critical categories the text and the author. Dryden's criticism promotes the place of Milton in English literary history in terms which describe a domain that increasingly comes to be considered autonomous and "literary."

CHAPTER 3

Imitating Shakespeare: gender and criticism

Declaring his love for Shakespeare in the *Essay of Dramatick Poesy*, Dryden praises him as England's Homer (XVII: 58); rewriting *Antony and Cleopatra*, he describes himself in the preface to *All for Love* (1678) as imitating the "Divine Shakespeare" (XIII: 18); and he not only lauds Shakespeare for his "Universal mind" in the "Grounds of Criticism in Tragedy," the essay that prefaces his version of *Troilus and Cressida* (1679), but he also claims that it is by enquiring "how far we ought to imitate" Shakespeare that he will disclose the grounds of criticism that essay's title promises (XIII: 229). Imitating Shakespeare offers Dryden the opportunity to articulate criticism as a vocation in the preface to *All for Love*; that preface is also the place where Dryden demonstrates a critical impartiality which underwrites his claims that criticism speaks to "all reasonable men" (XIII: 11). The first is a feature, and the second, a mode of address paradigmatic of later criticism. Dryden's most longstanding critical production, Shakespeare's "Universal Mind," allows him to cast the critical enterprise, derived from imitating Shakespeare, in philosophical terms.

Indeed, from Samuel Johnson to Gary Taylor, critics find in Dryden's extravagant appreciation of Shakespeare grounds for recognizing Dryden as an important critical predecessor. Johnson goes so far as to claim, in his *Life of Dryden*, that "[N]othing can be added" to Dryden's account of Shakespeare in the *Essay of Dramatick Poesy* by the subsequent critics whose practice he inaugurates.[1] In claiming Dryden as their progenitor, however, and affiliating themselves with Shakespeare through Dryden's ostensibly filial relation to him, these critics misrecognize Dryden's formation of a literary genealogy. For example, for Taylor, Dryden's filial relation to Shakespeare explains his ambivalence:

Some readers have concluded that Dryden's criticisms were conventional but his praise sincere; others decide that his praise was hypocritical and his contempt genuine. I suspect instead that a real admiration cohabited with a real contempt, and that the two attitudes tortured each other for the length of Dryden's life. In

1668 Dryden could say "I love Shakespeare" and mean it – in the same way that an adolescent can honestly abstractly say, "I love my parents" while in practice hating them much of the time. It was Davenant who liked to believe and let others believe that he was Shakespeare's bastard, but it was Dryden who acted like a son – or, rather, an orphan – a posthumous child of uncertain paternity constantly measuring himself against the image of his dead father, testing his legitimacy by his success, finding himself wanting, professing "respect" while chafing for some form of independence, hating what he loved, and hating himself for hating it.[2]

But Dryden's literary genealogy does not fully conform to such familiar oedipal configurations. As I show by taking up the connections Dryden himself draws between imitating Shakespeare and establishing the "grounds" of criticism, his transformations of Shakespeare's plays give a gendered structure both to Shakespeare's universality and to the critical neutrality to which subsequent critics have laid claim. In the first part of this chapter, I show how the domestication and sentimentalization of Shakespeare in *All for Love* contribute to the critical vocation Dryden articulates in that play's preface and to his feminization of literary judgment in its epilogue. In the second part, I analyze the ostensibly disembodying process of abstraction out of which Shakespeare's universality is produced, which derives from an extended comparison of Shakespeare with a feminized Fletcher; I also consider the ways Shakespeare's universality is inflected by Dryden's dramatization of the reversability of gendered attributes in his version of *Troilus and Cressida*.

By reading the ways Dryden treats Shakespeare across his critical and dramatic writings, I want to highlight the performativity of Dryden's critical writing in order to refine our sense of the place Dryden carves out for criticism's accomplishment. By calling into question the filial, oedipal and normatively masculinist terms which have been used to describe Dryden's relation to Shakespeare – terms which both the literary critical tradition and its histories have embraced – I find more precise ways to characterize the social and sexual aspects of literary genealogy that are derived from and embedded in Dryden. This characterization gives greater social and historical specificity to the later seventeenth-century critic's location between the court and the theatre. The domestic organization of the literary tradition that Dryden describes as an inheritance whose transmission is guaranteed by criticism forms a literary genealogy that provided women writers of the generation following Dryden an access to both the literary tradition and the critical practice it establishes.

These aspects of literary criticism have not yet been factored into its history.

As terms of literary evaluation, 'masculine' and 'feminine' have a long history in English criticism.[3] They are prominent in Dryden's critical enterprise, particularly so, I would argue, in his critical treatments of Shakespeare, for reasons which will become clear in the analysis that follows. Much of my sense of these terms' later seventeenth-century meanings, and their contributions to Dryden's consolidation of a native literary tradition that is as accessible to women critics as it is to their male counterparts, is informed by the body of recent scholarship devoted to the analysis of the varying historical meanings and status of gender.

Thomas Laqueur argues that the later seventeenth century witnessed a shift in the biological understandings of gender difference, claiming that an "opposite" sex model replaced the familiar one-sex model that had dominated understandings of biological difference.[4] Within the hierarchical model, gender is a relatively disembodied characteristic; it describes behavior rather than biology, permitting a certain amount of gender reversibility. Laqueur's formulation is suggestive because it enables an understanding of how gender can be flexible or mobile – men can be feminine when, for example, they weep, and women can be masculine when they behave heroically. What Laqueur does not fully describe, however, are the implications of the fact that such reversibility is not symmetrical: the man who cries is not valued equally with the woman who behaves heroically. Within the oppositional model, gender was increasingly understood to be an embodied state, and reversibility, when it occurred, came to signal something more problematic: by the middle of the eighteenth century, as Kristina Straub and others have shown, such reversibility came to be understood as perversion.[5]

Jonathan Goldberg has offered an important caveat to Laqueur, observing that "the history of a biological understanding of gendered bodies is [not] the same thing as a history of gender."[6] Referring to other definitional and institutional forms of gender, and thus reading gender as one social category among others, Michael McKeon offers a synoptic view of the development of gender difference on a patriarchal, rather than "patriarchalist," model which arises out of the seventeenth-century crises of succession. In "Historicizing Patriarchy," McKeon assembles later seventeenth-century political and legal writings about succession, marshalls evidence of socio-economic reorganization, and builds on materials gathered by historians of sexuality, including Laqueur, to argue that "the modern form of patriarchy depends upon the structural separation of the genders."[7] McKeon argues – rightly, in my view – that modern masculinity gets defined out of the interstices of femininity and effeminacy. Neatly encapsulating the researches of Alan Bray, Randolph Trumbach, Kristina Straub and others into a philology of "effeminacy," McKeon proposes that:

In the seventeenth century, "effeminate" referred to two distinct kinds of sexual overindulgence both of which were marked by male ingratiation with the female: it referred to men who *are like* women (in the sense of sodomitical transvestism), and to men who *like* women (in the sense of being sexually obsessed with them). By the middle of the eighteenth century, an adult effeminate man was likely to be taken only in the former sense, as an exclusive sodomite or molly. The word "effeminacy" had ceased by then to be able to bear both senses because effeminacy was held to signify a desire to emulate women that was plainly incompatible with sexual desire for them. (308)

By situating the history of the term "effeminate" in relation to the decline of aristocratic ideology, McKeon paves the way for an integration of the historicized terms of gender with other terms of analysis for seventeenth-century ideological change.

Dryden offers an interesting testing ground for the identification of the later seventeenth century as the switch-point in competing understandings of gender. Not only does he use gendered terms for literary evaluation in his critical writing, but his plays are also full of instances of troubling gender reversals that express the crisis Laqueur describes. For every time Dryden uses gendered terms that express a hierarchical relation, there is another instance in which such terms are relatively embodied, registering both the crisis in the hierarchical understanding and the emergence of an oppositional relation. In some instances, both models are present, even though they potentially contradict each other. The question is, how to read such seemingly paradoxical moments?

Using Laqueur to read Milton, John Guillory proposes that the references in *Paradise Lost* to the gender of the heavenly bodies are not metaphorical applications of the signs of gender to ungendered bodies but are expressions of a hierarchical relation that Milton expects to find both in nature and in the relations between the sexes.[8] For Guillory, Milton's use of gendered terms registers a moment of crisis in this hierarchy, a crisis reflected in changing understandings of the relations between the sexes. Like Milton's, Dryden's references to the gender of nonbiological matters are not metaphorical applications of the signs of gender. While for Milton, however, gendered terms are placeholders expressing nostalgia for the stability of the hierarchical relation, for Dryden and his immediate successors, hierarchical relations are increasingly under pressure and not necessarily guarantors of stability, and gender becomes increasingly an embodied sign of human sexuality.[9] As we have seen, although Dryden and Milton are contemporaries, Dryden nevertheless presents himself self-consciously as the new man to Milton's old-fashionedness. Dryden's interest in the embodiment of gender might be seen as an expression of this modernity. His use of 'masculine' and 'feminine' as terms to describe literary matters still elicits and expresses approval and disapproval respectively, a residual effect of the terms' expression of the hierarchical arrangement, but this use differs from Milton's desire for a stable hierarchy of relations. The literary content Dryden gives the terms reflects their reference to what are coming to be understood as incommensurable domains. Nowhere is this more clear than in Dryden's treatments of Shakespeare in *All for Love* and *Troilus and Cressida*.

But Dryden's gendered representations of Shakespeare are, perhaps, best approached by turning first to Dryden's earliest rewriting of Shakespeare. In the prologue to his collaboration with Sir William Davenant on *The Tempest: or the Enchanted Isle* (performed 1667, published 1669), Dryden's representation of Shakespeare reveals a complex imbrication of his relation to the literary past and his own theatrical practices with questions of gender. Dryden's strategic use of gender – it is both self-promoting and deferential, both to Shakespeare and to his royal patron – offers a pretext for his more complicated use of gender in his later treatments of Shakespeare and his articulation in them of a social space for criticism between the theatre and the court.

In this early prologue, Dryden exploits and reverses the set of connections between theatricality and gender on Shakespeare's stage. Whereas on the Renaissance stage, boy actors took women's parts, on the Restoration stage, actresses, new to that medium, often took male parts.[10] In their *Tempest*, Dryden and Davenant employ this casting practice for a character of their own invention, Prospero's adopted son, Hippolito. The prologue turns on this reverse casting-practice, capitalizing on it in its final lines to offer the actress, who has played the role of Hippolito, as a sexual gift to the King. This final turn, however, follows from a series of equally astonishing reversals: the prologue begins with Dryden's confidently asserting Shakespeare's immortality and ends with his apologizing for him. Shakespeare's exceptional status makes him the site of contradictions, and the prologue is structured by paradox giving way to paradox as each proves inadequate to Dryden's critical task.

Right from the start, Dryden tries to capture Shakespeare's unusual state of being: as something between alive and dead, Shakespeare is old dust out of which new things nevertheless grow. Almost immediately, however, this paradox is replaced by another: Shakespeare can teach others even though he was never taught himself. The prologue moves from one couplet to the next, searching for the paradox that best conveys Shakespeare's powers. This series is halted, however, when Dryden finds that Shakespeare's regenerative powers are better analogized to royal rather than to natural or botanical powers:

> As when a Tree's cut down the secret root
> Lives under ground, and thence new Branches shoot;
> So, from old Shakespear's honour'd dust, this day
> Springs up and buds a new reviving Play:
> Shakespeare, who (taught by none) did first impart
> To Fletcher Wit, to labouring Johnson Art.
> He Monarch-like gave those his subject law,
> And is that Nature which they paint and draw.[11]

Shakespeare's "Monarch-like" existence may be short-lived in the prologue, but, while the simile stands, it bridges royal power and nature: giving laws to subjects is like giving (natural) subjects to the artist. So fit a ruler is Shakespeare that his works become the nature that dictates Fletcher's and Jonson's art: if Jonson and Fletcher "have since outwrit all other men, / 'Tis with the drops which fell from Shakespear's Pen" (x: 6).

In order to make possible an imitation of Shakespeare that would approach the stature of his achievement as both royal and natural, Dryden qualifies the analogy between Shakespeare and the king. In fact, the prologue undergoes a reversal from being in praise of Shakespeare insofar as he resembles the king, to being apologetic to the king on his behalf. The successive small-scale reversals that have structured the prologue to this point are recapitulated on a larger scale by the transformation of praise into apology:

> I must confess 'twas bold, nor would you now
> That liberty to vulgar Wits allow
> Which works by Magick supernatural things:
> But Shakespear's pow'r is sacred as a King's.
> Those Legends from old Priest-hood were receiv'd,
> And he then writ, as people then believ'd.
> But, if for Shakespear we your grace implore,
> We for our Theatre shall want it more. (x: 6)

Shakespeare cannot be "monarch-like" in the presence of Charles II. As royal analogy turns into royal address, the grace that Dryden implores for Shakespeare and for his own play is that of His Grace Charles II, in front of whom the play was performed in November 1667.[12] The shift in modes of address, or, more accurately, the late appearance in the poem of the specific royal "you" to which it is addressed, reverses the position of Shakespeare from that of a writer who is the immortal king of literature into that of a writer who needs to be defended, excused – indeed, who needs to be rewritten.

Dryden complicates this otherwise familiar justification for the improvement present writers make on past texts by invoking His Grace's grace for his rewriting. Indeed, he needs it more than Shakespeare does, and the cause is the problematic "transformation" Dryden works in place of the now incredible and discredited magic of Shakespeare:

> But, if for Shakespear we your grace implore,
> We for our Theatre shall want it more:
> Who by our dearth of Youths are forc'd t'employ
> One of our Women to present a Boy.
> And that's a transformation you will say
> Exceeding all the Magick in the Play. (x: 6–7)

Dryden ventriloquizes the king's response: casting a woman in a boy's role exceeds the practice, in Shakespeare's theatre, of casting a boy in a woman's role. In the context of praising Shakespeare for everything *but* his magic, it seems clear that "exceeding" Shakespeare's magic is excessive. Dryden excuses the reversal that occurs in his theatre on the grounds that the "dearth of Youths" has forced it.

Exactly what, though, is excessive? At first, it seems excessive both to employ a woman and to transform her into a boy. In response, however, to the projected criticism of the king, who will find this transformation excessive, Dryden chides the viewers, suggesting that they modify their expectations since there may in fact be no transformation:

> Let none expect in the last Act to find,
> Her Sex transform'd from man to Woman-kind.
> Whate'er she was before the Play began,
> All you shall see of her is perfect man. (x: 7)

The king will say the transformation of woman to man in Dryden's play is excessive even though Dryden cautions his spectators to expect no further transformation (of man to woman; of woman revealed as woman). What transformation exceeds Shakespeare's magic if no transformation is to be expected? The answer to this implied question is, I would argue, his transformed *Tempest*. Furthermore, Dryden wants the words he scripts for the king to have opposite connotations when they are applied to Shakespeare and to himself. Dryden wishes the king to utter, "That's a transformation exceeding all the magic in the play" as a criticism of Shakespeare's magic and a positive valuation of Dryden's own. The prologue is structured to facilitate this answer. The gendering of the "transformation" is the feature of facilitation for which we need an account. Dryden is proposing that the practice of opposite cross-gendered casting epitomizes his relationship to Shakespeare.

Different relations hold between theatrical representation and gender in Dryden's and Shakespeare's theatres. In Dryden's play, theatrical illusion is not broken by the kind of self-referential gestures performed in some of Shakespeare's plays. (Not only does Cleopatra have a speech about her greatness being "boyed" in Rome (*Antony and Cleopatra*, v.ii. 218–20), but women such as Portia and Viola disguise themselves as men, thereby reminding the audience that they are male actors disguised as women.) The contrast between Shakespeare and Dryden epitomized by opposite cross-gendered casting is sustained in the texture of the representation in each writer's theatre: whereas Shakespeare's is discontinuous and self-referential, Dryden's is seamless and illusionistic.

Thus, notwithstanding his dismissal of the "real" – "Whate'er she was before the Play began" – Dryden challenges his spectators to see if they can detect the "real" woman under the male disguise. The spectators' visual perceptions smack up against limits which are also the limits of representation in Dryden's theatre, and a new understanding of gender identity is proposed that conforms to these perceptual limits: "All you shall *see* of her is perfect man [my emphasis]." Visually, theatrically, she is male, but epistemologically, linguistically (i.e. pronomially) she is female. The contradiction between what is seen and what is known is resolved in the appeal to physical contact where carnal "knowledge" provides the ultimate proof. The "real" is recuperated in the bawdy invitation to the king with which the prologue ends:

> Or if your fancy will be farther led
> To find her Woman, it must be abed.
>   (x: 7)

Whatever may have been lost in the "dearth" is thereby transformed into a gain, or, more precisely, into a sexual conquest, where no uncertainty as to "her true sex" will be sustained. The relation between gender and theatrical representation apparently resolves Dryden's relationship to Shakespeare: Dryden proposes that his literary achievement "exceeds" Shakespeare because he substitutes heterosexual opportunity in place of a "dearth of Youths."

But the seamless "real" of Dryden's theatre also displays its "seam" in this prologue: in exchange for the king's "grace," Dryden offers the sexual gift of the actress, but she also stands for another gift, that of his text to the king. In this way, although Dryden figures his text as "perfect man" and himself as Shakespeare's improver, text and author accomplish these feats insofar as they are best represented by a woman. Moreover, text and author are further conflated: the "perfect man" is Dryden's extension of his self-presentation as Neander, the new man of the *Essay of Dramatick Poesy* who admires Jonson but "loves" Shakespeare.

The substitutions of heterosexual opportunity for "dearth of Youths," of Dryden for Shakespeare, are complex and multivalent. They permit Dryden to depict his relationship to Shakespeare as an instance of cultural transmission in which Dryden both receives and improves Shakespeare. The substitutions inform his critical stance in relation to Shakespeare; to the extent that we accept Samuel Johnson's identification of Dryden as "the father of criticism in English," these substitutions also shape our own practices.[13] These substitutions, however, are not symmetrical, which suggests that under the smooth surface of patrilineal bequest lie complicated gender representations that potentially disrupt the filial relation. Indeed, the multivalent sexual overtones of his representation of his text as a gift to the king in the form of the actress are echoed, as I will show, in his dual representations of his relation to Shakespeare in *All for Love* and its prefatory essay, where it is both loving and competitive, figured both in the preface as a familial bond between men, and in the play as a competition between women over the title of legitimate "wife."

ALL FOR LOVE?: LOVING AND CRITICIZING SHAKESPEARE

All for Love is the only one of Dryden's plays that modern critics like without qualifications.[14] Nevertheless, much contemporary critical discussion evaluates the play in comparison to *Antony and Cleopatra*.[15] These discussions have, in part, been invited by Dryden himself, who remarks in the preface, "In my Stile I have professed to imitate the Divine Shakespeare" (XIII: 18); indeed, it is difficult to take account of the changes Dryden made to Shakespeare's plays and remain neutral to Shakespeare's elevated status.[16] In asking, however, not how Shakespeare enabled Dryden's dramatic practice, but how Dryden's relation to Shakespeare shaped his criticism, we should be able not only to appreciate better that Shakespeare's divinity is, in part, a product of Dryden's criticism, but also to specify the difficulty – and the desirability – of this neutrality as a legacy of the kind of criticism he practices.

The changes Dryden makes to Shakespeare's *Antony and Cleopatra* include a streamlining of the action and settings that brings the play into conformity with the neo-classical unities of time and place. These structural compressions make the heroic conflict between love and duty the pivotal center of the play, which is adumbrated through a number of thematic changes as well. Augmenting the theme of friendship between men, Dryden elaborates the character of Ventidius, whose exchanges with Antony highlight Antony's commitment to love over empire and friendship, and that of Dolabella, whose appearance as a competitor for Cleopatra's affections restages Antony's love–duty conflict in the register of rivalry. Dryden also introduces the character of Octavia, who is accompanied onstage by Antony's children. Her presence gives dramatic embodiment to Antony's dilemma; her confrontation with Cleopatra over the title of Antony's "wife" resituates the heroic conflict of Shakespeare's Cleopatra between the demands of empire and those of the heart at the domestic level.

Laura Brown understands the changes Dryden makes to Shakespeare in the context of a generic shift in Restoration drama from heroic to affective tragedy. Locating the development of affective tragedy in the social context of the decline of aristocratic ideology, Brown depicts the formal changes that ensue from the replacement of the drama of social status, exemplified by the heroic play and the Restoration comedy of manners, by the drama of moral worth. These plays feature the substitution of the unfortunate and undeserved situation of the central character for the aristocratic status of the heroic protagonist; the replacement of aristocratic heroes by private citizens, and, frequently, by women protagonists; and a turn to domestic material, and, ultimately, national as opposed to exotic history.[17] For Brown, the Restoration adaptations of Shakespeare are graphic illustrations of the process in which "pity replaces admiration, [and] a concurrent stifling of motivation and character complexity, which systematically substitute innocence for blame and simple misunderstanding for responsibility" result in "the substitution of pathetic situation for evaluation, and the subsequent denial of public reference and social or moral meaning" (100). Ultimately, Brown argues that the restrictive focus of the serious drama exemplified in affective tragedy contributes to the transition remarked in literary histories of the eighteenth century in which the drama yields its place to the novel.

Indeed, for Brown, *All for Love* is a "relatively pure example of the form" of affective tragedy, and, as such, almost every episode of the play "is calculated to increase our pitying responses to the plight" of its protagonists (81). Though Brown's terms are suggestive for understanding the consequences of the sentimentalization of Shakespeare for the decline of the drama, they do not explain Shakespeare's role in the process she analyzes. Curiously, Dryden's sentimentalization of Shakespeare abets his articulation of a critical vocation. By looking at the means by which Dryden's revisions of Shakespeare in *All for Love* contribute to his critical practice, we can see that pathetic situation replaces evaluation in the drama by relocating such judgments outside the play, thus producing evaluation *of* the drama. Significantly for the importance neutrality and impartiality come to have in criticism, in his preface to *All for Love* Dryden articulates a critical vocation on the basis of self-criticism. This self-criticism should, I want to argue, be understood as a paradigmatic critical gesture emerging from the sentimentalization of Shakespeare.

In the preface, Dryden singles out two moments of his own invention for special comment: a scene between Antony and Ventidius in which the two men declare their love for one another, and the introduction of the character of Octavia. The preface ends:

But since I may not be over-confident of my performance after him [Shakespeare], it will be prudence in me to be silent. Yet I hope I may affirm, and without vanity, that by imitating him I have excell'd myself throughout the Play and particularly, that I prefer the Scene betwixt *Antony* and *Ventidius* in the first Act, to any I have written in this kind. (XIII: 19)

Imprudently, perhaps, Dryden does not remain silent; remarkably, he praises a scene of his own invention. In this addition to Shakespeare's play, characters alternate between long set speeches and short, rapid interchanges in which each metrically finishes the other's lines. The scene begins when Ventidius announces his previously unnoticed presence to Antony, who, having wondered why he was born, has thrown himself down.

    ANT. *starting up*. Art thou Ventidius?
    VENT. Are you Antony?
        I'm liker what I was, than you to him
        I left you last.
    ANT. I'm angry.

> VENT. So am I.
> ANT. I would be private: leave me.
> VENT. Sir, I love you,
> And therefore will not leave you.
> ANT. Will not leave me?
> Where have you learnt that Answer? Who am I?
> VENT. My Emperor; the Man I love next Heav'n:
> If I said more, I think 'twere scarce a Sin;
> Y'are all that's good and god-like. (I.i. 246–54)

The emotions of the scene escalate to include tears and blushes:

> ANT. Now thou hast seen me, art thou satisfy'd?
> For, if a Friend, thou hast beheld enough;
> And, if a Foe, too much.
> VENT. *weeping.* Look, Emperor, this is no common Deaw,
> I have not wept this Forty year; but now
> My Mother comes afresh into my eyes;
> I cannot help her softness.
> ANT. By heav'n, he weeps, poor good old Man, he weeps!
> The big round drops course one another down
> The furrows of his cheeks. Stop 'em Ventidius,
> Or I shall blush to death: they set my shame,
> That caus'd 'em, full before me. (I.i. 259–70)

The scene climaxes when Ventidius, having declared his love, persuades Antony to rally his forces. Their mutual interruptive style measures their merger and the scene ends in their embrace.

This scene, which highlights Dryden's augmentation of sentiment in his portrayal of Antony, is dramatically impressive, but he singles it out on the basis of the critical expertise he has claimed for himself in the rest of the preface, primarily through his negative assessment of other features which escalate the pathetic impact of his play – through, more specifically, another of his own inventions, the introduction of the character of Octavia:

The greatest errour in the contrivance seems to be in the person of Octavia: For though I might use the priviledge of a Poet, to introduce her into Alexandria, yet I had not enough consider'd, that the compassion she mov'd to her self and children, was destructive to that which I reserv'd for Antony and Cleopatra; whose mutual love being founded upon vice, must lessen the favour of the Audience to them, when Virtue and Innocence were oppress'd by it. And, though I justified Antony in some measure, by making Octavia's departure, to proceed wholly from her self; yet the force of the first machine still remain'd; and the dividing of the pity, like the cutting of a River into many Channels, abated the strength of the natural stream. (XIII: 10–11)

His reservations about the effectiveness of the introduction of Octavia as a vehicle for heightening the pitiful plight of Antony aside, Dryden's comments indicate his awareness that the pathetic impact of his play relies on his representation of the characters' domestic relations. Indeed, he goes on to criticize at length his representation of Octavia and Cleopatra's confrontation over the title of Antony's "wife." In his "wifely" Cleopatra, who says of herself, "Nature meant me / A Wife, a silly harmless household Dove" (IV.i, 91–92), and who fights with Octavia for domestic legitimacy, Dryden seems to compress the changes he makes to Shakespeare's "riggish" queen.[18] He thus offers a synecdoche for his differences from Shakespeare, one which figures each playwright's play as his Cleopatra. Samuel Johnson would seem to have borrowed this technique from Dryden when he critiques Shakespeare's propensity for punning in the *Preface to Shakespeare*; significantly, though, he conflates Shakespeare's Cleopatra with Dryden's when he describes Shakespeare's "excessive" verbal play as "his Cleopatra, for whom he lost the world."[19] The subtitle of *All for Love* is *The World Well Lost*. Although it might be tempting, at this point, to chart the relative places of Johnson and his precursor critic, Dryden, on Harold Bloom's map of misreading, it would be premature to do so without further attention to the complicated gender dynamics of Dryden's treatment of Shakespeare that, one might argue, Johnson's conflation suppresses.[20] Moreover, to apply to critics the exclusively oedipal terms Bloom uses to describe the relations between poets will not further my project to describe the access which Dryden's treatments of Shakespeare provide to the generation of women critics who follow him.

For, in the preface to *All for Love*, Dryden offers a rather different representation of his relationship to Shakespeare. It begins:

The death of *Antony* and *Cleopatra*, is a Subject which has been treated by the greatest Wits of our Nation, after *Shakespeare*; and by all so variously, that their example has given me the confidence to try my self in this Bowe of *Ulysses* amongst the Crowd of Sutors; and, withal, to take my own measures, in aiming at the Mark. I doubt not but the same motive has prevailed with all of us in this attempt; I mean the excellency of the Moral: for the chief persons represented, were the famous pattern of unlawful love; and their end was unfortunate. (XIII: 10)

We should not let Dryden's displacement of the motive for rewriting the Antony and Cleopatra story from literary competition to "the excellency of the Moral" distract us from the curious gendering of an otherwise oedipal conception of literary relations. When Dryden discusses the motive for the "greatest Wits of our Nation, after Shakespeare" to treat the subject of Antony and Cleopatra's death, he proposes an analogy that captures the decided non-neutrality of literary competition.

At first glance, Dryden's proposal to take up the bow of Ulysses describes literary competition in terms of sexual competition and seems quite unexceptionable. However, a closer look brings to light a peculiar failure that the classical analogy builds in: as we know from Homer, no one else can wield Ulysses' bow. Moreover, if Shakespeare is Ulysses, who is the Penelope to whom the best writer will have literary or sexual access?

According to the analogy, none of the succeeding wits can successfully vie with Shakespeare for the body of his unnamed "wife." Although the analogy would thus seem to portray Dryden's self-insertion into the classical scene of rivalry, with Shakespeare as Ulysses in the *paterfamilias* position and Dryden in the role of Telemachus, rather than as one of the suitors, literary failure must, in any case, result.[21] When we turn to the scene from *All for Love* that Dryden characterizes as his literary failure, however, we can see that it resituates the patrilineal contest in other terms. The emotional and dramatic center of his play, the scene depicts the competition between Octavia and Cleopatra over the title of "wife." Indeed, I would argue that the scene Dryden calls attention to as a failure is the true scene of literary competition.

Dryden displaces the rivalry between male playwrights onto a rivalry between female characters. This scene of rivalry, however, is not only the sentimental centerpiece of the play, it is also a principal object of Dryden's critical attention in the preface. Identifying the introduction of Octavia, and the scene between women, which occurs immediately after her appearance with her children, as his flaws, Dryden has it both ways: he criticizes his domestication of Shakespeare even though he has dramatized it. By specifying the scene of women fighting which dramatizes his competition with Shakespeare as particularly worthy of criticism, he both figures and denies the competition.

But Dryden also gets something else out of the classical analogy: behind the conflict between Dryden's Octavia and Cleopatra lies another conflict – between Dryden's and Shakespeare's Cleopatras. Synecdochically identifying each playwright with his version of Cleopatra, and replacing Shakespeare's "riggish queen" by a paradigmatically wifely Cleopatra, embodying the virtue most closely associated with Penelope, Dryden's Cleopatra comes to signal domestic literary success of the sort that Dryden achieves for himself when he joins the ranks of "the greatest

Wits of our Nation." If Shakespeare is Ulysses, then Dryden's Cleopatra is his Penelope.

The generational levelling that this coupling permits suggests that the combined effect of Dryden's preferred scene, the loving scene between Antony and Ventidius, and his self-identified failure, the fight scene between Octavia and Cleopatra, functionally evacuates the position of *paterfamilias* offered in the classical analogy. I propose that Dryden identifies his own literary success with the domestic success of Cleopatra as a result of a double displacement: he displaces the competition between himself and Shakespeare from the generational model presented in the classical allusion of the preface onto the two scenes he singles out for comment – the preferred scene between men, which denies the rivalry and represents it as love, and the critiqued scene between women, which accentuates competition and figures literary superiority as domestic legitimacy. Dryden's significant preference for the scene between Antony and Ventidius, the scene of loving men, is permitted, I would argue, partly because of the ways the battle between women encodes matters of status instability in the homosocial sphere of courtly male interaction in matters of domesticity and gender. Further attention to his treatment of this scene in its social context is required in order to understand the ways domestication and sentimentalization inform Dryden's critical practices.

In the preface to *All for Love*, Dryden engages in a bitter battle with Rochester over the status of poetry as the privilege of the male aristocrat. Rochester, famed libertine poet and arbiter of wit, has put in question Dryden's self-inclusion among "the greatest Wits of our Nation."[22] In "The Allusion to Horace" (which circulated in manuscript in 1676), Rochester equates Dryden's criticism of Shakespeare and Jonson with arrogance.

> But does not Dryden find ev'n Jonson dull;
> Fletcher and Beaumont uncorrect, and full
> Of lewd lines, as he calls 'em; Shakespeare's style
> Stiff and affected; to his own the while
> Allowing all the justness that his pride
> So arrogantly has to those denied?[23]

In response, Dryden calls into question the access those men of "wretched affectation," drunken debauchery and privilege have to wit, clearly understanding Rochester's accusation of arrogance in the social register as pointing the finger at him as a social climber. Over and against wealth and libertinage, Dryden presents poverty and modesty as his poetic and critical qualifications.

And is this not a wretched affectation, not to be contented with what Fortune has done for them, and sit down quietly with their estate, but they must call their Wits in question and needlessly expose their nakedness to public view? If a little glittering in discourse has pass'd them on us for witty men, where was the necessity of undeceiving the World?... We who would write, if we want the Talent, yet have the excuse that we do it for a poor subsistence; but what can be urg'd in their defence, who not having the Vocation of Poverty to scribble, out of mere wantonness take pains to make themselves ridiculous? (xiii: 14)

The nakedness to which Dryden refers has a notorious historical referent: it is that of Sir Charles Sedley, one of Rochester's circle, and, particularly significant in this context, a "Wit" who wrote an *Antony and Cleopatra* that was performed the same year as Dryden's *All for Love*, and to greater popular acclaim.[24] Sedley had been arrested in 1663 for appearing nude on the balcony of a tavern to give a mock-sermon.[25] In Dryden's attack, public nakedness is a crime, but baring the absence of wit is an even greater one. He invokes poverty, and, with it, modesty, as corollary virtues that paradoxically permit the poor writer to dress better than the naked aristocrat.

The topic of modest dress comes up earlier in the preface, when, defending the propriety of representing women fighting, Dryden claims to have kept himself within the bounds of modesty.

'Tis true, some actions, though natural, are not fit to be represented; and broad obscenities in words, ought in good manners to be avoided: expressions therefore are the modest cloathing of our thoughts, as Breeches and Petticoats are of our bodies. If I have kept myself within the bounds of modesty, all beyond is but nicety and affectation; which is no more than modesty deprav'd into a vice: they betray themselves who are too quick of apprehension in such cases and leave all reasonable men to imagine worse of them, than of the Poet. (xiii: 11)

Expressions are the modest clothes available to the poor writer, preventing him from appearing naked out of either destitution or aristocratic vice. Nakedness, however, is not the only vice; so is the over-investment in modesty that depraves it: curiously both fashion and puritanism present such dangers. Despite the precariousness of the situation, Dryden keeps himself within the bounds of modesty by registering, apparently effortlessly, the difference between the obscene and the modest as the gender difference between breeches and petticoats. As we will see, he puts forward criticism as the discourse that best regulates these differences.

Counterpointing Dryden's ease is the figure of Sedley, who appears either naked or richly appointed in elaborate clothes, as another anecdote illustrates.

Edward Kynaston, one of the last male actors to take women's roles, was cast in a play that included a satirical portrait of Sedley. Not only did Kynaston appear on stage in the elaborate lace collars that were Sedley's sartorial signature, but he also paraded around St. James's Park so attired. In an exercise in threatened class-prerogative, that may also have been an early instance of "gay-bashing," Sedley had Kynaston beaten up by hired hands.[26] This anecdote tells as much about the changing theatrical casting practices as it does about changing class and gender boundaries in the Restoration. In view of Dryden's association of the obscene with the libertine and the modest with the poor writer, we might speculate that if Sedley provides an example of aristocratic anxieties about matters of both status and sexuality, Dryden appears to propose that in place of status anxieties, the prerogative of the poor writer is a mastery of reformed masculine codes.

Dryden locates himself within the bounds of modest dress in an attempt to neutralize status hierarchies, naturalize gender distinctions and decorum and appeal to "all reasonable men." The "bounds of modesty" rule out affectation and depravity as well as "broad obscenities," which, however natural, are "not fit to be represented." "All reasonable men" may imagine worse of obscene aristocrats and those who deprave modesty into a vice than of the poets who scribble out of a "Vocation of Poverty." Dryden thus proposes to overcome the qualitative distinctions supposedly provided by birth in the suggestion that proper gender distinctions will be drawn in the well-mannered critical discourse of those who are positioned within modesty's bounds.

Dryden often substitutes gender for status terms in order to facilitate his claim to critical expertise. His singling out of his representations of domestic femininity under stress for critical attention in the preface shows that for criticism to appeal to "all reasonable men," it needs both to distance itself from the libertinage associated with a declining aristocracy and to disavow the means by which this distance is accomplished. The scene of female rivalry that he added to Shakespeare's play is of such importance to Dryden that he founds his claims as a critic, including those of "modesty" and "poverty," on his understanding of it.

Dryden knows that the French poets would have criticized his choice to dramatize the domestic confrontation between Octavia and Cleopatra. They "would not, for example, have suffer'd Cleopatra and Octavia to have met; or if they had met, there must have only pass'd betwixt them some cold civilities, but no eagerness of repartée, for fear of offending against the greatness of their Characters and the modesty of their Sex" (XIII: 11). Drawing our attention to his awareness as the grounds for self-praise rather than self-condemnation, Dryden redirects the critique of his work against those who would object:

This objection I foresaw, and at the same time contemn'd: for I judg'd it both *natural* and *probable*, that Octavia, proud of her new-gain'd Conquest, would search out Cleopatra to triumph over her; and that Cleopatra, thus attacqu'd, was not of a spirit to shun the encounter: and 'tis not unlikely, that two exasperated Rivals should use such Satyre as I have put into their mouths; for after all, though one were a Roman, and the other a Queen, they were both Women. (XIII: 11)

Dryden's paradoxical reasoning is more remarkable than his self-promoting rhetoric. Part of the reason to condemn the spectacle is the whole reason that Dryden defends it: it is not suitable for *great women* to fight because they are great, that is they are highly placed, but nevertheless, "after all, though one were a Roman, and the other a Queen, they were both Women." Dryden replaces the social categories, "Queen" and "Roman," by the gender category "Women," and by subsuming matters of status and nation under matters of gender, he is able to maintain his status both as an imitator of "nature," and as a critic.

Although Dryden observes that what offends in the representation of Octavia and Cleopatra fighting is precisely that one is a Queen and the other a Roman, none of his contemporaries seems to have complained. Nevertheless, Dryden himself feels the need to comment: "But this is an objection which none of my Critiques have urg'd against me; and therefore I might have let it pass, if I could have resolv'd to have been partial to myself" (XIII: 11). Significantly, Dryden presents his critical qualification as his ability to remain impartial; he can observe what has escaped other people's attention. His ostensible indifference to his own flaws informs his claim to critical, indeed, moral superiority. The high cost of this claim, criticizing his own play, can be attributed in part to the ongoing status battle over who has access to literary judgment and, in part, to his understanding of the threat of competing with Shakespeare. The strategic insistence on the domestic – both in his elevation of scribbling as the "Vocation of Poverty" and in the representation of women fighting which displaces his competition with Shakespeare – results, oddly enough, in the proposal of neutrality as a critical prerequisite.

Feeling and indifference, pathetic response and impartiality, are both equally necessary to criticism, and gender is thus an important term in its operations.

For example, Dryden's criticism of the scene between Cleopatra and Octavia, which activates his claim to critical impartiality, underwrites his preference for the scene between Antony and Ventidius. From this point of view, it is significant that the friendship between Antony and Ventidius registers homoerotically. Both Antony's interactions with Ventidius and his more pronounced homoerotically charged relationship to Dollabella exemplify a hyper-desirability: both men and women compete over him.[27] Indeed, Dryden's noncritical representations of male–male eroticism may be facilitated by the scenes of fighting women.[28]

At this point, the connections between Dryden's depictions of male anxieties about both political and sexual power and the critical discourse he inaugurates can be made clear. *All for Love* focuses on the contest between *women* as the determinant of male political power and value, thereby displacing male rivalry onto a "safe" sphere in which castration is not possible. As we have seen, in the preface to *All for Love*, Dryden bases his critical claims on his own partiality. Castigating and defending his sentimental scene of female rivalry, Dryden stakes his claim to critical expertise by stating that he might have let his fault pass, "if I could have resolv'd to have been partial to myself" (XIII: 11). The condition is strange: if he could have resolved to be partial, he would have allowed his play to be uncriticized, that is to say, his play would have remained "whole" (or, uncriticized), if he had remained partial; but if he had remained partial, he would have lacked the reconstitution that criticism supplies. Criticism reconstitutes the fragmented play, with the added advantage of constituting Dryden as *im*partial, as "whole." His lack of resolve is dissolved in the reconstituted wholeness of authority that critical judgment expresses. The pathetic situation which, to return to Brown's terms, replaces evaluation in the play, produces, in Dryden's hands, evaluation of the play. The importance that neutrality comes to have in the critical discourse that is Dryden's legacy thus depends, ironically, on sentimental theatrical representation and on the sentimental gesture of self-criticism.

Dryden thus redeems his integrity as a playwright even as he passes critical judgment on his own play. He stakes out two roles which correspond to that of the playwright and the critic, one inside and one outside the play: on the inside, he is the wifely Cleopatra, a dramatist who can compete with Shakespeare; on the outside, he is Telemachus, a weak playwright but impartial critic and judge of Shakespeare/Ulysses. Threatened by competition with Shakespeare, he criticizes his innovative scene of fighting women which follows from his introduction of Octavia, and his negative criticism validates his critical expertise. It supplies the position out of which he can prefer his other innovative scene, the scene between men. Staging a scene of literary competition as rivalry between women, he creates an object of criticism, a fetish, which is significantly a fight in which there is no threat of castration. He can be critical of his own play because his self-criticism "remasculinizes" him.[29]

Dryden's epilogue to *All for Love* recapitulates the ways in which the scenes of fighting women and loving men mark the differences between the present and past theatrical practices to suggest other directions for criticism even as it reinscribes some of the same dynamics. When Dryden replays the relation between scenes of fighting women and loving men and literary evaluation, the paradigmatic literary judgments are performed by women.

Dryden aims his epilogue at wits and sparks by an indirect appeal on behalf of the playwright to "the Fair Sex."

> Yet, if he might his own Grand Jury call,
> By the Fair Sex he begs to stand or fall.
> Let Caesar's Pow'r the Mens ambition move,
> But grace You him who lost the World for Love.
> (XIII: 111)

Although the speaker of the epilogue appeals to the ladies, and thereby constitutes a "sentimental" audience who will grant grace to the playwright, he also deflects potential criticism by ventriloquizing it through a wrinkled, ugly antiquated lady. Making her the mouthpiece invites the audience to dismiss the charge that the new plays are not as good as the old ones:

> Yet if some antiquated Lady say,
> The last Age is not Copy'd in his Play;
> Heav'n help the Man who for that face must drudge,
> Which only has the wrinkles of a Judge.   (XIII: 111)

The speaker of Dryden's epilogue uses the difference between the haglike creature and the "fair" women who are moved to pity Antony over Caesar to draw the contrast between the last age, identifiably Shakespeare's, and the present moment.[30] The contrast between Shakespeare and Dryden necessitates an appeal to judges in any case, be they fair or wrinkled, and, in both cases, they are female. His appeal to female judges minimizes the threat of being judged in comparison to Shakespeare, a comparable act to staging the competition between himself and Shakespeare in the scene of fighting women. Significantly, in order to solicit the favourable judgment of the female judges, Dryden's epilogue establishes equivalences between Caesar, whose power moves men, and Shakespeare on the one hand, and between he "who lost the World for Love," that is, Antony, and Dryden on the other. Dryden assumes the role of Antony in the eyes of his female judges in the epilogue, risking the literary failure he has represented in the preface as "try[ing the]... Bowe of *Ulysses*," even though he has neutralized his competition with Shakespeare in the scene of rivalry between women in the play. He thereby lays the grounds for his own (and others') increasingly oedipalized critical treatments of Shakespeare. However, by representing his paradigmatic literary critics as women, Dryden's feminization of literary judgment facilitates the accession of women writers to criticism. In subsequent chapters devoted to the writings of Aphra Behn, Catharine Trotter and Delarivier Manley, I pursue this aspect of Dryden's critical legacy.

In the preface, Dryden had circumscribed the critical vocation within modesty's bounds, which, I argued, he represented as the proper, or non-aristocratic, recognition of gender difference; the feminization of literary judgment that occurs in the epilogue points to the strategic use of feminization as the means by which a declining aristocratic ideology is displaced and the space for the emergence of bourgeois masculinity carved out. I turn now to give further consideration to this conjuncture, for Dryden's universalization of Shakespeare in "The Grounds of Criticism in Tragedy," and the changes he makes to Shakespeare's *Troilus and Cressida*, provide a better view of these operations as they inform the practice of criticism Dryden inaugurates and the literary genealogy this practice produces.

UNIVERSALIZING SHAKESPEARE AND ITS CRITICAL CONSEQUENCES

In the prologue to his version of *Troilus and Cressida*, Dryden ventriloquizes Shakespeare's ghost, who praises the faithfulness of Dryden's version of the play to classical sources if not to Shakespeare himself. Dryden's emendations, the prologue establishes, elevate Dryden's play above Shakespeare's. As I suggested earlier, Dryden bases his claim of "faithfulness" to Shakespeare (even though this involved "improving" him) on having made Cressida faithful to Troilus. A more detailed consideration of the changes Dryden makes to Shakespeare's *Troilus and Cressida* brings out the importance of gender to Dryden's production of Shakespeare's "universality" in the "Grounds of Criticism in Tragedy," the critical essay which prefaces this play.

In Shakespeare's version of *Troilus and Cressida*, the valor of the Trojans is conspicuously absent; not only is the idea of valor drastically undercut, but fidelity and heroism are functionally made impossible. In Dryden's play, Trojan valor is augmented by making Cressida faithful to Troilus. Turning *Troilus and Cressida* into a pathetic tragedy, Dryden has Cressida commit suicide at the end of the play.[31] The "faithful Scene" of the prologue that exemplifies Dryden's faithfulness to Shakespeare thus occurs, I would argue, *in* Dryden's play, in his scene of Cressida's faithfulness to Troilus. Establishing the fidelity of the woman, the contingency upon which male valor, as it is measured by genealogical continuity, depends, Dryden aligns his own "faithfulness" to Shakespeare with Cressida's faithfulness to Troilus, in order to secure the literary inheritance which Dryden's female followers take up.

Dryden represents the reunion between the faithful Cressida and Troilus at the end of his version of the play, just before they both die. Cressida, who has stabbed herself to vindicate her innocence, rejects Diomedes' help and turns to Troilus:

> CRESSID. Stand off; and touch me not, thou Traitor, Diomede.
> But you, my only Troilus, come near:
> Trust me, the wound which I have giv'n this breast
> Is far lesse painful, than the wound you gave it.
> Oh, can you yet believe that I am true?
> TROIL. This were too much, e'ev if thou hadst been false!
> But, Oh, thou purest, whitest innocence,
> (For such I know thee now, too late I know it!) (v.ii. 263–70)

Notwithstanding the gains accrued on the basis of the "faithful Scene" – the retroactive elevation of Shakespeare above Homer by means of Dryden's "faithful" revision – Cressida's loyal behavior has quite different effects on Troilus. When Troilus discovers that Cressida has been faithful all along, the characters exchange gender positions: when Cressida kills herself, Troilus experiences her action as feminizing. He complains:

> She's gone for ever, and she blest me dying!
> Cou'd she have curs'd me worse? she dy'd for me;
> And like a woman, I lament for her. (v.ii. 281–83)

What makes Cressida's blessing a curse is not only the fact of her death, but also its feminizing effect on him. In dying for him, Cressida is masculinized; in crying for her, he is feminized.[32] If, however, Dryden feminizes Troilus in order to ensure the excellence of Trojan valor, and the transmission of a British literary tradition which, in the logic of the prologue, depends upon it, he does so at the risk of feminizing Shakespeare.

It is necessary to correlate Dryden's dramatization of the reversibility of gender in the play with the the status of the gender terms in the critical essay, in Dryden's production of Shakespeare's "Universal mind." The reversibility of gender implied by Troilus and Cressida's exchange of positions indicates that gender is a question of behavior rather than being. Dryden's manly Andromache, true to the etymology of her name, provides another instance of his preoccupation with the relations between gender and behavior in this play. In striking contrast to Shakespeare's Andromache, who appears in only one scene to try to dissuade Hector from the heroics that lead to his death (v.iii), Dryden's Andromache wants her husband to supplement his heroic behavior – she suggests that Hector issue a challenge to the Greeks (II.i). These representations of the reversibility of gendered attributes, in which there is a relative lack of embodiment, attests to the perpetuation of the traditional hierarchical relation Laqueur describes: both men and women are manly when they behave heroically; both men and women are feminine when they weep. The degree of concern Dryden manifests, however, over questions of gender and its meanings in both the critical and dramatic texts suggests that this hierarchical relation is in crisis.

The centerpiece of "The Grounds of Criticism in Tragedy," Dryden's sustained comparison of Shakespeare and Fletcher, is elaborated through an account of their different literary practices in the terms of gender. Dryden's comparison derogates Fletcher as feminine, soft and derivative, and elevates Shakespeare as masculine, omnicapable and original: "Shakespear generally moves more terror, and Fletcher more compassion: For the first had a more Masculine, a bolder and more fiery Genius; the Second a more soft and Womanish." (XIII: 233). At first, the gender terms seem designed to distribute the labor of literary reproduction between Shakespeare and Fletcher; however, the gender difference also selects which poet is to be recognized as having patriarchal status, which is the "father" figure from whom the literary tradition will be inherited. The terms of the comparison are directed to answer the question posed at the beginning of the essay, of "how far we ought to imitate our own

Poets, Shakespear and Fletcher, in their Tragedies" (XIII: 229); they specify which one is to be imitated and why:

[T]he excellency of that Poet [Shakespeare] was, as I have said, in the more manly passions; Fletcher's in the softer: Shakespeare writ better betwixt man and man; Fletcher, betwixt man and woman: consequently, the one describ'd friendship better, the other love: yet Shakespeare taught Fletcher to write love; and Juliet and Desdemona are Originals. 'Tis true, the scholar had the softer soul; but the Master had the kinder. Friendship is both a virtue, and a Passion essentially; love is a passion only in its nature, and is not a virtue but by Accident: good nature makes Friendship; but effeminacy Love. Shakespear had an Universal mind, which comprehended all Characters and Passions; Fletcher a more confin'd, and limited: for though he treated love in perfection, yet Honour, Ambition, Revenge, and generally all the stronger Passions, he either touch'd not, or not Masterly. To conclude all; he was a limb of Shakespear. (XIII: 247)

The gendered terms seem to point to different domains, as Dryden ascribes to each poet his area of expertise: Shakespeare excels at writing scenes of friendship between men, and Fletcher's talent is the love scene between a man and a woman. As the paragraph progresses, however, a new term is introduced into the comparison, which repositions the opposition of "masculinity" to "femininity" in a hierarchy: Dryden focuses on priority, on who learned what from whom, which, as a consequence, turns "masculinity" into "mastery." Shakespeare's talent, which is located on one side of the comparison at the beginning (he is "masculine" to Fletcher's "feminine"), expands to take over what was initially described as Fletcher's territory. When Shakespeare is uncloaked as the master to Fletcher's student, scenes in which Shakespeare has instructed Fletcher, between men and women, are revealed to be always becoming, or to have been already, scenes between men.

Indeed, Dryden arrives at Shakespeare's "Universal mind" only after he has discussed Shakespeare's most famous scene of male friendship, the quarrel between Brutus and Cassius, and dismissed its influence on his own scene between Hector and Troilus. According to Jonathan Goldberg, the quarrel between Brutus and Cassius should be understood as a representation of homoerotic love between men. However, Dryden introduces two elements into his quarrel scene which significantly reduce the homoeroticism in Shakespeare's scene: the blood relation that, by virtue of the taboo on incest, insists on heterosexuality, and the woman, Cressida, who provides grounds for the quarrel and mediates between the brothers.[33] It is important to note this subterranean homoeroticism: Dryden may "correct" this aspect of Shakespeare's work, but it calls into question neither his masculinity in relation to Fletcher nor his universality.

Dryden's production of Shakespeare's "Universal mind" would seem to create an abstract pattern of literary excellence, retrospectively a state beyond, or before, gender. Shakespeare's universality would seem to abstract the gendered body, and reinforce the hierarchical relation of sexual difference in which the male could be said to include the female, to be its "more perfect" model. However, the comparison between Shakespeare and Fletcher also clearly depends upon the incommensurability of femininity and masculinity: regardless of the pains Dryden takes to subsume the gender differences in this abstraction, they nevertheless leave their trace in the image of Shakespeare's bodily appropriation of Fletcher – he is his "limb." Though Dryden only arrives at the transcendent universality of Shakespeare's "mind" once the gender differences that have been used to guarantee the connections between masculinity and mastery have been expressed and then suppressed, the technique of abstracted embodiment which results in Shakespeare's "Universal mind" belongs to Laqueur's regime of incommensurability.

There are also, however, further differences between the gendering of Fletcher and the gender-reversibility Dryden dramatizes in *Troilus and Cressida*. Two astute readers of Fletcher, Robert Markley and Jeff Masten, provide some suggestive contexts for understanding Dryden's feminization of Fletcher, and why it would work differently than his feminization of Troilus. In his analysis of the ideologies of "wit" in seventeeth-century drama, Markley points out that Fletcher becomes the exemplar of a stylistic grace and aristocratic assurance in James Shirley's preface to the first folio collection of Beaumont and Fletcher's plays (1647). Shirley's identification of Fletcher with "an idyllic past of wit, courtly grace, youthful pleasures, and the joys of the theatre," is echoed in the commendatory poems, which extol Fletcher as the dramatist who brought the "conversation of gentlemen" to the stage.[34] In discussing the ways in which Fletcher comes to subsume and stand for his collaboration with Beaumont, Masten looks at the emergence of a singular author-function modeled on patriarchal absolutism from a field of possibilities that includes collaborative authorship based on eroticized male friendship.[35] The feminization of Fletcher, on the basis of his aristocratic courtliness (whether it is perceived, as Markley argues, or real) and his queer collaborative authorship (as elaborated by Masten), amounts to a dismissal of him as a literary model, and underwrites Dryden's elevation of Shakespeare as the transcendent and masculine ideal to be imitated.

What though of Dryden's feminization of Troilus, which enables his imitation of Shakespeare and Dryden's faithfulness to him? To describe the differences between Dryden's feminization of Fletcher, which he uses for derogation, and his feminization of Troilus, which enables imitation, in terms of Laqueur's two models of gender difference will only get us so far. Dryden's different feminizations of Troilus and Fletcher reflect the possibility, increasingly available with the emergent cultural dispensation of opposition and incommensurability, that one can slide down the scale from masculine to feminine, but that one cannot acquire masculinity. In Dryden's use, the ascent from femininity to masculinity presents the prospect of increased privilege at the same time as it raises anxieties about status. The affiliation of masculinity with aristocracy, in the context of the decline of aristocratic ideology and the contest between hierarchical and oppositional understandings of sexual difference, means increasingly, to paraphrase De Beauvoir, that a woman may be made but a man must be born.

Indeed, Dryden's alternate feminizations of Fletcher and Troilus suggest that masculinity shares features with aristocratic ideology in its emphasis on birth, and that femininity shares features with progressive ideology in its emphasis on worth.[36] From this point of view, Dryden's hostility towards aristocratic ideology is a contributing factor in his feminization of Fletcher, and he castigates him as its representative. Viewed as an instance of what McKeon calls "progressive ideology," Dryden's feminization of Troilus provides an alternative "femininity" to the castigated aristocratic kind, producing the "softening" effects that permit Dryden's imitation of Shakespeare. It is from this point of view that we can also appreciate the modernity of Dryden's feminization of literary judgment in the epilogue to *All for Love*. This analysis suggests that even as masculinity and femininity come to signify incommensurable spheres in an emergent bourgeois culture, masculinity retains the privileged veneer of a residual aristocratic code. Bourgeois femininity would seem to have appeared earlier than bourgeois masculinity, and perhaps the comparatively slower emergence of bourgeois masculinity can help to explain why the new men of the first half of the eighteenth century – from Addison and Steele through to the "Men of Feeling" – look so feminine.[37]

Dryden's different feminizations, to use McKeon's terms, produce not a patriarchalist but a patriarchal Shakespeare. The emendatory critical practice and its consolidation of a native literary inheritance on the basis of Dryden's fidelity to Shakespeare is underwritten by a faithful Cressida and a feminized Troilus. The combination of this fidelity, Dryden's propensity for representing – as he does in *All for Love* – status anxieties in gendered terms, the use of gendered terms for representing his relations to Shakespeare, and the critical neutrality to which they give rise produce a patriarchal Shakespeare who proves to be extremely productive for a younger generation of women writers. They claim critical access to Shakespeare and the native literary tradition through Dryden. Shakespeare's "Universal mind" thus both registers the privileged place Shakespeare continues to occupy within literary studies as England's untutored genius and reveals the underlying reconfigurations of gender definitions that make this privilege possible.

CHAPTER 4

The female playwright and the city lady

When the topic of women playwrights arises in *A Comparison Between the Two Stages*, an anonymous dramatic dialogue that satirically reviews English drama between 1695 and 1702, it provokes the wrath of Chagrin the critic.[1] His fellow interlocutors, Sullen, a dissenter, and Ramble, a beau, share his concern with the number of women writing for the stage. Such concern was, no doubt, prompted by the remarkable theatrical season of 1695/96, which Paula Backscheider heralds as the high-water mark of female-authored contributions to the English stage. As she notes, over one-third of all the new plays that season were written by women or adapted from women's work. The theatre at Drury Lane produced Delarivier Manley's *The Lost Lover* and *The Royal Mischief*, as well as Catharine Trotter's dramatic adaptation of Aphra Behn's *Agnes de Castro*, and two plays by Mary Pix, *Ibrahim* and *The Spanish Wives*; the Lincoln's Inn Fields Company produced *She Ventures, and He Wins* "by a Young Lady" who called herself Ariadne, Thomas Southerne's adaptation of Behn's *Oroonoko*, and it gave Behn's own *The Younger Brother* its posthumous premiere.[2]

As if railing could halt this deluge, Chagrin exclaims:

What a Pox have the Women to do with the Muses? I grant you the Poets call the Nine Muses by the Names of Women, but why so? not because the sex had anything to do with Poetry, but because in the Sex they're much fitter for prostitution. I hate these Petticoat-Authors; 'tis false Grammar, there's no Feminine for the Latin word, 'tis entirely of the Masculine Gender, and the Language won't bear such a thing as a she-Author. (26)

When Chagrin refers to "the Language," he appeals to the authority of Latin, and invokes the fact that women, as a rule, did not have access to classical learning, inferring they should therefore be barred from writing. In contrast to Dryden, who, as we have seen, mediates the classical and vernacular languages to produce a national literary tradition that is accessible to both men and women, Chagrin resurrects the classical standard to regulate vernacular literary production along gendered lines. Notwithstanding his desire for the classical to govern the vernacular, the English language bore increasing numbers of female authors in the years following Aphra Behn's death in 1689.

Chagrin asserts the grammatical impossibility of such women as Catharine Trotter, Delarivier Manley, Mary Pix and Susannah Centlivre by desiring that the social organization of gender would match the structure of Latin grammar. His concept of criticism, however, in which he would serve as the legislator of such a correspondence, depends, ironically, on the instances of its failure that these women writers signify. Chagrin, who is interchangeably called "Critick," thus represents a regulatory relation between criticism and gender at the moment when professional critical practice emerges: for him, criticism is a discourse that maintains writing as an exclusively male activity, but, ironically, a discourse that only comes into being when such exclusivity is threatened.

Probably a generation younger than Dryden, Chagrin depicts writing as belonging exclusively to the masculine domain, a portrait strikingly at odds with Dryden's representation of a national vernacular literary tradition whose standard is set by an ideal writing which expresses both feminine and masculine traits, exemplified by the "Universal Shakespeare." According to James Winn's recent study of Dryden's organization of the "sister" arts, Dryden understood music and painting, as well as poetry, in terms of gendered interactions (both across media and within any single one); moreover he responded generously to his female contemporaries' artistic achievements, in verse (for example, "The Ode to Anne Killigrew") as well as in personal letters (as his correspondence with Elizabeth Thomas attests).[3] Commenting on Aphra Behn's contribution to the translation of Ovid's *Heroïdes* in his "Preface to Ovid's Epistles," Dryden wrote, "I was desir'd to say that the Authour who is of the Fair Sex, understoode not Latine. But if she does not, I am afraid she has given us occasion to be asham'd who do."[4] As the most important writer of his age, and a translator of a significant number of classical texts, Dryden was an important enabler of the very women writers Chagrin objects to.

"What a Pox have the Women to do with the Muses?" indeed. A number of women writers associated themselves with the Muses when they contributed to the first volume of poetry written by women, a volume commemorating Dryden's death in 1700. *The Nine Muses*, compiled by Manley, includes elegies by her, Trotter, Pix, Sarah Fyge, Lady Sarah

Piers and others.[5] Each poem ventriloquizes a Muse; the collection thus substantiates Dryden's support as well as the terms in which Chagrin expresses his concern. Indeed, the terms of Chagrin's opposition to women writing reveal that, like Dryden's, his views of literary authority and of criticism are structured by the concepts of masculinity and femininity. Whereas Dryden's views, however, did not secure authorship as an exclusively masculine – or male – venue, Chagrin's assertion of the grammatical falsity of women writers lines up authorship with masculinity, and femininity with prostitution. This alignment represents, perhaps, a more clearly "incommensurate" model of gender difference than the one depicted by Dryden that I elucidated in the previous chapter. It supports the professional critical practice that emerges over the course of the eighteenth century and that has, until recently, dominated contemporary forms of literary criticism as well.[6] Indeed, Chagrin's wish that the English language would bear only male authors acknowledges the, to him, lamentable fact of women writers, and suggests that the criticism these women write is itself a privileged site for the exploration of the relations between authorship and gender. However, while recent feminist accounts of literary criticism undertake to restore women's writing to its history, the status of gender in these interpretations remains occluded.

As Laurie Finke rightly observes, "the assumption that women have no tradition of literary criticism is an illusion created by the particular practices that have constructed this history in the first place." However, when she turns to the criticism of Aphra Behn, it is as a way to establish that a woman's critical writing, because it is situated at the margins, provides the privileged vantage point from which to identify the ideology of Restoration literary theory – that is, according to Finke, its local enmeshment in the politics of court and patronage. As a non-aristocratic woman writer, Behn's relation to court politics would have been more attenuated than was Dryden's, who was laureate, and a relation of the Howards through marriage, but Dryden's criticism can as easily as Behn's "expose the cultural work and partisan interestedness masked by the abstractions of seventeenth-century critical orthodoxies."[7] The editors of *Women Critics*, a recent and groundbreaking anthology of criticism by women, set out to correct the literary history of criticism, and, laudably, their aim is "not to forge from this group of writers a distinctly female critical tradition."[8] Indeed, as I have been arguing, it would be impossible to produce a pure, feminocentric genealogy, considering that the very terms of genealogical inheritance derive from Dryden's use of them to ground the national literary tradition.

As the editors of this collection point out, acknowledging the contributions of women writers to the history of literary criticism broadens our understanding of criticism itself by extending our expectations of where to find it. The historical reliance of critical practice on the mutually constituting ideas of gender and authorship then becomes visible. However, the editors note with surprise the number of women who theorized about dramatic literature and performance, "associat[ing] this involvement with the licensing agreements enacted in England after 1660 which required that only women play female roles," which, they speculate, eventually prompted women actresses too to write plays (xiv).[9] This speculation overlooks a number of things: the numbers of women playwrights who were not actresses (including Behn, Trotter and Manley); and the longevity of cross-gendered performance through the beginning of the eighteenth century in which actresses not only took male roles in mixed productions, but also participated in a popular tradition of all-female performance, both at court, as John Crowne's masque *Calisto* exemplifies, and in the public theatre, as the performance which opened the Haymarket Theatre in 1705, a production of Congreve's *Love for Love* "Acted all by Women," attests.[10] However, the association of women writers with actresses does offer the opportunity to elaborate the significance of the theatre to both male- and female-authored criticism, a significance that has not been taken into account in any history of literary criticism. The Restoration stage, as Dryden's example attests, mediates the emergence of criticism (and literary culture with it) into the "public sphere," which it helps to constitute by providing a platform.

Interestingly, Catherine Gallagher cites Chagrin as an authority in her influential work on Behn's strategies for negotiating the literary marketplace, but not in order to bring Behn into relation with Dryden.[11] Gallagher uses Chagrin's words to establish the prevailing misogynist notion that prostitution is the only possible profession for women, which, she argues, Behn reappropriates and transforms, presenting herself and her sexualized text as infinitely exchangeable commodities, rather than as the wifely property of a single (male) consumer. However, whereas her essay on Behn specifically locates the redeployment of prostitution as a metaphor for self-authorization within the context of the theatre, when she extends the implications of her argument in her book about the shaping contributions women writers make to the development of "fiction," the theatre drops out of her account of the growth of the literary marketplace, and its role is never fully elucidated.[12]

The theatre/market matrix has been brilliantly delineated by Jean-Christophe Agnew, whose focus on the transition from Renaissance to Enlightenment modes of exchange suggests both the affinities between the theatre and the market and the processes through which they come to appear "worlds apart" from each other.[13] Attention to emergent practices of literary criticism as they shape the transition from a theatrically based literary culture to one both supported, and represented, by prose, makes apparent the ways in which Gallagher's idea of the literary marketplace is anachronistic: firstly, her centralization of "fiction" in the development of that market fails to take fully into account its origins in the theatre, if, indeed, fiction has origins that can be easily specified; and secondly, the literariness of the literary marketplace is thus falsely hypostatized, prematurely granted the autonomy it will only fully achieve in the second half of the eighteenth century in England.[14] In the following pages, I look at the criticism of Behn, Trotter and Manley (that of the first two in this chapter, and of the last in the next), and at the uses to which they put Dryden's writing. Like Dryden's, their criticism is appended to their theatrical texts in prologues, epilogues, prefaces and letters of dedication. Examining it allows us to complete our analysis of the emergence of a professional critical practice out of the transition from a court-sponsored literary culture centered on the theatre to a more bourgeois literary culture focused on prose writing (both fiction and journalism), and dependent on a reading public.

As we have seen, Dryden's critical writing registers the fully transitional nature of the Restoration as a political and cultural moment, a transition recapitulated in "The Secular Masque" (1700), a poem written at the end of his life. The title of that poem perfectly captures the ambivalence of the later Stuart court culture, which would have resuscitated the forms of an earlier absolutism, represented by the masque, even though these were understood, in the wake of the regicide and the demystification of the divine right of kings and inherited monarchy (complete with the Glorious Revolution), as secular. Eleanor Boswell's detailed study of one of the last court masques, John Crowne's *Calisto* (1675), establishes the central role of Charles II's court in setting the agenda for the public theatre.[15] As R. O. Bucholz notes, Charles II was the last monarch to spend so lavishly, and, as a result, his court attracted in numbers authors, like Dryden and Behn, who could expect the remuneration that turned their talents into service. As theatre historian Robert Hume notes, the Lord Chamberlain's books reflect Charles II's intense personal interest in the theatre (he spent accordingly), as well as chronicling the drama's loss of status under his successors. Over a period of three years, Queen Anne sponsored only four command performances. Bucholz, too, documents the ways in which religious polarization at the courts both of James II and of William and Mary increased military spending and decreased sponsorship of court ritual and entertainment, contributing to the decline of court culture.[16]

Curiously, although they were adolescents at the time, both future queens, Mary and Anne, had the central roles in the court production of Crowne's *Calisto*. Although Queen Anne might have proved disappointing as a patron of the theatre, her youthful investments in theatrical performance – she also had a leading role in a court performance of Nathaniel Lee's *Mithridates* – suggest that she may also have provided such female playwrights as Trotter with royal sanction.[17] Moreover, her reign provided real opportunities for some women (most notoriously including her favorites, Sarah Churchill, Duchess of Marlborough, and Abigail Masham Hill) to act on their political ambitions. Women's critical writing between the reigns of Charles II and of Anne not only reflects the changing status of the theatre but also problematizes Jürgen Habermas's description of the "bourgeois public sphere," along lines already drawn by feminist political theorists such as Nancy Fraser. While this material can be used to bolster the by-now-familiar critique of Habermas, I am less interested in backdating the emergence of "public sphere" discourse from the early decades of the eighteenth century and the periodical essays of Addison and Steele to the later decades of the seventeenth century, than I am in specifying the contributions to critical discourse made by the exploitation of the intersections of gender and the theatre by female critics writing in Dryden's wake, namely by Behn during Charles's reign and then by Trotter between 1696 and 1706.

APHRA BEHN, THE CRITIC

Aphra Behn's critical writing surrounds her plays in dedicatory letters, prologues, epilogues and prefaces addressed to readers. Behn's most sustained critical discussions occur in the texts that preface *The Dutch Lover* (1673) and *The Lucky Chance* (1687), in which she takes up the topics of writing as a woman and her relation to her female audience. These are the concerns addressed in two recent critical essays about Behn's criticism. However valuable they may be in certain respects, though, by overstating the differences between Behn and her closest contemporary, Dryden, both accounts give a distorted sense of criticism, retrospectively finding it to be more fully formed than our examination of Dryden's writing would suggest. Moreover, neither account has much to say about Behn's critical judgments.[18]

Laurie Finke portrays Behn's critical development as a shift from an initial insistence that plays can only divert but not instruct (in the preface to *The Dutch Lover*), a rejection of the Horatian dictum associated with an assertion of the power of female writing in the absence of classical learning, to an acceptance of the morality of the stage (in the preface to *The Lucky Chance*), which Finke depicts as a retreat into orthodoxy by an older, more successful author who nonetheless retains her special ability to expose the imbrication of criticism with politics and patronage (20–21). In these prefaces, however, Behn also situates herself in a social field, in relation to her dramatic precursors and contemporaries, and the terms in which she does so are all the more interesting when compared to those Dryden uses.

As Finke notes, Behn addresses the inequality between male and female access to learning in the preface to *The Dutch Lover* only to make moot the relevance of the classics to literary achievement:

For waving the examination why women having equal education with men, were not as capable of knowledge, of whatsoever sort as well as they: I'll say only as I have touch'd before, that Plays have no great room for that which is men's great advantage over women, that is Learning; We all well know that the immortal Shakespeare's Plays (who was not guilty of much more of this than often falls to women's share) have better pleas'd the World than Jonson's works, though by the way 'tis said, that Benjamin was no such Rabbi neither; (sufficient indeed to rob poor Salust of his best orations).[19]

Behn affiliates Shakespeare with women on the basis of their shared lack of classical training, thus claiming his literary legacy for herself even while she indicates that access to learning may be more complicated than one might suppose. The parenthetical illustration of Jonson's classical borrowings that wittily offsets her disclaimer of familiarity with the classics comes, as she makes explicit, from hearsay rather than from firsthand knowledge. Behn's casual phrasing invites us to share the higher value she places on the social acumen required to distinguish which witty coffee-house anecdotes, heard secondhand, might be worth repeating, than on book-learning. Her condemnation of pedantry recalls Dryden's condemnation of Jonson's Truewit for speaking more like a university pedant than a courtly wit in his *examen* of *Epicene* in *Essay of Dramatick Poesy*. She thus locates herself alongside Dryden in the milieu Erich Auerbach describes as "the court and the town."

Behn then turns her affiliation with Shakespeare into a sign of her present accomplishment. She exposes the affected learning inflicted on her by the "wit" who rejects her play as an instance of women's writing, as the passage I cited above continues:

[I]t has been observ'd that they are apt to admire [Jonson] most confoundedly, who have just such a scantling of it as he had; but affectation hath always had a greater share in both the action and the discourse of men than truth and judgment have; and for our Modern ones, except our most inimitable Laureat, I dare to say that I know none that write at such a formidable rate, but that a woman may well hope to reach their greatest heights. (162)

It is curious that Behn locates Dryden, the "inimitable Laureat," beyond the range of other writers, regardless of their sex, considering that she associates her own writing with Shakespeare's, but presumably this affiliation is less risky because as a past (and dead) writer, Shakespeare cannot disavow her. Her extravagant praise of Dryden, however – he is inimitable, the very term Dryden uses to praise Shakespeare – also suggests that her affiliation with Shakespeare is routed through Dryden. Moreover, her deference to Dryden also invites comparison to him, a comparison warranted by the Drydenesque gesture of exceptional self-affiliation, as well as by the fact that she was, after him, the most prolific playwright of the period. In the preface to *The Lucky Chance*, in which Behn defends her play against charges of indecency levelled at her with particular ferocity because she is a woman writer, the first example she uses to vindicate herself is Dryden's *Oedipus*.

As Jessica Munns notes, Behn's preface to *The Lucky Chance* is her most challenging text, as far as her representation of the relations among gender, writing and criticism is concerned. Charged with having written an obscene play, Behn interrogates the custodians of decency in whose name the charge is laid: "the ladies." Forced to defend her particular vulnerability to this charge because she is a woman writer, Behn uses her sense that her writing is no more obscene than that of her male counterparts to call into question the existence of these ladies. Throughout most of the preface, she suggests that "the ladies" should be seen as the rhetorical sleight of hand produced by irate and jealous male would-be wits who seek to police her literary output. Poets jealous of her success, "[W]hen they can no other way prevail with the Town, they charge it with the old never failing Scandal – That 'tis not fit for the Ladys."[20]

After defusing some of the particular charges by comparing her play to others', Behn states provocatively,

Had I a Day or two's time, I would sum up all your Beloved Plays, and all the Things in them that are past with such Silence by; because written by Men: such masculine Strokes in me, must not be allow'd. I must conclude those Women (*if there be any such*) greater Critics in that sort of conversation than my self, who find any of that sort in mine, or any thing that can be justly reproached. (216, my emphasis)

David Roberts acutely understands Behn's remarks to establish beyond doubt that ladies did patronize the theatre, though he follows Behn's lead in speculating upon the relations between these actual patronesses and the "ladies" addressed in so many prologues, epilogues and other writings appended to theatrical texts.[21] Perhaps more noteworthy is Behn's claim that "those Women" with expertise in "that sort of conversation" may be figments of a male imagination with a predilection for obscenity.

Using her critical expertise to identify the discrepancies between the ventriloquized ladies and the ladies to whom she goes on to appeal, Behn's tone becomes much more solicitous: "Ladies, for its further justification to you, be pleas'd to know, that the first Copy of this Play was read by several Ladys of very great Quality, and unquestioned Fame, and received their most favourable Opinion, not one charging it with the crime, that some have been pleas'd to find in the Acting" (217). Having covered all the bases, Behn ends the preface with the proclamation which the editors of *Women Critics* claim demonstrates the importance of the critical voice to women writers (xvi–xvii):

All I ask, is the priviledge for my Masculine Part the Poet in me, (if any such you will allow me) to tread in those successful Paths my predecessors have so long thriv'd in, to take those Measures that both Ancients and Moderns have set me, and by which they have leas'd the World so well: If I must not, because of my Sex, have this Freedom, but that you will usurp all to yourselves; I lay down my Quill, and you shall hear no more of me, no not so much as to make Comparisons, because I will be kinder to my Brothers of the Pen, than they have been to a defenceless Woman; for I am not content to write for a Third day only. I value Fame as much as if I had been born a Hero; and if you rob me of that, I can retire from the ungrateful World, and scorn its fickle Favours. (217)

For Behn, the use of the quill both to invent and to make comparisons, that is, both the poet and the critic in her, belong to her masculine part. She claims that writing gives her access to this masculine part, associating the possession of the quill with a performance of masculinity. For Behn, however, the quill is not unilaterally phallic; instead, as the theatrical resonance of the term "part" suggests, writing is an act which allows cross-gendered performance. This attitude towards writing is evident again when she proceeds to expose the double standard that permits her brother writers to usurp all to themselves the privilege of cross-gendered identification even while they would restrict her to a singular femininity. Behn ironically turns her unwillingness to remain a "defenceless Woman" into the accusation that they access their feminine parts, through which they condemn her writing in the name of "the ladies," at the expense of the very commitment to chivalry that should prohibit attacking her as such.

For Behn, writing is not gender-neutral; rather it is a medium through which imaginative self-translation across gendered lines becomes possible. It should surprise us neither that this performative understanding of writing is facilitated by its proximity to the stage, nor that this attitude is misrecognized by Behn's contemporaries as "looseness," and by our own, in a slightly different register, as "transgressive."[22] This characterization, which bespeaks the ways female authorship was circumscribed along similar lines to those regulating women's sexual behavior, should not allow us to collapse, as Gallagher does through her focus on Behn's metaphor of prostitution, the one into the other. Otherwise, "gender" threatens to become the exclusive term of analysis, and we lose sight of its intersections with the ways other social and political factors situate the writer in question, thus risking repeating the marginalization of women writers that has already occurred through the exclusion of "gender" as a term in the first place.

THE GENDER OF LITERARY GENEALOGY

In an economical account of the emergence of female authorship that looks at the manufacture of two alternative models, the "chaste Orinda," Katherine Philips, and the "loose Astrea," Aphra Behn, Paula Backscheider provides a salutary proviso that prevents any simple understanding of these apparently heavily gendered qualifiers.[23] As Backscheider points out, the "chaste" propriety of Philips's reluctance to appear in print sharply contrasts with the "loose" professionalism of Behn's bawdy writing only until we recognize Philips's construction as an "author-function" (74). Backscheider's examination of Philips's translation of Corneille's *Pompée* reveals a dramatist intent on publication as well as production, and the posthumously published *Letters from Orinda to Poliarchus* (1705) make it clear that Philips's reluctance to appear in print is a pose that masks her commitment to a literary career. Thus while Philips and Behn offered succeeding women writers models of authorship unquestionably but differently gendered, to extrapolate gender from the writing is more complicated than it might appear.

The difficulties of extricating questions of gender and writing are exemplified in "To the Excellent Orinda," an anonymous appreciation of Philips's *Pompey* by a woman who signed herself "Philo-philippa." The poem opens by setting up an opposition between male writing, sponsored by Phoebus, and female writing, sponsored by Orinda, who acquires the laurel directly from Daphne:

> Let the male Poets their male Phoebus chuse,
> Thee I invoke, Orinda, for my Muse;
> He could but force Branch, Daphne her Tree
> Most freely offers to her Sex and thee,
> And says to verse, so unconstrain'd as yours,
> Her Laurel freely comes, your fame secures:
> And men no longer shall with ravish'd Bays
> Crown their forc'd Poems by as forc'd a praise.
> (1–8)[24]

The poem instances the genealogizing impulse that so often informs the appreciation and legitimation of women's literary ambitions, an impulse we have seen Dryden turn into what comes to be the critically commonplace vocabulary of familial relations between poets. As it proceeds, however, the poem obscures the difference between men and women that supposedly grounds the separate traditions:

> Train'd up to Arms, we Amazons have been,
> And Spartan Virgins strong as Spartan Men:
> Breed Women but as Men, and they are these;
> Whilst Sybarit Men are Women by their ease.
> (63–66)

Philo-philippa seeks to neutralize "masculinity" and "femininity" as evaluative criteria, and legitimate her own writing, by making the case that the soul has no sex:

> If Souls no Sexes have, as 'tis confest,
> 'Tis not the he or she makes Poems best:
> Nor can men call these Verses Feminine,
> Be the sense vigorous and Masculine.
> (91–94)

No sooner has she jettisoned the applicability of gender as a social mode of organization to writing (and other spiritual activities), however, than the persistence of gender reasserts itself. These lines continue:

> 'Tis true, Apollo sits as Judge of Wit,
> But the nine Female learned Troop are it.
> (95–96)

The poem vacillates between these two positions for another hundred lines. Philo-philippa asserts, on the one hand, that Corneille's *Pompeé* and Orinda's translation of it make the two authors indistinguishable from one another in their achievements:

> And yet ye both are so the very same,
> As when two Tapers join'd make one bright flame.
> And sure the Copier's honour is not small,
> When Artists doubt which is Original.   (161–64)

On the other hand, she argues that Orinda writes under fettering conditions:

> But if your fetter'd Muse thus praised be,
> What great things do you write when it is free?
> (105–6)

These vacillations record the difficulties of fixing in any final sense the relation between gender and writing for Philo-philippa, if not for Orinda herself.[25]

What does emerge clearly, however, is the insistent pressure that the social terms of gender exert over Philo-philippa. This, in conjunction with other end-of-the-century social pressures, the results of a century's worth of crises of succession, impact on Trotter, who writes a generation later in a moment in which court culture is in full decline. Literature and literary criticism reflect this decline, as they turn away from aristocratic patronage towards an emergent reading public, but they also become factors in the development of the public sphere, as is attested by Richard Steele and Joseph Addison's career-making gestures of shaping the reading public.[26] For Trotter, as for Dryden and Behn, criticism still depends on the theatre (textually, in the sense that it occurs in texts appended to plays, and substantively in the sense that dramatic texts are under discussion), but while, like Chagrin (whose presence in a dramatic dialogue evokes Dryden's *Essay of Dramatick Poesy*), Trotter orients her criticism towards a consuming public, partly as a result of Dryden's availability as a model, she does so out of a social position of a "city lady," whose place is emphatically not at court. In this sense, Trotter, like Chagrin, more closely resembles the city-centered Addison or Steele than she does the more court-oriented Dryden or Behn.

THE CITY LADY AS CRITIC

Although she was a precocious sixteen-year-old when she adapted Aphra Behn's *Agnes de Castro* for the stage, Trotter is less easily located in the "school" of Astrea than her translation might suggest. Indeed, her treatment of femininity, inaugurated in that work, sustained in her later plays and important to her critical writing as well, might prompt some to situate her more firmly in the "school" of Orinda. Instead of categorizing Trotter in the terms of a feminist literary genealogy, in the following pages I argue that Trotter's treatment of femininity should be understood as a focal point around and through which other social pressures constellate and get expressed, allowing her to contribute to the formation of genealogy as a literary-critical category.

Two of her female contemporaries seem to have understood her literary achievements in this way when they characterize her as mediating between Orinda and Astrea. Delarivier Manley's commendatory poem "To the Author of *Agnes de Castro*," heralds Trotter as joint heir to both Orinda and Astrea:

> Orinda, and the Fair Astrea gone,
> Not one was found to fill the vacant throne:
> Aspiring Man had quite regain'd the Sway,
> Again had Taught us humbly to Obey;
> Till you (Nature's third start, in favour of our Kind)
> With stronger Arms, their Empire have disjoyn'd,
> And snatcht a Lawrel which they thought their Prize,
> Thus conqu'ror, with your Wit, as with your Eyes.

Sarah Piers's commendatory poem, prefaced to Trotter's *The Unhappy Penitent* (1701), also describes how Philips and Behn paved the way for Trotter's achievement:

> Thus like the Morning Star Orinda rose
> A Champion for her sex and wisely chose,
> Conscious of female weakness, humble wais
> T'insinuate applause, not storm the Bays.
> Next gay Astrea briskly won the Prize,
> Yet left a Spacious room to criticise.[27]

However, Trotter's own appeal to precedent as a strategy to legitimize her literary ambition does not restrict itself along gendered lines; in her self-genealogizing, Trotter looks to Behn, as is evident in the choice to rewrite her, but also to Shakespeare and Dryden, as we will see when we examine other features of her self-presentation in her subsequent plays and their prefatory material. Indeed, as in Dryden's critical practice, the self-genealogizing gesture of legitimation is paradigmatically a critical one insofar as it inscribes a literary history that gets taken up in the vocabulary of "ages" and "schools," even as it records the crises of inheritance that inform the formulation of a vernacular national literary tradition. Because Trotter's adaptation of Behn offers a vantage point on the imbrication of gender and writing in Trotter's own career, it is the appropriate place to begin investigating its role in her criticism.

A tragic romance, the story of Agnes de Castro routes a circuit of triangulated desire through Constantia, the princess of Portugal, who loves her husband, Don Pedro, heir to the throne, who adores Agnes de Castro, the loving and loyal friend of Constantia. Subsidiary points of triangulation drive the plot: Don Alvaro is Don Pedro's rival for Agnes's affections, and Don Alvaro's sister, Elvira, competes with Agnes for the heart of Don Pedro. Both Trotter's and Behn's texts explore the conflict between those who would regulate love according to the demands of alliance (notably Don Alvaro and the king), and those who accept that love is determined by a higher power regardless of worldly considerations or individual self-control (Don Pedro, Constantia and Agnes).

The affective impact of Behn's novelistic version derives from her presentation of the equanimity with which the main characters accept the vicissitudes of an emotional life without letting it call their virtue into question. Reminiscent of Mme. de Lafayette's *The Princess of Cleves* in this respect, Behn's text nevertheless does not eschew melodrama. The plot is set in motion by Elvira, who discloses to Constantia her husband's passion for Agnes. Were it not for her machinations, however, the three members of the central triangle would simply persist in their situation. Though no one attains satisfaction or reciprocation for his or her passion, all three exhibit a touching willingness to accept their triangulated relations. Once it is brought to their attention, they even desire to preserve it, recognizing that other alternatives are more dangerous. Agnes does not seek to leave Coimbra until Don Alvaro's advances become overwhelming, and even then Don Pedro and Constantia persuade her to stay.

Perhaps because she feels the need to make her central characters less passive for the purposes of the stage, Trotter alters the onset of the action, making Constantia more actively inquisitive into the recesses of Don Pedro's heart. Although to the great disappointment of Elvira and her maid, Bianca, Constantia exhibits no jealousy when she finds out that Don Pedro loves Agnes, her epistemological drive to identify the object of Pedro's affections from the outset makes her more clearly Elvira's counterpart. In Behn's version, by contrast, Constantia's acceptance that Don Pedro does not return her affections undermines her position as rival either to Elvira or to Agnes.

By adding Bianca as Elvira's servant and helper, Trotter doubles the sources of female villainy and provides her play with a parallel to the heroic friendship of Agnes and Constantia. In the second act, Elvira and Bianca discuss the duplicitous nature of women, offsetting the exchanges in the first and second acts in which Constantia and Agnes discourse on the merits of a friendship which allows Constantia to trust that Agnes has not and will not betray her with Don Pedro. As Elvira says,

> 'Tis the peculiar cunning of our Sex,
> To make Good, Ill, and Ill for Good appear;
> And things which seem directly contrary,
> We turn, and use to compass our designs.[28]

None of the rumination on the ways in which characters are emblems of their gender is present in Behn's version. Although in Trotter's version the "female natures" of Elvira and Bianca, on the one hand, and Constantia and Agnes, on the other, differ radically, together they register the play's almost obsessive interest in depicting women's actions as reflections of their gender. Thus, in contrast to Behn, who at the end of her career (in the preface to *The Lucky Chance*) exploits the disjunctions between poetry, criticism and gender, Trotter dramatizes the conjunctions between them, both at the level of character – so that actions reflect gendered "natures" – and at the level of authorship – so that Trotter presents her own writing as the reflection of her gender. If Behn's disjunctions are enabled by her situation at the crux of the two models of gender difference identified by Laqueur, Trotter's conjunctions point to the waning of the older hierarchical model and the consolidation of the newer incommensurable model of gender difference. Indeed, the conjunctions among poetry, criticism and gender, which Trotter explores more fully in later works, are not the privileged terrain of the female author; they also provide the "Manly" William Wycherley (so called by his contemporaries after the outspoken hero of his play, *The Plain Dealer*) with the ground upon which to appeal to the audience to recognize *Agnes de Castro*'s dramatic success in the prologue he wrote "at the author's request."

Nominally addressed to the "Ladies and Gallants" of the audience, Wycherley's prologue turns from one group to the other, but as it specifies each one's relations to the authoress, the types of men diversify: there are "Men of Honour," "Men of Wit" and "Beaux." Despite the multiplication of male types, they are all defined by their reactions to female behavior. Wycherley requests that the audience

> will not your Displeasure to her show,
> Who your scorn Ventures, but to pleasure you,
> Nay, her own pleasure does for you forego;
> And like the Pregnant of her Sex, to gain,
> But for your pleasure, more Disgrace and Pain.[29]

Wycherley's prologue particularizes the reasons each contingent should refrain from censuring the play: Men of Honour should not speak ill of those women they do not know; Beaux should never silence others, particularly women, to hide their own want of wit; and Wits are enjoined to appreciate with patience "Our Female Wit." The prologue ends:

> Nay, though it shou'd not please, th'Intention praise,
> 'Tis merit only, to desire to please;
> Then be not, as Poor Women often find,
> Less kind to her because she's more inclin'd,
> At venture of her Fame, to please Mankind.

The figures of the pregnant woman and the fallen woman analogize the pleasure provided by the woman writer to a female sexuality whose sole purpose is to satisfy men. Wycherley reduces women's gender to a set of sexual, rather than more abstract, attributes, and thus women's sexuality forms the basis of socially regulatory ideals of gender that the categories "Men of Wit," "Men of Honour", and "Beaux", represent. In other words, for Wycherley, women's behavior reflects their sexuality, and men's behavior reflects their reactions to women. A woman's writing, understood, as the woman herself, as a potential source of pleasure, can thus become the paradigmatic and generative instance of gender organization.

Michael McKeon observes a similar consequence of the ways Richard Steele uses effeminacy "in the experimental construction of masculine norms" in several early numbers of the *Tatler*: he and his contributors make "a minute and searching discrimination of the 'distinct Classes' of men encountered at the London coffee houses" by focusing on gender characteristics – "to the exclusion of professional and status discriminants."[30] As McKeon notes, "This effect is achieved by characterizing the several male types largely according to their disparate relations to women. In other words, it is as though the general rule of patriarchy, by which women are defined in terms of their relation to the father and the husband, at this particular moment takes on a certain gender reciprocity" (313). For McKeon, the early eighteenth century offers a view of the surprisingly positive (if temporary) contributions both effeminacy and femininity made to "the early modern experimentation with masculinity" (313). I will return to McKeon's argument about the emergence of gender difference in England between 1660 and 1760 when I examine the role that effeminacy and femininity play in Trotter's literary criticism. For now, it is enough to note that Trotter capitalizes on the possibility McKeon notes for gender reciprocity when she rewrites Wycherley's concept of pleasure in her prologue for *Love at a Loss: or Most Votes Carry it* (1701):

> Fain wou'd our Authoress please, and please you so,
> That to herself you shou'd the pleasure owe,
> We think she's safe by forces of her own,
> And like her Nature, she depends on none.[31]

Although the prologue is intertextually dependent, the "Authoress" asserts that she is "naturally" independent. Accepting Wycherley's assertion that women's sexuality is the basis for the social organization of gender, Trotter expands the concept of female sexuality to reflect her status "independent" of men. The play is dedicated to Lady Sarah Piers, with whom Trotter apparently exchanged love letters.[32] Curiously, the play finds no other way to marry off its heroine, named Lesbia, than by majority vote, as the subtitle indicates. Although marriage signals female dependence, Trotter attempts to revalue the conventional comic conclusion by dramatizing the possibility that Beaumine, the rake, will be reformed by marriage to a virtuous woman. Trotter's presentation of women as virtuous agents of reform relies on an optimistic version of Wycherley's view that women's sexuality provides the basis for the social organization of gender; for Trotter, this view underwrites her authorial choices, and, as we will see, her critical practice as well. Interestingly, this view includes the extension of women's erotic options to include homosocial friendship in the name of female independence. This independence, however, may depend, after all, on the monarch; Trotter comes to refer women's capacity to inspire virtuous action to Queen Anne, whose youthful theatrical investments also may have licensed Trotter's representation of women's independence in terms of homoerotic friendship between women.[33]

In the prologue to *The Revolution of Sweden* (1706), Trotter's last play, she expands her understanding of the role of the woman writer as that of a social reformer. It begins:

> Invited by a Woman, every Guest,
> No doubt expects a soft Effeminate Treat,
> Has set his appetite for tender strains
> Of Maids forsaken, or Despairing swains...
> But she by other means to please design'd...
> To publick Virtues she'd your Souls incite,
> A woman thus may give you safe Delight.[34]

Trotter divides femininity from the false expectations of the audience for some "Effeminate Treat." The division is marked by the contrast between the results of "a Woman['s]" invitation, and what "A woman" gives. The prologue suggests that, shedding the false generic expectations associated with the writer's gender, the audience will discover a truer association: as a female-authored play, it will incite the public to virtue. Moreover, the prologue concludes by situating Trotter's claims about gendered expectations under the aegis of political power:

> Nor can the vainest, haughtiest Man, disdain
> A Woman's precepts in great Anna's Reign;
> If by a woman you tonight are taught,
> Think on that Source from whence th'Instruction's brought.

Trotter thus elaborates her role as a woman writer into a claim to be a defender of her sex.[35] Like Mary Astell, in her argument against the subordination of women, Trotter appeals to the practical and symbolic significance of Queen Anne as ruler of the country. As Astell argues, the notion of man's natural superiority to woman is ridiculous, since it would mean that "the greatest Queen ought not to command, but to obey her footman."[36] Trotter's presentation of Anne's royal power as the framework within which a female author might incite her audience to "publick Virtues" complicates Habermas's distinction between the "literary" and the "critical" or "political public spheres."[37]

The dedication of *The Unhappy Penitent* (1701) to Charles, Lord Halifax, is Trotter's most recognizable literary-critical text. There, according to her editor and biographer, Thomas Birch, "She draws the characters of the most eminent of her predecessors in tragic poetry with great judgment and precision."[38] The dedication to *The Unhappy Penitent* expresses her conviction that her writing appeals to the softer passions by virtue of her being a member of the "softer" sex.

We should not be surprised to find that Dryden is a subject of Trotter's criticism, considering that, by including extensive critical comments in a dedicatory letter, Trotter follows Dryden's critical model. Trotter's remarks begin:

> The most Universal genius this Nation ever bred, Dryden himself, did not excel in every part[.] [T]hrough most of what he has writ there appears a distinguishing greatness, that Elevation of Thought, that Sublime which transports the Soul; he commands our Admiration for himself, but little moves our concern for those he represents; his Genius seems not to work upon the softer Passions, tho' some of his last Translations are excellent in that kind, nothing more lively, more tender or more moving, but there the *Words*, alone are his, of which it must be confess'd he had on all Subjects the exactest Propriety, the most Expressive, and dispos'd into the sweetest Numbers.[39]

Borrowing her terms of approval from Dryden's extolling of Shakespeare for his "Universal mind," Trotter praises Dryden in the style he uses for others. Moreover, she adopts another of Dryden's trademarks: she describes his virtues in order to excuse his flaws, thereby calling attention to his flaws in order to make room for herself as a superior critic and playwright. All that is tender and moving in Dryden's writing are his words. Her remarks suggest that to elicit softness is desirable, and she proceeds to consider how other playwrights fare on this count. She finds that both Thomas Otway and Nathaniel Lee, two of Dryden's contemporaries, also fall short of the mark: Otway is compassionate but too limited, and Lee could have been great, but he aimed instead at the sublime, which made him extravagant.

As the dedication proceeds, however, it becomes clear that Trotter is not only interested in placing herself in a tradition of sentimental writers, succeeding at eliciting softness where they have failed. She also describes the flaw her own play shares with those writers, offering a critique of the tradition she delineates, which, in turn, validates her judgment as a critic. By taking love as its subject, *The Unhappy Penitent* extends the tradition that includes Dryden's *All for Love*, Lee's *The Rival Queens* and Otway's *Venice Preserv'd*; like them, it reproduces the effeminate taste of the age:

> [T]he Distress is not great enough, the Subject of it only the misfortune of Lovers, which I partly design'd in compliance with the effeminate taste of the Age; notwithstanding which, and the right of Possession, it has long held on the Modern Stage, I have ventur'd to propose a Doubt whether Love be a proper Subject for it; seems to me not Noble, not solemn enough for Tragedy, but I have a much greater Objection against it, at least as 'tis generally represented ... the most that can be allow'd that passion is to be the Noblest frailty of the Mind, but 'tis a Frailty, and becomes a Vice, when cherish'd as an exalted Vertue. (A2v–3r)

Trotter's attack on the subject of love seems strange: it appears to threaten the status of her own play, calling into question her judgment and therefore potentially undermining her appreciation of her predecessors as well. The main flaw for which she faults these writers, that they do not properly elicit the softer emotions, seems either redundant or irrelevant in light of the problem of subject matter, where the flaw would lie instead in the very attempt to elicit the softer passions in the first place.

To view Trotter as undermining her own critical credibility, however, requires that we equate taking love as the subject with appealing to the softer passions, an equation underwritten by our own association of a sentimental subject – love – with feminine (and feminizing, or "effeminate") taste. When Trotter calls the age "effeminate," she condemns the choice of love as the subject of plays, but, as her remarks on Dryden, Otway and Lee make clear, she considers appealing to the softer passions to be a virtue – moreover, one at which she is more successful than her male counterparts. Trotter may criticize effeminacy, but her elevation of softness implies a valuation of "femininity" that makes her realization of softness more successful.

Where Dryden presents a sliding scale between femininity and effeminacy, Trotter's doubts about the nobility of love as a subject of tragedy, in conjunction with her praise for plays that "work upon the softer passions," put a wedge between femininity and effeminacy in the name of virtue. The comparison between Dryden and Trotter is sharpened by McKeon's account of the emergence of gender difference in England. McKeon observes the shift in meanings that "effeminacy" undergoes between 1660 and 1760 from indicating men who like women (in the sense of being sexually obsessed with them), to indicating men who *are like* women (in the sense of sodomitical transvestism) (308). McKeon uses the figure of the corrupt and unproductive aristocrat who comes to be associated with that of the sodomite in order to propose that we understand this shift in relation to the decline of aristocratic ideology (311–12). For Dryden, effeminacy threatens masculinity, but not because it is associated with sodomy, as the counter-example of Rochester, the aristocratic masculine rake as sodomite, makes clear; Trotter's elevation of femininity above effeminacy may be seen as a step in the process that affiliates effeminacy with sodomy, construing it as a "failure" of both "true" femininity and "true" masculinity. The distance of Trotter from the court milieu, and the distance of William's court – condemned in the 1690s (after Mary's death) as excessively hospitable to sodomites – from aristocratic ideals, are both important factors in Trotter's literary-critical articulation of bourgeois gender codes.[40]

Trotter's understanding of the sentimental and its affects intersects with her critical practice, and in this respect she also displays her debt to

Dryden. Dryden uses the production of tears and partiality to consolidate his role as an impartial critic; as we have seen, the connections he draws between scenes of partiality and critical impartiality owe a great deal to the ways he represents Shakespeare, particularly in *All for Love* and its preface. Interestingly, in Trotter's preface, she comments on Shakespeare and her remarks fulfill a similar function; they anchor her understanding of softness and thus enable her to use the criterion of self-consciousness where Dryden has used impartiality, to empower her critical judgment. It is also noteworthy that in her comments on Shakespeare, Trotter sounds the most like Dryden himself:

The inimitable Shakespeare seems alone secure on every side from attack, (for I speak not here of Faults against the Rules of Poetry, but against the natural genius) he had all the Images of nature present to him, Study'd her throughly, and boldly copy'd all her various Features, for tho' he chiefly exerted himself on the more Masculine Passion, 'tis as the choice of his Judgment, not the restraint of his genius, and he seems to have design'd those few tender moving Scenes he has giv'n us, as proof he cou'd be every way equally Admirable. (A2v)

Like Dryden, Trotter characterizes Shakespeare in gendered terms. He excells at the representation of "Masculine" passions, and the fact that he writes more such scenes than those that are tender and moving is the result of judgment, not ability. Trotter thus associates Shakespeare's judgment with his masculinity, which she characterizes as both singular ("inimitable," "alone") and natural. Moreover, her Shakespeare includes the capacity for femininity.

Trotter's preface clearly echoes Dryden's preface to *Troilus and Cressida*, in which his initial contrast between Shakespeare's "masculinity" and Fletcher's "femininity" (XIII: 233) is subsumed by his production of Shakespeare's universality. Trotter borrows Dryden's association of Shakespeare with a state beyond gender that testifies to his paradoxical (in)imitability; both Trotter and Dryden thus maintain Shakespeare's excellent masculinity. However, Trotter's deference to Dryden's criticism is not complete. Although, like Dryden, Trotter connects the subject of love to effeminacy, she does not share Dryden's association of softness with effeminacy. As we have seen, Trotter inserts "femininity" as the term to be associated with softness, thus redeeming softness as a writerly virtue, and castigating the "effeminacy" of love. As I argued in the previous chapter, Dryden uses the gender terms to facilitate his representation of the literary tradition as a patrimony, which can then be inherited from a universal and classicized Shakespeare. When Trotter diverges from

Dryden on the question of softness, she inserts "femininity" as a term independent from "effeminacy." Unlike Behn, who affiliates Shakespeare with female authorship on the basis of a shared lack of classical schooling, Trotter insists that the affiliation should be understood on the grounds of softness.

Trotter's self-presentation as a woman writer stems both from her understanding of gender as following from biological sex and from her association of femininity with virtuous reform. Ironically, when she presents this position out of an apologetic stance, it seems as if she has taken the paternalistic advice of George Savile, the Marquis of Halifax. In his conduct manual addressed to women, *A Ladies New Years Gift*, Halifax suggests that women turn their weakness and tears to their advantage:

> You [women] have it in your power not only to free your selves, but to subdue your Masters, and without violence to throw both Natural and legal Authority at your feet. We [men] are made of differing Tempers, that our Defects may the better be mutually supplied: Your Sex wanteth our reason for your conduct, and our Strength for your Protection: Ours wanteth your Gentleness to soften and to entertain us. You have more strength in your Looks, than we have in our Laws, and more Power in your tears, than we have by our Arguments.[41]

Trotter justifies her critical assertions as follows:

> I know not how, my Lord, in designing only to hint an obstacle to perfection in our Poets, I have unawares launch'd into a Subject which I fear your Lordship will think unbecoming in me to touch; but if Presidents may be admitted as a plea, several wretched Poets before me have had the priviledge of passing their censure on the best; however I may be allow'd to urge that the Fault which I have caution'd against, is not mine, I know too well the Bounds of my stinted talent, and I fear I may rather be accused of not having exerted the little strength I have, than of aiming beyond it in this weak performance, which I presume not to offer your Lordship but as an object of your mercy. (A2v)

Trotter's syntax, with its many negative constructions and qualifiers, serves a purpose: overwhelmingly deferential and self-minimizing, it masks her assertions as excuses. Trotter underlines through repetition her lack of control – she does not know, she is unaware – but she also "know[s] too well." What she knows, however, is "the Bounds of my stinted talent." Self-consciousness is her distinguishing mark – it testifies to her critical virtues. Knowing her self-worth validates her judgments and vindicates her from the flaws of the others who pass judgment. Thus, if her predecessors have passed censure, she has a double right to do so – because of precedent and because she is more virtuous. Although she claims access to her precedents, their arrogance and self-overestimation recast her appeal to them, proportionately strengthening her claims to virtue and self-consciousness. Whereas Dryden justifies finding fault with Shakespeare in terms of his own critical strength, that is, his impartiality, Trotter strategically represents her critical judgment in terms of knowing her own worth.

Trotter empowers her assertion of self-consciousness by means of the powerful historical affiliation with Shakespeare. Self-consciousness as a critical virtue is, perhaps, no stranger a precursor to neutrality or objectivity than impartiality, though it lacks the latter's conspicuous potential for a magisterial perspective, situated as it is in the private domain. Yet impartiality also registers as private, as Ros Ballaster observes when she contrasts impartiality to the political partisanship conveyed by the phrase, "being a party man." Ballaster describes Addison and Steele's affiliation with women as connected to their non-participation in party politics, especially considering that they define their impartiality through the feminized activities of "spectating" and "tattling."[42] If self-consciousness is Trotter's "improvement" on Dryden's impartiality, it is noteworthy that Trotter only puts it forward, following Dryden's model, once she has adopted an apologetic tone.

Trotter reorients the private (and Protestant) criterion of "self-consciousness" towards the public. She thus aims to incite in her audience virtue in the name of social reform, and she does so out of a social position she describes in an interesting analogy that allows us to situate her critical innovations in relation to the transition of literary culture away from a court-subsidized scene of patronage to one more oriented towards a consuming public:

[L]ike some City Ladies, who are content to be the jest at court rather than not appear there, I feel a Satisfaction in the Honour of being known to your Lordship, tho' only by my Faults. The knowledge of our Transgressions may be a considerable Step towards amending them for the Future, but 'tis certainly a great aggravation of them in the Committing, which I must confess my self guilty of in Writing this Play. (A2v)

Trotter clearly signals her non-aristocratic social standing: her father, Captain David Trotter, had held a prestigious post in the Royal Navy under Charles II until his death in 1684. He left his family dependent on a pension bestowed by the Admiralty, which was stopped after Charles's death, obliging his wife and two daughters to depend on the charity of friends and relations.[43] A professional writer from the city but not of it, her identification as a "City Lady," accompanied by her witty acknowledgment of the foibles of "City Ladies" operates as another example of the workings of self-consciousness: it exempts her from the vanities of these ladies but it also gains her access to people, such as her patron, within the courtly orbit.

Self-consciousness thus constitutes Trotter's major qualification as both a playwright and a critic. It allows her to stake a claim to a literary inheritance and she portrays it as the result of her femininity. However, when Trotter develops self-consciousness into a platform for promoting women's writings in the letter dedicating *The Revolution in Sweden* to Lady Harriet Godolphin, she inadvertently registers the limitations of this model for connecting gender and writing.

Having elaborated her role as a woman writer into a claim to be a defender of her sex, she calls for more patronage of women by women, and invokes the French as a model not for their "Fopperies" but for their "illustrious Women." She goes on, however, in an apologetic mode, to indicate that she cannot do justice to her patron Lady Harriet's merits: "I dare only Venture Superficially to touch [them]. An Addison shou'd draw that Prudence of your Conduct, that Delicacy of Judgment..." (A3r). As my ellipsis signifies, Trotter goes on to enumerate Lady Harriet's virtues. She pays court to her patroness, but wary of being the city lady who would rather be the jest in court than not appear there, she protects herself from being laughed at by ventriloquizing Joseph Addison. Curiously, her consciousness of her own questionable courtliness overrides the oddness of deferring to Addison in the context of a call for more opportunities for English women. "An Addison" can negotiate the social distinctions between city and court with greater ease and more propriety than she can, or so she implies.

The disparity between Trotter's feminist agenda and the tactics she uses to pursue it, which, however inadvertently, reinscribe women in an inferior position to men like Addison, draws our attention to the correspondences between gender and writing that Trotter finds enabling; it exhibits the same understanding of the relation expressed by Chagrin the critic. As we have seen, Chagrin experiences a failure of correspondence between grammar and gender and seeks, through criticism, to legislate its maintenance. Trotter, by contrast, portrays the success of this correspondence; it enables her literary and critical achievement. Although they each regard the correspondence differently, both Trotter's and Chagrin's critical practices are designed to enforce it. However, the correspondence which Trotter finds enabling cannot transcend the social distinctions that circumscribe women's mobility, limiting their access to the courtly sphere and its literary traditions. Interestingly, the performative understanding of the relations between gender and writing exhibited by Behn, and elaborated, as we shall see in the following chapter, by Manley, provides critical access to this courtly sphere, although in ways that revalue its status. Moreover, their exploitation of the disjunctions among poetry, criticism and gender that they find so enabling ultimately invites the charges that come to be levelled against their sexual morality (their "looseness"). If Trotter's critical position as a city lady provides an exception to Habermas's description of the emergence of bourgeois public sphere culture as male, it is one that proves the rule – or at least, in her deference to "an Addison," points to its consolidation.

CHAPTER 5

Scandals of a female nature

Although Delarivier Manley was born to the Lieutenant Governor and Commander of all His Majesty's castles, forts and forces within the Isle of Jersey, with the appropriate aristocratic connections for a position at court, her hopes to be appointed a maid of honour to Mary of Modena, wife of James II, were thwarted by the Glorious Revolution. Manley went on to be "ruined" by her cousin, John Manley, who seduced her into a bigamous marriage, and with whom she had a son in 1692. For the rest of her life, Manley supported herself by her writing. She began her literary career in 1696, with the publication of *Letters Written on a Stage Coach Journey to Exeter* and two plays, *The Lost Lover, or: The Jealous Husband* and *The Royal Mischief*.[1] Jonathan Swift sponsored her authorship of Tory pamphlets, and invited her collaboration on the *Examiner*, of which she became the editor in June, 1711.[2] Although she continued to write intermittently for the stage, she is remembered chiefly for her scandal chronicle, *The New Atalantis* (1709), in which she put to use as Tory propaganda the episodic romance, modeled after the French courtly *roman à clef*.[3]

The New Atalantis is a political satire consisting of episodes of sexually scandalous behavior perpetrated by thinly disguised "persons of quality." Representing political "abuses" as sexual "abuses," Manley relies on the sexual scandal's being understood as political allegory.[4] These "persons of quality" were clear political targets who were, quite explicitly, meant to be recognized – and indeed they were, as her arrest for libel soon after the book's appearance indicates. Manley aims her satire mainly at the group of powerful Whigs at Queen Anne's court. Depending on how much political power one wants to attribute to such satire, and the degree of credence one gives to Sarah Churchill's correspondence, *The New Atalantis* may well have helped to precipitate the collapse of the Whig ministry in 1710, a year after its publication.[5]

The New Atalantis, however, also functions as literary criticism, an aspect of the text that emerges when we observe that many targets of its satire were literary figures. For example, Manley, who had edited the collection of poems by women writers published to commemorate Dryden's death, attacks these figures in *The New Atalantis*. As Rosalind Ballaster notes, "The four women who contributed poems to *The Nine Muses* of 1700 – Sarah Fyge Egerton, Mary Pix, Catharine Trotter and Susannah Centlivre – are all satirised in *The New Atalantis* both for their Whig politics and for their disloyalty as friends" (xiii). Indeed, Manley sustained a critique of Trotter almost from the outset of her career.[6] Although she wrote a commendatory poem for Trotter's *Agnes de Castro* that hailed her as the joint heir to the literary legacies of Katherine Philips and Aphra Behn, in the preface to her play, *The Lost Lover*, she quickly retracted her praise, stating:

> They object the verses wrote by me before *Agnes de Castro* where, with Poetick vanity I seemed to think myself a Champion of our Sex; some of my Witty Critticks make a Jest of my proving so favourable an Enemy, but let me tell them then, this is not design'd as a Consequence of that Challenge, being writ two years before, and cannot have a smaller Share in their esteem than it does in mine.[7]

In the following pages, I begin with an examination of Manley's portrait of Trotter in *The New Atalantis* to establish the ways it works as both literary criticism and political satire. I then move back to Manley's critique of Trotter in her theatrical writings, and to a consideration of Dryden's influence on them, which permits me to conclude my argument about the role of women in the emergence of criticism out of the transition from its dependence on the theatre to its orientation, in prose, towards a reading public.

The New Atalantis begins with the reunion of Virtue and her daughter, Astrea, named, significantly, in homage to Aphra Behn.[8] Astrea, who had abandoned the world but revisits it to see if "humankind were still as defective as when she in disgust forsook it" (4), hears her mother's complaint that she has found "no sanctuary among the lovers of this age" (5). Virtue, abandoned and outwardly in tatters, explains that the degeneration of the age stems from its exclusive pursuit of bodily pleasures at the expense of those of the heart. She illustrates the "diabolical way of argument" that insists "love resides not in the heart, but in the face" (5), by citing Rochester's poem, "A Letter from Artemisia in the Town to Chloe in the Country":

> To an exact Perfection they have brought
> The Action Love, the Passion is forgot. (5)

Exploiting Rochester's ventriloquism of his critique of court vice through aristocratic female epistolarity, Manley uses female allegorical figures to redirect the critique. As Jonathan Kramnick points out, whereas Rochester aims his critique of the court at a court-affiliated, aristocratic, coterie audience, Manley aims hers towards the broader audience of the town.[9] Moreover, her exposé of aristocratic sex-scandal embraces literary figures in the same vocabulary, regardless of their provenance. The difficulty of distinguishing political from literary critique in Manley's satire points to a feature it shares with that of her male contemporaries: it occurs in a field of cultural production in which the literary is not yet clearly demarcated from other kinds of writing. Yet the path her critical career takes from the composition of theatrical writing to that of prose satire allows us to specify the social relations of literary and political criticism, and aristocratic and popular tastes, both as Manley represents them in her texts and as she comes to represent them for her male contemporaries. After looking at the ways Manley's satire emerges out of her exploration of the conjunctions and disjunctions among writing, gender and social position in the theatrical writing, I conclude by situating the critical satirical practice of *The New Atalantis* in relation to that of her male contemporaries.

MANLEY'S SATIRICAL CRITICISM

In a brief episode in the ongoing debasement of virtue that *The New Atalantis* chronicles, Intelligence, another of Manley's allegorical female narrators, tells of Daphne's (Trotter's) literary career, which is prompted by the lack of generosity of her lover, Fortunatas (the Duke of Marlborough). An exchange of favors allows Daphne to veil her modesty in the pretense of business, but Intelligence wonders why Daphne does not grow rich as a result. Marlborough and his duchess had grown notoriously wealthy as a result of Queen Anne's favor; part of Intelligence's political satire thus stems from her comments on Marlborough's stinginess:

It appears strange to me, that considering the Count's Power and Riches, she did not make her fortune by his Fondness. But I think there yet wants an Example of elevated Generosity in him, to any of his Mistresses, tho' the World can't dispute that he has had many: His way to pay the favour, being to desire the Lady to study if there is anything in his Power, by which he may oblige any Relation or Friend of hers; and that he will not fail to grant it. Thus every way a Husband of his Money, his reputation and grandeur procure him the good Fortune he desires; Tho' were the ladies with whom he has a mind to converse of my taste, they would think his own very handsome Person a Reward sufficient for all the Charms they can bestow. (159)

Catherine Gallagher interprets Intelligence's ironic announcement of her willingness to make love to Fortunatas for free as an authorizing sign of her taste and cultivation.[10] As the portrait continues, however, Intelligence zeros in on the main target of this portion of her satire: Daphne's career.

After the first run of the Count's Favour, Daphne was forced to descend: All were not Fortunatas's, that she saw herself oblig'd to endure. Then it was, that she wrote for the Stage sometimes with ill fortune, sometimes with indifferent, and but once with success; for which she was oblig'd to the long Experience and good Judgment of that excellent tragedian Roscius [Betterton]. (159)

Although Daphne writes as a consequence of her failed love affair, her erotic career does not stop when she begins writing. Depicting Daphne's failure to relinquish her sense of herself as virtuous despite her erotic adventures, Intelligence makes the point that Daphne's literary and erotic careers, are, in practice, indistinguishable:

See what it is, to be so great a Man as is the Count Fortunatas, whose Favour is esteemed such a piece of good Fortune, that the very ladies can't possess it without boasting: they who disdain to have their Virtue so much suspected as any other, do not forbear to proclaim the Sacrifice they have made to him; how else had the World been acquainted with his affair with Daphne, and others? (159–60)

Intelligence implies that even Daphne, who guards her virtue more zealously than some, has been willing to advertise her involvement with Fortunatas.

The force behind Intelligence's critique of Daphne's self-advertisement comes from its pastiche of an early piece of writing by Trotter – the romance, *Olinda's Adventures*.[11] An epistolary tale, the romance is made up of the letters of an impoverished but educated young woman who withstands the trials of her virtue by her much older and much more powerful lover. Intelligence continues: "I could enumerate, were it not too tedious, many of Daphne's Adventures; by which she has become the Diversion of as many of the Town as found her to their Taste, and would purchase: yet still she assum'd an Air of Virtue pretended, and was ever eloquent (according to her stiff manner) upon the Foible of others" (160). Manley thus represents Catharine Trotter's career in two senses. The events of her life are chronicled: like Daphne,

Trotter marries a vicar, gives up writing for the stage, and produces religious and philosophical tracts. The "plot" of Daphne's/Trotter's life, however, is also intertwined with the plot of *Olinda's Adventures*. Manley thus implies that Trotter has scripted her own life in a form of proleptic autobiography:[12]

But Daphne's marriage cross'd her delights: How does she exclaim against that breach of Friendship in the Fair? how regret the Authority of a Husband, who has boldly dar'd to carry his Wife into the Country? where she now sets up for regularity, and intends to be an ornament to that religion, which she had formerly abandon'd, and newly again profess'd. She will write no more for the Stage; 'tis profane, indiscreet, unpardonable: Controversie engrosses all her Hours; the Muses must give place: If she have any fancy or Judgment, we may justly expect to see something excellent from a hand so well fitted (if experience can fit) to paint the defects and beauties of those many Opinions she has so often, and so zealously embrac'd. (160)

Though marriage has altered the course of Daphne's career, her new professions of morality do offer another kind of writing opportunity, one to which, Intelligence suggests, she is equally suited. By innuendo, Intelligence implies that Daphne embraces as many opinions as she has men. If her "experience[s]" have "fit" her, they also call her aspirations to virtue into question, casting doubt on her fancy and judgment. By highlighting the way Daphne's life intertwines with her writing, Manley's satirical rewriting of Trotter's romance functions as literary criticism. As Patricia Köster observes:

Mrs. Manley appears to claim that *Olinda's Adventures* is fictionalized autobiography and that it includes too much self-praise. In debunking it, she caricatures both Daphne and Daphne's book. Once we realize the double intent of the passage, we must recognize the skill with which Mrs. Manley obtains her ends. Without any direct reference to *Olinda's Adventures* but only to Daphne's wild hypocrisy, she makes the whole passage serve as literary criticism.[13]

Manley uses this literary criticism to deflate Trotter's claims that her writing reflects her gender, suggesting that instead it reflects her sex-life.

Manley's literary criticism here works the same way as her political satire: in both, she characteristically deflates a person's public stance by playing on his/her private (erotic) actions. Trotter's writing makes her a public figure in much the same way as being a general does for Marlborough. Manley's equation of a woman's writing with her sexuality can sound like a most retrograde version of Swift or Pope on women, but the leveling of Trotter's and Marlborough's status makes both equally matters of public concern. Her criticism thus registers the sustained imbrication of literary and political discourses even as they are reoriented from the court towards the town.

MANLEY'S THEATRICAL CRITICISM

When Manley retracted her praise for Trotter's *Agnes de Castro* in the preface to *The Lost Lover*, she had every reason to feel embattled: quarrels within the Drury Lane company over the production of another of her plays, *The Royal Mischief*, had prompted her to take it to Betterton at Lincoln's Inn Fields, and this unprecedented maneuver had provoked the actors at Drury Lane to mount a satire, *The Female Wits* (performed 1696, published 1704), about the rehearsal of a play by a woman writer, aimed clearly at Manley.[14] Much of the preface of *The Lost Lover* thus aims to safeguard the success of *The Royal Mischief*, which also appeared in print in 1696. Indeed, in the "Epistle to the Reader" which prefaces *The Royal Mischief*, Manley defends herself for rewriting the heroic play from the perspective of its female heroic characters.

According to Manley, the critics have difficulty with her play because of the "warmth" of its central character, Homais, a royal princess whose sexual desires and ambition wreak havoc on the nation, and who, as Lucyle Hook points out, "out-hectors and out-loves all the restoration Alexanders, Montezumas and Drawcansirs written for and by men."[15] They fail, however, to recognize the precedent of Dryden, whom Manley invokes as her model both for writing a heroic play in blank verse and for her female heroine. She states, "Leonora in the Double Discovery and part of Areng-Zebe, have touches as full of natural fire as possible." (Interestingly, she does not mention *The Conquest of Granada*'s Lyndaraxa, who most closely resembles Manley's Homais, but she probably omits this play because it is in rhyme.)

Indeed, the influence of Dryden on women writers at the end of the century is evident not only in their criticism, in which he frequently features as a subject, but also in their participation in the revival of the heroic play, with which he had been personally identified by Buckingham *et al.* in the satiric portrait of Bayes in *The Rehearsal*. Trotter's *The Fatal Friendship* (1698) and *The Unhappy Penitent* (1701) are tragedies of love closer in spirit, perhaps, to Otway's *Venice Preserv'd* and Dryden's *All for Love*, than to, say, *Aureng Zebe*, but both *Agnes de Castro* (1696) and *The Revolution in Sweden* (1703) incorporate love and political intrigue on the heroic model; and Manley's *The Royal Mischief* announces its affiliation with earlier heroic drama in its cast, which featured Elizabeth Barry and Ann Bracegirdle, actresses who had paired off in many heroic plays, most famously in Lee's *The Rival Queens*.[16]

The revival of the heroic drama, no longer rhymed in the 1690s, has, however, seemed anomalous to historians of the theatre. Both Robert Hume and Laura Brown have been hard-pressed to explain what each sees as a self-conscious but misguided attempt to recuperate for a weakening theatrical culture the spectacular appeal of extravaganzas like Dryden's two-part, ten-act *The Conquest of Granada*. Judith Milhous's history of the actors' rebellion that led to the creation of rival theatre companies, the Lincoln's Inn Fields company and the theatre at Drury Lane, asserts that such spectacular productions were put into the service of this theatrical competition. Milhous uses this rivalry to explain many features of the drama of the 1690s, including the greater opportunities it availed to women playwrights. But concentrating on the figure of Dryden, for a moment, allows us to identify more specifically what in the heroic drama might have appealed to the playwrights of this decade.

As a package that provided the terms for negotiating competing social forces in the generic love–duty conflict, the heroic play, particularly in Dryden's hands, often came accompanied by prefatory critical writing that put these same tensions into the service of establishing a form of literary and critical authority.[17] The essay prefacing *The Conquest of Granada*, "Of Heroic Playes," for example, contains Dryden's defense of rhyme against Sir Robert Howard's attack, and, as George McFadden has shown, it is impossible to abstract the literary debate over rhyme from the political allegiances encoded, which formed around such non-literary issues as Clarendon's policies and the Duke of York's succession.[18] And the "Epilogue to the Second Part of *The Conquest of Granada*," in which Dryden articulates the concept of "the age," prompts the "Defense of the Epilogue," appended to the play's second part, in which, apologizing for taking both Ben Jonson and Shakespeare to task for their lack of refined language, Dryden excuses his critique (justifying it as a production of a literary-historical narrative), claiming that it and his dramatic accomplishments flow from the newly accessible wit and conversation available at court and chiefly exemplified by Charles II. As a prototypical heroic play, *The Conquest of Granada, Parts I and II* thus offers a model in which, I would suggest, the playwrights of the 1690s could find resources for negotiating their own social conflicts. They transpose Dryden's terms for representing the conflict over aristocratic ideology that surfaced in the 1670s in the variegated crises over patrimonial inheritance – expressed both in the factionalizing over questions of succession at court, and in the treatment of the inheritance of a literary patrimony – onto the tensions between the court and the town as sites of cultural and political value. They also seek to carve their own critical positions out of this social field with Dryden as their model. The women playwrights, in particular, depend on his use of gender to do so, using him both as a source and as a counter-example.

In the preface to *The Royal Mischief*, having regendered the heroic play female, Manley complains that she has not received the praise she might have expected from women. Like Behn in the preface to *The Lucky Chance*, she finds that female solidarity does not function as an adequate basis for criticism: "I am sorry those of my own Sex are influenced by them [her critics], and receive any character of a Play upon trust without distinguishing Ill nature, Envy and Detraction in the Representation."[19] Although Manley entertains the idea that gender should shape literary matters, her language suggests the opposite: echoing Behn, Manley concludes by suggesting that gender is an effect produced by writing. Unduly influenced by (male) critics who dislike Homais, women will "receive any character of a Play." Objecting to the degree to which women's critical opinions are influenced by men, Manley uses the term "character," which, even though it refers to the play, also conveys women's impressionability. As such, the preface to *The Royal Mischief* resonates with the preface to *The Lost Lover*, in which Manley announces that she is "satisfied the bare name of being a Woman's Play damn'd it beyond its own want of Merit," writing, "Had I confin'd my Sense, as before, to some short song of Phillis, a tender Billet, and the freedom of agreeable Conversation, I had still preserved the Character of a Witty Woman."[20] Punning on the literal meaning of "character" as a letter, Manley suggests that her character, as in her reputation, is determined by her writing. The status Manley gives to writing, evident in these uses of the term "character," is contradictory: much like letters printed on the page, characters are impressed upon women, but Manley writes in excess of her assigned character. Women both are and are not characterized by writing. Like Behn, who makes recourse to the theatrical vocabulary of "parts" in her preface to *The Lucky Chance*, Manley uses the term "character" to exploit a confusion about the critical repercussions of women's gender which she leaves unresolved: complaining that women let their critical judgments be determined by men, she proposes that criticism would be more properly governed by a stricter correspondence between gender and genre; at the same time, however, her attitude towards "a Woman's Play" seems derisive, and she situates her criticism beyond the gender/genre matrix by writing outside the genres assigned to women and subverting the notion that "feminine nature" expresses itself in women's writing.

As "To the Reader" proceeds, her descriptions of *The Royal Mischief* become increasingly inextricable from her description of her character, Homais:

> [A]s a Woman, I thought it Policy to begin with the softest, and which is easiest to our own Sex. Ambition etc. were too bold for the first flight; all would have condemn'd me if venturing upon another I had fail'd, when gentle Love stood ready to afford an easy Victory. I did not believe it possible to pursue him too far, or that my laurel should seem the less graceful for having made an entire Conquest. ([A]3v)

The simple contrasts between love and ambition are belied by the fact that *The Royal Mischief* tackles both; indeed the play explores their indistinguishability in the character of Homais. More significantly, perhaps, when Manley describes her choice, her identification with her character becomes clear: pursuing love too far is Homais's fault, which Manley here transcribes as a feature of her writing by writing heroic drama.

At the end of the preface, in another appeal to her female audience, the conflation of references to her play with references to its main character is overlaid by a conflation of Manley's writing with the performance of the actress, Elizabeth Barry:

> I do not doubt when the Ladies have given themselves the trouble of reading, and comparing it with others, they'll find the prejudice against our Sex, and not refuse me the satisfaction of entertaining them, nor the leasure of Mrs. Barry, who, by all who saw her, is concluded to have exceeded that perfection which before she was justly thought to have arrived at; my Obligations to her were the greater since against her own approbation, she excell'd and made the part of an ill Woman not only entertaining but admirable. ([A]4r)

Manley claims that Barry's theatrical performance might help female readers of the play to appreciate her own literary achievement, but the logic of this claim rests on the combination of the identification of *The Royal Mischief* with Homais and that of the writer with the actress. The theatre is thus revealed as the site which grounds Manley's literary and critical authority, and the performance of the actress becomes the basis of her authorial appeal.

Manley makes the satisfaction she would receive from entertaining the ladies analogous to the pleasure Elizabeth Barry gave (and presumably took) in her highly touted performance of Homais. Both Manley and

Barry thus depend on the audience. The identification of the writer with the actress, however, does not cancel out the identification of the writing (and the writer) with the character. Like the ladies in Manley's audience, Barry too has had to overcome her initial reservations about taking the part of an "ill Woman." Moreover, Barry takes Manley's "part" in the sense both of performing the role she has written, that of Homais, and of taking Manley's side in "the prejudice against our Sex." In this double claim, Manley identifies both herself and her writing with her character, Homais, as she is performed by Barry.

If Barry provides the model for Manley, however, Manley also wants Barry to prove exemplary for her lady readers. Barry is thus the intermediary through whom Manley will interact with her audience. The slippery substitutions – performer for character for writing for writer – also coexist, suggesting that the basis for Manley's authorial appeal is performative in a philosophical sense, and grounded in the theatre in a historical sense.[21] Manley makes her authorial appeal to an audience of ladies whose ability to constitute her as a writer also depends on the performance of the actress.

Manley's representation of the author's dependence on the actor or the actress locates critical authority in a theatrical context, but the status of the theatre in her formulation is markedly different than in Dryden's. Whereas he situates himself between precursor dramatists such as Shakespeare and Jonson, on the one hand, and courtly patrons, on the other, her focus on the performers registers the new status of the audience as a public: no longer full of potential patrons, it is nonetheless to be serviced – both entertained and morally guided – by spokespeople (actor or author, or actor on behalf of author) for the theatrical performance or text. The spokesperson position can as easily be occupied by what we would call a narrator as by the actor or actress, and is closer to an authorial persona in the criticism Manley appends to her prose. Manley's later critical writing measures the receding importance of the theatre in literary culture, although it nevertheless retains a residual status that informs the critical vocabulary she uses.

The address "To the Reader" that prefaces *The Secret History of Queen Zarah and the Zarazians* (1705) – Manley's satirical account of Sarah Churchill, the Duchess of Marlborough, and her rise to power – emphasizes the techniques the "historian" must use to attract and pleasure the reader, advising against excessive digression, moralizing commentary when the action is coming to a climax, and unnatural conversation, in order to cater to the taste of the English:

These little Pieces [histories] which have banish'd Romances are much more agreeable to the Brisk and Impetuous Humours of the English, who have naturally no Taste for longwinded Performances, for they have no sooner begun a Book but they desire to see the End of it: the Prodigious Length of the Ancient Romances, the Mixture of so many Extraordinary Adventures, and the great Number of Actors that appear on the Stage, and the Likeness which is so little managed, all which has given a Distaste to persons of good Sense, and has made Romances so much cry'd down, as we find 'em at present.[22]

The pleasure that the author can supply is no longer analogized to that which the actress gives, but rather is proportionate to the suspense generated by the text and the involvement which the intrigues of a "true history" solicit from the reader. Using a theatrical vocabulary to describe the faulty construction of romances ("the great Number of Actors that appear on the Stage"), the preface identifies romances with the theatre, but nevertheless retains the theatrical vocabulary, using "character" and "actor" interchangeably, to describe what the authors of "historical novels" should do.

Although the preface to *Queen Zarah* has long been taken as Manley's, John L. Sutton Jr., has shown that it is actually a translation of a French essay by Abbé Morvan de Bellegarde contained in a 1702 courtesy book, *Lettres curieuses de litterature*, which is itself a paraphrase of the second part of the Sieur du Plaisir's *Sentimens sur les lettres et sur l'histoire* (1683).[23] Notwithstanding the lack of originality, however, Manley's use of the translated text to preface *Queen Zarah* attests to the investments the development of a critical vocabulary for prose had, in both England and France, in the theatre. Manley's use of this text also bespeaks her shift in focus from a theatre-going audience to a reading public.

The changing status of the theatre is marked in a distinction between the "Character of the Historian" and that of the "Heroe":

[T]here is nevertheless a distinction to be made between the Character of the Historian and the Heroe, for if it be the Heroe that speaks, then he ought to express himself Ingeniously, without affecting any Nicety of Points or Syllogisms, because he speaks without any Preparation; but when the Author speaks of his Chief, he may use a more Nice Language, and chuse his Terms for the better expressing his Designs; [However] Moral Reflexions, Maxims and Sentences are more proper in Discourses for Instructions than in Historical Novels, whose chief End, is to please; and if we find in them some Instructions, it proceeds rather from their Descriptions than their Precepts.

This passage describes the awkward placement of the aristocratic hero of the stage in the non-aristocratic novel. The technical advice for achieving a naturalism of conversation concentrates on modulating the distance from which the author (and the authorial persona, the historian) manipulates the action or the reader. By contrast, for Dryden, naturalism in conversation is partly achieved through rhyme, which may strike us as counter-intuitive, but Dryden defends this "naturalism" when he identifies Charles II's courtly conversation as the model for the rhymed exchanges of his heroes, in "Of Heroique Plays" and "Defense of the Epilogue," the preface and appendix to *The Conquest of Granada*. Manley's interest in criteria appropriate to narrative, in contrast to performance, like that of her French sources, thus indicates the turn away from the theatrically based, court-sponsored literary culture (although the theatrical vocabulary is never completely abandoned), towards a new set of concerns about reading. Indeed, the vocabulary registers this turn towards the public sphere in the insistence that "Every Historian ought to be extreamly uninterested" (that is, above the interests of party) – and yet Manley's propagandistic satire is far from impartial. It is in her understanding of satire, and the ways her satire functions as literary criticism, that Manley mediates the shift from a theatre audience to a reading public.[24] It is thus to her satirical writing that I now return, to examine the ways in which it displays her contributions to an emergent critical practice, as well as to the political discourse of her immediate context.

MANLEY'S SCANDALOUS CRITICISM

One of the few episodes of *The New Atalantis* not narrated by Intelligence is related by another of Manley's spokeswomen, the midwife, Mrs. Nightwork. Nightwork describes the deniability of her own scandalmongering as a professional talent which she calls narration "under the Rose." Intelligence, worried that Nightwork's presence will render her services to Astrea and Virtue obsolete, challenges Nightwork's right to promulgate scandal: "But is not that something against Conscience? I thought Mrs. Nightwork you had been sworn to secrecy." (138). Nightwork replies,

> Directly but not Indirectly; as for Example, I must not say I delivered my Lady such a One of a lovely Boy in such a place, and at such a Time; that is being directly forsworn. But I may say, I did such a sort of Lady (describing her person as well as I can) the good Office, but can't for my Life imagine who she is. This is all under the Rose; and without this indirect Liberty, we should be but ill Company to most of our Ladies, who love to be amused with the failings of others, and would not always give us so favourable and warm a Reception, if we had nothing of Scandal to entertain them with. (139)

Nightwork insists that her access to scandal is not only a consequence of her business – she delivers illegitimate children – but also a factor that contributes to its flourishing. More people employ her because she entertains them at the same time. Mrs. Nightwork's narration "under the Rose" also describes Manley's own satirical practice, which might be understood as a joke version of Dryden's and Behn's vernacular affiliation with Shakespeare in which women, who could not be expected to understand *sub rosa*, would roughly translate it into something about female genitalia. Manley thus locates her status as a professional writer in terms of female sexuality, but later scenes of sapphism prevent any simple identification of female sexuality with reproduction.

Mrs. Nightwork's description of her indirect liberty shares key features with Manley's description of her role as the "translator" of the tales published in *The New Atalantis*: like Mrs. Nightwork, she eschews direct and prefers indirect or veiled tales; like her, she relishes the contradiction in which she both asserts and disavows the connections between the stories told and the familiar world. Manley's ironic self-presentation in the dedicatory letter to the second part of *The New Atalantis* displays her characteristic use of disavowal – now of literary precedent – which allows us to specify another of its critical functions:

> Were not the Scene of these Memoirs in an Island with which those of ours are but little acquainted, I should, my lord, say something in the Defence of them, as they seem guilty of particular Reflection, defending the Author, by the President of our great Fore-fathers in Satire, who not only flew against the general reigning Vices, but pointed at individual Persons, as may be seen in Ennius, Varro, Lucian, Horace, Juvenal, Persius, etc. (132)

"Were not the Scene" in a distant island, then she would need to defend herself; however, the island is foreign and therefore its scenes do not "particular[ly] Reflect" on our own. Manley actively denies that her stories "reflect." Yet, the term is specifically associated with satire: as Dryden notes in his "Discourse Concerning the Original and Progress of Satire" – "in English, to say satire is to mean reflection."[25] Thus, even though she rejects any need to defend herself, Manley introduces a preemptive defense strategy: precedent, and specifically the precedent of Dryden. In *The New Atalantis*'s dedicatory letter, Manley states: "The New Atalantis, seems, my Lord to be written like varonian Satyrs, on different Subjects, Tales, Stories and Characters of Invention, after the Manner of Lucian, who copy'd from Varro. In my Opinion, nothing can be added to Mr. Dryden's learned Discourse of Satire, in his Dedication of Juvenal" (132). She then quotes Dryden twice. Notable in the passages Manley cites is Dryden's concern to justify satire as a moral genre, and to associate it with poetic vocation. In the first passage, Dryden states, "he who instructs most usefully will carry the palm," and, in the second, he calls satire the "Poet's Office." When Manley has one of her narrators, the midwife Mrs. Nightwork, refer to her profession as the "Good Office," she offers a feminized version of the "Poet's Office," suggesting that the services she performs include telling scandalous tales as well as delivering illegitimate children, thus also revising Wycherley's equation of women's writing with their sexual status in the prologue to Trotter's *Agnes de Castro*.

Using Dryden to authorize her writing, Manley proposes both that she has access to precedents for defense (Dryden, and through him the classics),[26] and that she is exempt from the need to defend herself: "Were not the Scene of these Memoirs...I should say...something in the Defence of them." The conditional mood permits this contradictory treatment of her forefathers. She claims to need neither a defense nor Dryden, but refers to him anyway in her own defense. Manley's relation to literary precedent is thus both affirmed and disavowed. Like Dryden, she makes a claim for her own unprecedentedness while boosting her claim with precedent.

In her depiction of the inscription of the generic markers of femininity in Manley's *The New Atalantis*, Rosalind Ballaster misleadingly distinguishes Manley's satire from that of her male counterparts.[27] According to Ballaster, when Manley invokes Varro in the dedicatory letter to *The New Atalantis*, she does so as a way out of the dichotomous alternative – Horace or Juvenal – which Dryden has sexualized in order to give Juvenal the pride of place in the "Discourse Concerning Satire":

[Horace] may ravish other men; but I am too stupid or insensible to be tickled...His urbanity, that is, his good manners, are to be commended, but his wit is faint; and his salt, if I may dare to say so, almost insipid. Juvenal is of a more vigorous and masculine wit; he gives me as much pleasure as I can bear; he fully satisfies my expectation; he treats his subject home: his spleen is raised, and he raises mine: I have the pleasure of concernment in all he says; he drives his reader along with him; and when he is at the end of his way, I would willingly stop with him. If he went another stage, it would be too far; it would make a journey of a progress, and turn delight into fatigue.[28]

As Ballaster notes in "Manl(e)y Forms," "The foppish, emasculated gentleman lazily tickling his reader/lover into laughing submission is no match for the consummate sexual artistry of the angry misanthropist, whose powerful thrusts rapidly bring his reader/lover to full satisfaction" (222). According to Ballaster, "By citing Varro, Manley successfully conveys her critical difference [i.e. her femininity], from her contemporaries in satire, without placing herself outside of the politically over-determined debate on the form in general" (223–24). Moreover, she argues that Manley's invocation of Varro is paradigmatic of her writing as a woman (237).

Manley, however, has not cited Varro; she has invoked him through Dryden's "Discourse Concerning Satire." Indeed, her affiliation with Varro has a precedent in Dryden: despite his own preference for Juvenal, Dryden associates his own satirical practice with that of Varro. Although he remembers no English examples of satire in which verse is mixed with prose, another aspect of Varronian satire – its featuring subjects that are "tales or stories of [the poet's] own invention" – is illustrated "(if it be not too vain to mention anything of my own) [by] the poems of *Absalom and MacFleknoe*" (115). As the terms of Dryden's comparison of Horace and Juvenal make clear, Manley's sexualized understanding of satire also has a precedent in Dryden. Whereas Dryden works out his own relation to the classical satirists in sexual scenarios between men, Manley works out her relation to precedent, represented by Dryden, in erotic scenes between women.

Catherine Gallagher contextualizes Manley's disavowal of direct referentiality in *The New Atalantis* as partly motivated by the prevalent use of libel law to regulate printing between the lapse of the Licensing Act in 1695 and the death of Queen Anne in 1714.[29] For Gallagher, Manley's unwillingness to accord her text political transparency, is, by implication, an embrace of fiction – an embrace she associates with Manley's femininity. Although such a reading is compelling, it nevertheless fails to acknowledge one of Manley's crucial agendas. Her writing is, after all, satire and therefore openly relies on referential recognition despite any familiar gestures of disavowal that are, as they all must be, also acknowledgments. We have already seen this double gesture at work in Manley's treatment of literary precedent, represented for her by Dryden, when she bases her claim that her writing is unprecedented upon a critical rejection of his influence. By accepting Manley's disavowal of referentiality at face value, Gallagher overlooks the ways that Manley's satirical portraits of other writers function as both literary criticism and political satire.

Both Ballaster's and Gallagher's readings of Manley rely on the feminist association of gender with genre, but no matter which genre, fiction or satire, this association produces a familiar yet problematic literary history, one that renders invisible both the relations between gender and sexuality and the contributions of female critics, such as Manley, Trotter or Behn, to the history of criticism. By accepting the affiliations between gender and genre, both Ballaster and Gallagher insist on finding textual markers of femininity only within the "appropriate" generic confines where they might be expected to appear.[30]

Indeed, Manley's recurrent, and, I would suggest, signature gesture of affirmation and disavowal contributes to criticism a paradigmatic maneuver, one that recasts Trotter's feminist revision of Dryden's claims for his own impartiality (in the preface to *All for Love*) when she puts forward self-consciousness as the hallmark of her critical judgment and expertise. Like Trotter, Manley associates her critical authority with her female nature, which conditions the disavowals of referentiality and precedent upon which her texts, at the same time, openly rely. The complexity of this double stance, however, also distances her from any straightforward evocation of femininity. She exploits her access as a woman writer to the sexual scandals associated with female power (casting her talents, in the figure of Mrs. Nightwork, as a form of midwifery), at the same time as she deplores them. The ways this double gesture contributes to criticism become clearer when we consider her redefinition of satire in the episode of the New Cabal.

If, in the midwife, Manley has associated writing with reproductive female sexuality, in the New Cabal she makes quite a different association. The court of Queen Anne is not, after all, primarily a site of reproductive power; rather it is a site of female political power – a power explicitly dissociated from reproduction (by the fact that Queen Anne had seventeen pregnancies, and only one child who survived infancy) and from marriage (by the fact that, in contrast to her sister Mary who had ruled alongside her husband, William, Anne ruled alone).[31] Manley's satire on the New Cabal brings narration "under the Rose" – that is, simultaneous affirmation and disavowal – into explicit relation to sapphism. Indeed, the literary-critical portrait of Daphne discussed earlier is part of Manley's extended critique of the New Cabal, and it is signaled as such when Intelligence calls Daphne's marriage a "breach of Friendship in the Fair." This critique, which, as we shall see, presents political commitments as homoerotic bonds supported by a feminist-separatist ideology, damns the women as hypocrites if they interact with men and as perverts if they do not. While such representations of sapphism were a frequent feature of political pamphlets directed by different hands against both

Whigs and Tories during Queen Anne's reign, in Manley's treatment sapphism is also represented as generative of satire.[32]

As Virtue, Intelligence and Astrea wander around St. James's Park, a notorious site for assignations, Astrea wonders about the ladies whose voices she hears emanating from three coaches. Intelligence answers her:

[T]hese Ladies are of the new cabal; a Sect (however innocent in itself) that does not fail from meeting its share of Censure from the World. Alas! what can they do? How unfortunate are women? if they seek their Diversion out of themselves and include the other Sex, they must be Criminal? If in themselves (as those of the new Cabal) still they are Criminal? Tho' Censurers must carry their Imaginations to much greater length then I am able to do mine, to explain this Hypothesis with Success; they pretend to find in these the Vices of old Rome reviv'd; and quote you certain detestable Authors, who (to amuse Posterity) have introduc'd lasting Monuments of Vice, which could only subsist in Imagination; and can in reality have no other Foundation, than what are to be found in the Dreams of Poets, and the ill Nature of those Censurers, who will have no Diversions Innocent but what themselves advance! (154)

Introducing the New Cabal to Virtue and Astrea, Intelligence cannot help but introduce the accusations they have been charged with, despite her disclaimer that to explain or even imagine these accusations lies beyond her capabilities. Moreover, her stream of anecdotes filled with sexual innuendo establishes the sexual nature of the Cabal members' involvements with one another.

For example, Intelligence tells the story of Armida, whose tryst with her male lover is interrupted by a surprise visit by her female favorite. Insinuating that the man's jealous rage indicates that the women have an erotic relationship, Intelligence comments, "'Tis true, some things may be strain'd a little too far, and that causes reflections to be cast upon the rest" (154). Intelligence's cautionary words point to the supposed unfoundedness of Armida's sexual criminality, but by granting that these "reflections" have a cause, she also signals her satiric intent.

As Intelligence explains, stories such as these have provoked the Censurers:

Detestable Censurers, who after the manner of the Athenians, will not believe so great a Man as Socrates cou'd see every hour the Beauty of an Alcibiades without taxing his sensibility... Since then it is not in the Fate of even so wise a Man to avoid the Censure of the Busy and the Bold, Care ought to be taken by others (less fortify'd against the occasion of detraction, in declining such unaccountable intimacies) to prevent the ill-natur'd World's refining upon their mysterious innocence. (155)

The analogy between the Cabal members' same-sex activities and those of Socrates is produced nominally to acquit the Cabal of sexual criminality, but it is characteristic of Intelligence's (and Manley's) satire that the very same classical analogy to male sodomitical activity meant to rescue the women from censure is the means by which she reinjects sexual content into their activities. By invoking Socrates as a precedent for the New Cabal, Intelligence both establishes the reality of their sexual criminality and exposes their intellectual aspirations to classical status as pretentious. Her two-edged satire rejects their access to the classical precedent of Socrates even though she has just invoked him. This doubled invocation and disavowal offers a parallel to Manley's treatment of literary precedent in the sexual register.

When Astrea reflects on the "mysterious innocence" which Intelligence attributes to the Cabal, she elaborates Intelligence's attitude towards censure and redefines satire:

It is something so new and uncommon, so laudable and blameable, that we don't know how to determine; especially wanting light even to guess at what you call the Mysteries of the cabal. If only tender Friendship, inviolable and sincere, be the regard, what can be more meritorious, or a truer Emblem of their Happiness above? ... But if they carry it beyond what nature design'd, and fortifie themselves by these new-form'd Amities against the Hymenial Union, or give their Husbands but a second place in their Affections and Cares; 'tis wrong and to be blam'd. Thus far as to the Merit of the Thing it self. But when we look with true regard to the world, if it permit a shadow of Suspicion, a bare imagination, that the Misteries they pretend, have anything in 'em contrary to Kind, and that strict Modesty and Virtue do not adorn and support their Conversation; 'tis to be avoided and condemn'd; least they give occasion for obscene Laughter, new invented Satyr, fanciful Jealousies and impure Distrusts, in that nice unforgiving Sex: Who Arbitrarily decide, that Woman was only created (with all her beauty, Softness, Passions and compleat tenderness) to adorn the Husband's Reign, perfect his happiness and propagate the Kind. (161)

It looks as though Astrea cannot make up her mind what to think of the Cabal. Although she seems to endorse the "regard [of] the world" because, otherwise, the Cabal would risk provoking men, she depicts "that nice unforgiving Sex" as incapable of perceiving women as anything other than wives and mothers. Emphasizing the arbitrariness of men's decision that "Woman was only created ... to adorn the Husband's Reign, perfect his happiness and propagate the Kind," her conclusion ironically conceals a brief for sapphism. Moreover, the reason to defer to male judgment has nothing to do with men's inherent virtues; it consists of the possibility that the Cabal will "give occasion for obscene Laughter, [and] new invented Satyr," that is to say, that their behavior will produce a new kind of writing. Significantly, the person writing this "new invented Satyr" which both affirms and disavows its precedents is Manley. Her "new invented Satyr," partly because it is neither wholly new nor (presumably) wholly invented, helps to produce the spectacle of the New Cabal's sapphism, which is then associated with "female" rule and with "women's writing." Astrea claims that men may be provoked to write by the women's behavior, but Manley calls the chain of referential provocation into question by her endorsement and practice of writing "under the Rose." Indeed, Manley seems to assert that she has beaten the men to the punch: at the same time as she lashes female sexual crime, she flaunts her access to it as a woman writer. In her hands, the spectacle of female homoeroticism and its association with "female" rule does not primarily provoke men; it produces her own claims to unprecedentedness.

As we have seen, these claims are powerfully conditioned by Dryden's criticism – both his characteristic gestures in his treatments of his own literary forebears and his sexualization of satire. Manley's association of her satire with the unprecedented sexual criminality of the New Cabal forges fresh links between female writing and female sexuality, between criticism and gender. Dryden's claims to impartiality as a critic in the preface to *All for Love*, as I have argued, are underwritten by his feminizing representation of his relationship to Shakespeare in that play as the competition between Octavia and Cleopatra for the title of Antony's "legitimate" wife. Manley collapses the gestures Dryden offers serially in the generically differentiated locations of preface and play to offer, at one and the same time, both critical distance (disavowal, impartiality, the satirical condemnation of female vice) and critical proximity (affirmation, participation, her access as a woman writer to the scenes of female vice and her assertion that her satire is produced by it). Critical practice continues to depend on the double gesture of disavowal and avowal that we might find more recognizable in its twin imperatives: the attainment of distance (impartiality, objectivity) by means of close reading (intimate involvement with and attachment to texts). Manley's writing telegraphs the paradoxical aspects of this undertaking so clearly because she associates their congruence with female sexuality.

That Manley's satiric reduction of everything to sex has political effects is not suprising; what is remarkable is that she uses this reduction to empower her literary and critical, scandalous, authority, thus suggesting that there is something scandalous about critical authority. The links she forges between female writing and sexuality, between gender and criticism may not further the separation of literary criticism from political critique, but they become the grounds upon which she is dismissed as a woman writer.[33] I would suggest that this dismissal is partly motivated by the difficulty of distinguishing the literary-critical from the political in her writing, which can make the critical components within it appear trivial. As Paula McDowell points out, however, this overlay is the hallmark of the writing of her period.[34] Rather than using it to dismiss her, we should instead let it draw our attention to the ease with which scandal can be avoided when critical principles are extracted from the writings of her male contemporaries.

MANLEY AMONG THE MEN

A brief look at Manley's representation of Richard Steele in *The New Atalantis* helps us to contextualize Manley's satirical criticism in relation to that of her male contemporaries. In another instance of literary figures appearing alongside those with social and political power, Manley depicts Steele as Monsieur l'Ingrat (101–05). Intelligence's anecdotes about him emphasize that his genius for "wit and genteel repartee" secures him only the trappings of a social position beyond his humble beginnings as an Irish common trooper, which he has acquired through marriage. From the start, she wonders whether the "pert chariot" on which he first appears belongs to him, assuring her listeners, "he cannot yet sure pretend to that" (101). When he falls in with a con-man alchemist who exploits his venal desires, his poetic achievements are shown to rest on social blindness. He is repeatedly rescued from disaster by women who look out for his interests, but he never returns the favor, even after he becomes wealthy. Manley holds aristocratic ideals over Steele's head, using the gallic name to underline his failure to embody the virtues of *noblesse oblige*. Intelligence's summarizing claim, "he pays nor obliges no body, but when he can help it," aims to appeal to both aristocratic and popular concepts of fair exchange. Apparently Steele betrayed their friendship when he failed to lend Manley money when she was in need, but, personal motivations aside, the accusations of covetousness and hypocrisy take aim at Steele's Whig principles in the name of a gallant and heartfelt generosity that bridges aristocratic and popular concepts of virtue.

The New Atalantis unfolds story after story of pathetic women who are victims of male avarice and sexual predation, in which Manley dramatizes Tory virtue set in opposition to Whig hypocritical principle, and meshes aristocratic, popular and feminine features in the style that authorizes her critical satire; in episodes describing the female abuse of privilege, she foregrounds her access, as a woman writer, to the truths that may elude her male contemporaries, whose vanities occlude their vision, especially when it comes to perceiving women's participation in and contribution to political life.[35] The intertwining of politics with gender in her writing might be seen to guarantee Manley's obscurity in the history of criticism, for it is difficult to assess, from the current perspective in which literary criticism is readily distinguished from politics, how gender functions in her work. Her male contemporaries' takes on this matter can provide us with a sense of how to proceed. Indeed, the lines in which Alexander Pope memorialized Manley's novel mediation of hack and courtly writing are, perhaps, more familiar today than either Manley or her writing.

Pope uses *The New Atalantis* as an index of literary and aristocratic fashions when he has the Baron proclaim his victory over Belinda in the third canto of *The Rape of the Lock* (1714):

> While Fish in Streams, or Birds delight in Air,
> Or in a Coach and Six the British fair,
> As long as *Atalantis* shall be read,
> Or the small Pillow grace the Lady's Bed,
> While Visits shall be paid on solemn Days,
> When numerous Wax-lights in bright Order blaze,
> While Nymphs take Treats, or assignations give,
> So long my honour, Name and Praise shall live!
> (III: 163–70)

In these lines, however, Pope deflates the Baron's heroism by showing him hitching his fame to ephemeral aristocratic and feminine tastes which are, in turn, feminizing. As Kristina Straub and Ellen Pollack have persuasively argued, Pope obtains his own canonic immortality, in contrast to the Baron's, by the joint castigation of women and "effeminate" men.[36]

Significantly, Manley's writing retains its aristocratic veneer for Pope despite the obstacles her status as a political pamphleteer and hack would seem to present. Pope uses Manley to exemplify an aristocratic taste that is portrayed as both feminine and popular in order to clear the way for an elevated classical ideal that is ancient, pure and more aristocratic.[37] Bringing together in an odd compression political satire and literary criticism, aristocratic and popular fashions, Manley's writing amalgamates the features her male contemporaries, whether Whig or Tory, attempt to realign, often using gender, and sometimes Manley (as Pope's example illustrates), as a lever to do so. Pope capitalizes on Manley's combination of aristocratic, popular and feminine features when he has his Baron hitch his fame to her star, but he revises this legacy, consigning it to a "libertine" past in his critique of aristocratic popularity as feminizing.

Whigs like Steele and Addison share with the Tory Pope the tendency to use gender as a lever to accomplish their preferred alignments among political and literary criticism, aristocratic and popular tastes. Addison and Steele bring wit and learning out of the universities and into the coffee houses (*Spectator* 10), by embracing the standpoint of a virtuous, impartial femininity. Like Manley, they too use stories of pathetic women (see *Spectator* 11, for example) – although to Whig ends – but these are set against a critique of aristocratic satire, which they associate with the overvaluation of birth above worth and with "decadent" sexualities. The final number of the *Tatler* makes explicit Steele's understanding of the limited efficacy of satire as an agent of moral reform. The *Spectator* comments repeatedly on the moral importance of esteeming virtue above wit (see numbers 209 and 169 for examples), and warns of the dangers of malicious and party-oriented satire (34, 125, 270).[38]

Locating Swift in the context of Restoration culture, Robert Phiddian emphasizes the ways what he calls "Restoration enterprises" – the attempts of political, religious and scientific writers to restore coherent moral order to knowledge in the wake of the English Revolution – provide Swift with the pre-texts for parody.[39] Phiddian does not, however, discuss the ways Swift, like Pope, establishes elite literary culture by alternately associating both the aristocratic corruption of court culture and the *arriviste* mentality of newer denizens of public culture with femininity *tout court*.[40] In the writings of Steele, Addison, Pope and Swift, social, political and literary factors are as intertwined as they are in Manley's. Although Addison and Steele move to dissociate themselves from satire, Pope's and Swift's criticism often describes literary abuses in terms of the bodily, the sexual and the scandalous. Accounts of the Augustan contributions to the history of literary criticism, however, have recorded only the principles of criticism their writing can be made to exemplify. The example of Manley recontextualizes this history.

By ushering sexual scandal and innuendo from the court and the playhouse into the critical satirical prose associated with the town, the example of Manley brings into visibility a line of criticism, extending back to Dryden and on through to our own day, from which it might prove impossible to extract critical principles. There is a theatricalized bitchiness found in Dryden, Manley, Pope, Byron, Wilde, Beerbohm and Vidal that is an integral part of the critical judgments they express, no matter how temporally fleeting their targets. As Chris Baldick has shown, it only becomes a requirement of critical practice to identify the principles by which it operates with the advent of the study of English literature in the schools, codified in accordance with scientific models most famously by I. A. Richards.[41] Indeed, this extra-curricular line of criticism might make us re-evaluate the extraction of critical principles from the often nasty and often witty but always telling maneuvers by which critics – both canonical and non-canonical, both male and female – accrue cultural authority. I would hope that *Gender, Theatre and the Origins of Criticism from Dryden to Manley* thus permits the possibility of reclaiming a venerable history for the scandals of criticism.

By so clearly negotiating the transitions from court-centered to public-oriented literary production and from theatre to reading audience, Manley's writing marks the terminal point of the critical stage, that is, of criticism's dependence on the stage. In her aftermath, critical writing in English is increasingly free-standing or appended to prose fiction, though the theatre continues to be important. The traces of its former centrality can be found in the continued use of dramatic dialogue as a critical form, and in the sustained attention to drama as a critical subject. We even find remnants of this stage of criticism's development in the self-staging routines of contemporary academic criticism.

As this book has shown, it is no accident that recovering the place of the theatre in criticism's history has located the specific socio-historical coordinates of the critic – coordinates among which those of gender and sexuality are paramount. The incorporation of women writers' critical achievements into the history of criticism, as I hope to have demonstrated, alters our sense of the critical enterprise by making us more attuned to how its performative dynamics work along two axes: diachronically, as we account for early criticism's dependence on the stage and its retention of traces of this dependence even after it comes into its own; and synchronically, as we see most clearly in the function of self-staging as a way to access critical authority and its connections to gender and sexuality in the women whose critical writings I have treated.

The argument of this book has been that it is only by forgetting the aspects of Dryden's critical legacy that his female heirs found most useful that we can maintain the high-mindedness of the critical enterprise. The writings of Behn, Trotter and Manley make it obvious that it is only by ignoring the performative features of criticism that it can be elevated above the social scenes of its production. Reincorporating them into the early phase of criticism's history thus indicates some ways in which its history might be reconceived.

Notes

INTRODUCTION. THE CRITICAL STAGE

1. The most prominent of these accounts is Terry Eagleton's *The Function of Criticism: From The Spectator to Post-Structuralism* (London: Verso, 1984).
2. *British Dramatists from Dryden to Sheridan*, 2nd edn., ed. George Nettleton and Arthur Case, rev. George Winchester Stone Jr. (Carbondale: Southern Illinois University Press, 1969), 40.
3. For an acute account of the current "crisis" which analyzes the anti-intellectualism of the debates around "political correctness" by situating it in the context of the historical relations between eighteenth-century literary scholarship and engaged journalism, see Jonathan Brody Kramnick, "Origins of the Present Crisis," *Profession* (1997), 84–92.
4. Michael Fried, *Absorption and Theatricality: Painting and the Beholder in the Age of Diderot* (Berkeley: University of California Press, 1980); David Marshall, *The Figure of the Theater: Shaftesbury, Defoe, Adam Smith, and George Eliot* (New York: Columbia University Press, 1986).
5. Jean-Christophe Agnew, *Worlds Apart: The Market and the Theater in Anglo-American Thought, 1550–1750* (New York: Cambridge University Press, 1986). This evenhanded treatment of the anxieties provoked by the theatre and the market, and the shared vocabulary that expresses them, makes it apparent that by not situating their analysis of theatricality in relation to the market, Fried and Marshall, each endorsing his own version of antitheatricality, inadvertently inscribe the market as transcendent. We may be in a better position to assess the ambivalence of Diderot, Adam Smith and Shaftesbury, and their eighteenth-century contemporaries, towards the theatre in the context of the emergence of criticism's aesthetic discourses out of the shifting fortunes of the theatre.
6. Jürgen Habermas, *The Structural Transformation of the Public Sphere: An Inquiry into a Category of Bourgeois Society*, trans. Thomas Burger (Cambridge, Mass.: MIT Press, 1991), 32, 40–42.
7. For such accounts, see Eagleton, *The Function of Criticism*, and also Trevor Ross, *The Making of the English Literary Canon: From the Middle Ages to the Late Eighteenth Century* (Montreal: McGill-Queens University Press, 1998) and Jonathan Brody Kramnick, *Making the English Canon: Print-Capitalism and the Cultural Past*

1700–1770 (Cambridge University Press, 1998). See Pierre Bourdieu, *Distinction: A Social Critique of the Judgement of Taste*, trans. Richard Nice (Cambridge, Mass.: Harvard University Press, 1984), which registers both the social struggles accompanying the emergence of an autonomous aesthetic domain and the processes by which they are submerged and misrecognized.

8. Michael Ragussis has recently argued that the theatre, rather than the press, comprises the fourth estate of eighteenth-century British culture in "Jews and Other 'Outlandish Englishmen': Ethnic Performance and the Invention of British Identity under the Georges," *Critical Inquiry* 26 (2000), 776–77.

9. See Douglas Lane Patey, "The Eighteenth Century Invents the Canon," *Modern Language Studies* 18 (1988), 17–37; Trevor Ross, "The Emergence of 'Literature': Making and Reading the English Canon in the Eighteenth Century," *ELH* 63 (1996), 397–422; and Jonathan Brody Kramnick, "The Making of the English Canon," *PMLA* 112 (1997), 1087–101.

10. Like Kramnick, Trevor Ross characterizes Dryden's production of lineal genealogies as "accept[ing] without embarrassment the paradox of permanence and change," in *The Making of the English Literary Canon*, 168–69.

11. John Dryden, "Epilogue" to *The Conquest of Granada, Part II* in *The Works of John Dryden*, vol. XI, ed. John Loftis and David Stuart Rodes (Berkeley: University of California Press, 1978), 201.

12. For analyses of Dryden's poetry that include comments on the historicism of his critical writings, see Earl Miner, "The Poetics of the Critical Act: Dryden's Dealings with Rivals and Predecessors" in *Critical Essays on John Dryden*, ed. James Winn (New York: Simon and Schuster MacMillan, 1997), 33–47; David Bruce Kramer, *The Imperial Dryden: The Poetics of Appropriation in Seventeenth-Century England* (Athens: University of Georgia Press, 1994); and Achsah Guibbory, *The Map of Time: Seventeenth-Century English Literature and the Idea of History* (Urbana: University of Illinois Press, 1986).

13. Samuel Johnson, "Life of Dryden" in *Lives of the Poets*, ed. George Birbeck Hill (1905; New York: Octagon Books, 1967), 1: 410 and 342–46.

14. Harold Bloom, *The Anxiety of Influence: A Theory of Poetry* (New York: Oxford University Press, 1973) and *A Map of Misreading* (New York: Oxford University Press, 1975).

15. Johnson, "Life of Dryden," 410. Other critics have responded to Bloom's omission. In *Regaining Paradise: Milton and the Eighteenth Century* (New York: Cambridge University Press, 1986), Dustin Griffin argues that Bloom's terms for understanding Milton's influence on poets of the eighteenth century are not helpful. Jennifer Brady seeks to explain Dryden's lack of anxiety in "Dryden and Negotiations of Literary Succession and Precession" in *Literary Transmission and Authority: Dryden and Other Writers*, ed. Earl Miner and Jennifer Brady (New York: Cambridge University Press, 1993), 27–54.

16. According to Owen Ruffhead's *Life of Alexander Pope* (1769), Pope thought to "pen a discourse on the rise and progress of English poetry" and classed them by schools as a first step. Ruffhead is cited in *John Donne: The Critical Heritage*, ed. A. J. Smith (Boston: Routledge and Kegan Paul, 1975), 181.
17. Sandra Gilbert and Susan Gubar, *The Madwoman in the Attic*, 2nd edn. (New Haven: Yale University Press, 2000); Dale Spender's *Mothers of the Novel: 100 Good Women Writers before Jane Austen* (New York: Routledge and Kegan Paul, 1986). See Margaret Ezell, who provides an important corrective to this stumbling block of much feminist literary history in *Writing Women's Literary History* (Baltimore: Johns Hopkins University Press, 1993).
18. For three such treatments, see Kristina Straub, "Women, Gender and Criticism" in *Literary Criticism and Theory: The Greeks to the Present*, ed. Laurie Finke and Robert Con Davis (New York: Longman, 1989), 855–76; Laurie Finke, "Aphra Behn and the Ideological Construction of Restoration Literary Theory" in *Rereading Aphra Behn: History, Theory and Criticism*, ed. Heidi Hutner (Charlottesville: University Press of Virginia, 1993), 17–43; and Jessica Munns, " 'Good, Sweet, Honey, Sugar-Candied Reader': Aphra Behn's Foreplay in Forewords" in *Rereading Aphra Behn*, ed. Hutner, 44–64.
19. *Women Critics: An Anthology*, edited by the Folger Collective on Early Women Critics (Bloomington: Indiana University Press, 1995). The standard anthologies of critical writings of the seventeenth and eighteenth centuries contain no critical writing by women. See J. Spingarn (ed.), *Critical Essays of the Seventeenth Century*, 3 vols. (1908; New York: Oxford University Press, 1957), and Scott Elledge (ed.), *Eighteenth-century Critical Essays*, 2 vols. (Ithaca, NY: Cornell University Press, 1961).
20. Michael McKeon, "Historicizing Patriarchy: The Emergence of Gender Difference in England, 1660–1760," *Eighteenth-Century Studies* 28 (Spring 1995), 301.
21. Kristina Straub gives a finely nuanced account of how Pope establishes his literary authority by means of a complexly sexualized series of interactions with Colley Cibber in *Sexual Suspects: Eighteenth-Century Players and Sexual Ideology* (Princeton University Press, 1992), 69–88; in his historicization of the modern understanding of gender, Michael McKeon suggests that femininity and effeminacy have crucial, definitional roles to play in the construction of bourgeois masculinity in the writings of Richard Steele. See McKeon's "Historicizing Patriarchy", 295–322.
22. Ros Ballaster, Margaret Beetham, Elizabeth Frazer and Sandra Hebron, *Women's Worlds: Ideology, Femininity and the Woman's Magazine* (London: Macmillan, 1991), 39–40. Erin Skye Mackie's recent work on Addison and Steele argues that gender and sexuality are also important concepts for the proper understanding of their achievement. See *Market à La Mode* (Baltimore: Johns Hopkins University Press, 1998). Moreover, Mackie's book opens up the possibility for considering Addison and Steele's critical writings in relation to their dramatic works.

23. Thomas Laqueur, *Making Sex: Body and Gender from the Greeks to Freud* (Cambridge, Mass.: Harvard University Press, 1990).
24. Whereas Winn looks at different aspects of Dryden's life and artistic development in order to understand more fully his life and work, Runge "investigates Dryden's use of gender as a model of difference upon which he establishes literary judgment with the intent to prove the extent to which critical discourse intersects with the culturally specific ideology of gender." James Winn, *"When Beauty Fires the Blood": Love and the Arts in the Age of Dryden* (Ann Arbor: University of Michigan Press, 1992), 7. Laura Runge, " 'The Softness of Expression and the Smoothness of Measure': A Model of Gendered Decorum from Dryden's Criticism," *Essays in Literature* 20 (Fall 1993), 198.
25. Laqueur's very useful account of the shift from a hierarchical one-sex model of gender to an oppositional two-sex model is flawed, as Jonathan Goldberg acutely points out, by the assumption that the history of biological descriptions of gendered bodies amounts to a history of gender. See Goldberg, *Desiring Women Writing: English Renaissance Examples* (Palo Alto: Stanford University Press, 1997), 46, 201 n. 9. See also Alan Bray *Homosexuality in Renaissance England* (London: Gay Men's Press, 1982); Randolph Trumbach, "Are Modern Lesbian Women and Gay Men a Third Gender?" in *A Queer World: The Center for Lesbian and Gay Studies Reader*, ed. Martin Duderman (New York University Press, 1997), 87–99; Kristina Straub, *Sexual Suspects*; and Michael McKeon "Historicizing Patriarchy." These authors argue that the concomitant understandings of femininity and masculinity are realigned in conjunction with the decline of aristocratic culture, which is reflected in the association of male sodomitical behavior with effeminacy. See also *History Workshop Journal* 41 (Spring 1996), a special issue devoted to the history of gender and sexuality in seventeenth-century England.
26. On the philosophical necessity for understanding the construction of gender identities in relation to those of sexuality, see Judith Butler, *Gender Trouble: Feminism and the Subversion of Identity* (New York: Routledge, 1990), and Eve Kosofsky Sedgwick, *Epistemology of the Closet* (Berkeley: University of California Press, 1990). Their work meshes nicely with that of Joan Wallach Scott and Denise Riley, who insist on a historical understanding of gender. See Scott, "Experience" in *Feminists Theorize the Political*, ed. Judith Butler and Joan W. Scott (New York: Routledge, 1992), 22–40, and Riley, *"Am I That Name?": Feminism and the Category of "Women" in History* (New York: Macmillan, 1988).
27. For the speech act definition of the performative, see J. L. Austin, *How to Do Things with Words*, ed. J. O. Urmson and Marina Sbisa (Cambridge, Mass.: Harvard University Press, 1975); for the recent recuperations of the performative and its implications for theories of gender and sexuality, see Butler, *Gender Trouble*, and Eve Kosofsky Sedgwick, "Queer Performativity: Henry James's *The Art of the Novel*," *GLQ* 1 (1993), 1–16.

1. "EQUAL TO OURSELVES": JOHN DRYDEN'S NATIONAL LITERARY HISTORY

1. John Dryden, "The Secular Masque" in Dryden, *Works*, vol. XVI, ed. Vinton A. Dearing, XVI: 270–73.
2. Robert Hume, *Dryden's Criticism* (Ithaca: Cornell University Press, 1970), 150–86; Edward Pechter, *Dryden's Classical Theory of Literature* (London: Cambridge University Press, 1975), 59–61.
3. Miner, "Poetics of the Critical Act," 35.
4. Ralph Cohen, "John Dryden's Literary Criticism" in *New Homage to John Dryden* (Los Angeles: William Andrews Clark Memorial Library, 1983), 70. Miner, "Poetics of the Critical Act," 41.
5. John Dryden, "Preface to the Fables" in *Of Dramatic Poesy and Other Critical Essays by John Dryden*, ed. George Watson (London: J. M. Dent, 1962), II: 270.
6. See Miner, "Poetics of the Critical Act," 35–36. See also James Winn's introduction to *Critical Essays on John Dryden*, 3–4, where he summarizes the attention that a number of essays in that volume pay to the "Lineal Descents and Clans" passage. Winn, however, understands Dryden here to be expressing a "fluid and transformative theory of literary identity" that makes Dryden an early advocate of what we might call intertextuality (3). By contrast, Kramer understands the strategic power of Dryden's genealogies in terms derived from Harold Bloom in *The Imperial Dryden*, 23–24.
7. Benedict Anderson discusses the formation of a "national print language" in *Imagined Communities: Reflections on the Origin and Spread of Nationalism*, rev. edn. (London: Verso, 1991), ch. 3.
8. John Dryden, *Troilus and Cressida* in Dryden, *Works*, vol. XIII, ed. Maximillian E. Novak, 222. Further citations from this edition of the *Works* are given in the body of the text by volume and page number.
9. As Anderson puts it, "[P]rint-capitalism [gives] a new fixity to language, which in the long run helped to build that image of antiquity so central to the subjective idea of the nation." See *Imagined Communities*, 44.
10. Kramer, *The Imperial Dryden*, 16–62, 107–14.
11. René Wellek, *The Rise of English Literary History* (Chapel Hill: University of North Carolina Press, 1941), 25.
12. Eagleton, *The Function of Criticism*; Ross, *The Making of the English Literary Canon*; Kramnick, "The Making of the English Canon."
13. Johnson, *Lives of the Poets*, I: 410.
14. Joseph M. Levine, *The Battle of the Books: History and Literature in the Augustan Age* (Ithaca: Cornell University Press, 1991), 274–77.
15. See Howard Weinbrot, *Britannia's Issue: The Rise of British Literature from Dryden to Ossian* (New York: Cambridge University Press, 1993), 25–32, for a discussion of "Augustan" writers' ambivalent attitudes towards the examples of Greece and Rome. On Dryden's attitudes, see pp. 1–30, 114–43 and 150–92.

16. Dryden, "Epilogue" to *The Conquest of Granada, Part II*, 201–2. Further citations to this edition are given in the body of the text by volume and page number.
17. John Dryden, *Astrea Redux* in Dryden, *Works*, vol. 1, ed. Edward Niles Hooker and H. T. Swedenberg Jr., 22. In *Dryden, the Public Writer: 1660–1685* (Princeton University Press, 1978), 38–39, George McFadden discusses this poem in relation to Dryden's criticism.
18. Erich Auerbach, "La Cour et La Ville" *Scenes from the Drama of European Literature* (Manchester University Press, 1984), 133–82.
19. See Ian Donaldson, "Fathers and Sons: Jonson, Dryden and 'MacFlecknoe'" *Southern Review* 18 (1985), 314–37.
20. On "wit" as a sublimation of the relations between economic and political positions of prestige in the Restoration, see Eve Kosofsky Sedgwick's reading of *The Country Wife* in *Between Men: English Literature and Male Homosocial Desire* (New York: Columbia University Press, 1985), 62–63.
21. On the pedant versus the gentleman, see Kramnick, "The Making of the English Canon," 1091–92, and Eagleton, *The Function of Criticism*, 24–25.
22. For a parallel account of the importance of conversation to Robert Boyle's establishment of experimental science, see Steven Shapin, *A Social History of Truth: Civility and Science in Seventeenth-Century England* (University of Chicago Press, 1994).
23. Gerard Langbaine, *An Account of the English Dramatick Poets* (1691; Los Angeles: William Andrews Clark Memorial Library, 1971), 1: 133.
24. John Dryden, *Essay of Dramatick Poesy* in Dryden, *Works*, vol. XVII, ed. Samuel Holt Monk, 57. Further citations from this edition are given by volume and page number.
25. The four speakers, Crites, Eugenius, Lisideius and Neander, travel by boat first down the Thames towards Greenwich, and then back from the City of London to the Somerset steps. In his recent treatment of the *Essay of Dramatick Poesy*, David Haley accepts that Neander and Crites clearly stand in for Dryden himself and his brother-in-law, Sir Robert Howard, but calls into question critics' longstanding identifications of Eugenius and Lisideius with Buckhurst, the *Essay*'s dedicatee, and Sedley. Haley proposes instead that Eugenius is actually Davenant, and that Lisideius is Orrery. See *Dryden and the Problem of Freedom: The Republican Aftermath 1649–1680* (New Haven: Yale University Press, 1997), 165–72.
26. By the time Dryden published the *Essay*, the war had resulted in the exposure of massive corruption concerning the funding of the English navy, the impeachment and exile of Clarendon, and the Dutch had burned the English fleet. In *Country and Court: England 1658–1714* (Cambridge, Mass.: Harvard University Press, 1978), 96–101, J. R. Jones chronicles the events of the Second Dutch War.
27. Dryden's attempts, however, to capitalize on the national commercial superiority achieved in battle for his own independent status and for the empowerment of English aesthetic achievement are indeed wishful. In 1665,

the English naval victory over the Dutch was hardly complete; the Second Dutch War went on until 1667; and there was also a Third Dutch War (1672–74) which "exploded the mercantilist thesis on which all the Dutch wars had been based. There was no profit, actual or potential, to offset the money spent on the wars. Heavy taxation and higher customs, the pressing of ships and seamen, prohibitions on trade and the closure of the Baltic had all affected the economy adversely" (J. R. Jones, *Country and Court*, 109). On Dryden, Buckhurst and the relation between the aesthetic debates and their commercial context, see Cedric D. Reverand III, "Dryden's 'Essay of Dramatic Poesie': The Poet and the World of Affairs," *Studies in English Literature* 22 (1982), 375–93.

28. Cloth was the most important English export. The industry's interests were anti-Dutch and to encourage its profits, "dyeing and dressing of cloth in England became the rule, and the quantity of undressed cloth exports fell sharply. In 1666 came the famous statute enacting that the dead were to be buried in woollen, and not in imported textiles" (Christopher Hill, *The Century of Revolution: 1603–1714* (New York: Norton, 1961), 176).

29. Kramer's reading of Dryden's vexed debts to Corneille in the *Essay of Dramatick Poesy* goes a long way towards making sense of his masking his assertion of English literary ascendancy over the French in terms of English naval victory over the Dutch. See *The Imperial Dryden*, 33–46.

30. Jennifer Brady proposes that Dryden's ambivalences towards both his literary forefathers and his literary sons should prompt us to revise Harold Bloom's "Anxiety of Influence" model of literary history in "Dryden and Negotiations of Literary Succession and Precession."

31. In the light of Crites's claim that Eugenius loves Jonson, it is worth noting that the name "Eugenius" may be a derivation of the name of Eugenie Dauphine, the nephew who is restored to his uncle Morose's wealth in Jonson's *The Silent Woman*, the play that Neander examines in "Essay of Dramatick Poesy."

32. On Jonson's antitheatricality see C. H. Herford and P. Simpson's introduction to *Ben Jonson's Works*, vol. 1 (Oxford: Clarendon Press, 1925), 396; Timothy Murray, *Thetrical Legitimation: Allegories of Genius in Seventeenth-Century England and France* (Oxford University Press, 1987); and Jonas Barish, *The Antitheatrical Prejudice* (Berkeley: University of California Press, 1981), 132–54.

33. See Jones, *Country and Court*, 97.

34. Weinbrot discusses the attraction of the tale of Brutus, grandson of Aeneas, as the founder of Britain to seventeenth- and eighteenth-century poets in *Britannia's Issue*, 559–67. He suggests that Shakespeare's "hostility to the brainless and bloody Greeks in *Troilus and Cressida*" exploits this myth (559). For the way this mythic genealogy inflects Shakespeare's play, see Eric S. Mallin, "Emulous Factions and the Collapse of Chivalry: *Troilus and Cressida*," *Representations* 29 (Winter 1990), 153. See also Maximillian Novak's commentary on Dryden's *Troilus and Cressida* (XIII: 549).

35. See John Kenyon, *The History Men: The Historical Profession in England Since the Renaissance*, 2nd, edn. (London: Weidenfeld and Nicolson, 1993), 19–41, which discusses seventeenth-century English historians' use of and departure from Geoffrey of Monmouth. It is interesting to consider that even though Milton rejected the Brutus story, he retold it in his *History of Britain*.
36. Richard Helgerson explores the Elizabethan Humanist opposition between classic and vernacular languages expressed in Roger Ascham's *The Schoolmaster* (1570), and taken up by Spenser, Hervey, Sidney, Dyer and others, in *Forms of Nationhood: The Elizabethan Writing of England* (University of Chicago Press, 1992), 28–39.
37. As James Grantham Turner points out, long after the play stopped being performed, Oedipus' love speeches to Jocasta, written by Lee, had a strange afterlife: they were often quoted by the libertine seducers of the novel, most notably by Lovelace in Richardson's *Clarissa*. See Turner, "The Libertine Sublime: Love and Death in Restoration England," *Studies in Eighteenth-Century Culture* 19 (1989), 99–115.
38. Dryden specifies his contribution in the *Vindication of the Duke of Guise* (1683): the first and third acts of the play, its prologue and epilogue, and a prefatory essay. See *Works*, XIII: 443, where *Oedipus*' editor, Maximillian Novak, notes that Dryden's "scenery" "no doubt included the opening scene of the plague, second-act apparitions, third-act incantation, fifth-act leap from the tower, busy ghost." Of interest is the music for the raising of Lajus' ghost in Act 3: Henry Purcell's song "Music for a While." On Dryden and Lee's association, which spawned a number of other texts, see James Winn, *Dryden and His World* (New Haven: Yale University Press, 1987) – hereafter *DHW* – 116, and 381–84.
39. Dryden and Lee's play was performed at the Duke's Company theatre in Dorset Garden, which was built for the kind of spectacle that included apparitions, ghosts and the final leap from the tower. *Oedipus* marked Dryden's break with the King's Company and with his publisher Henry Herringman (XIII: 443–47).
40. As Jean-Joseph Goux argues, when, in Sophocles' *Oedipus at Colonus*, Oedipus promises to reveal the secret of his power to Theseus, "Oedipus becomes the founder of a symbolic lineage, a lineage that will not pass from father to son, but from sovereign to sovereign" (*Oedipus, Philosopher*, trans. Catherine Porter (Stanford University Press, 1993), 187). Goux offers an interpretation of the Oedipus story as a failed initiation which, paradoxically, inaugurates an "anthropocentering" era of philosophy.
41. See Kramer, *The Imperial Dryden*, 16–62, which analyzes Dryden's critique of the French in terms of his difficulties in acknowledging the influence, rather than as having any legitimacy of its own. On the connections between French neo-classicism and absolutism, see Mitchell Greenberg, *Subjectivity and Subjugation in Seventeenth-Century Drama and Prose: The Family Romance of French Classicism* (New York: Cambridge University Press, 1992).

42. Nathaniel Lee, *Lucius Junius Brutus: Father of his Country* (1681), ed. John Loftis (Lincoln: University of Nebraska Press, 1967).
43. *Ibid.*, xii–xiii. Loftis points out that the play is "by implication, a statement of the Whig constitutional position during the Exclusion controversy" (xiii). While it is easy to see Lee's play as a recommendation for constitutional monarchy, we must keep in mind the violence and brutality which the play dramatizes as the basis upon which the republic is founded.

2. STAGING CRITICISM, STAGING MILTON: JOHN DRYDEN'S *THE STATE OF INNOCENCE*

1. *The State of Innocence* and its preface, "The Author's Apology," in Dryden, *Works*, vol. XII, ed. Vinton A. Dearing, 81–146. Further references to these texts are given parenthetically in the body of the text. James Winn notes that the Stationers' Register contains an entry for *The State of Innocence* dated April 17, 1674, in *DHW*, 262; On the opera's composition, see 262–69.
2. Bourdieu, *Distinction*; David Marshall, "Arguing By Analogy: Hume's Standard of Taste," *Eighteenth-Century Studies* 28 (1995), 323–43.
3. For an account of these matters in Milton, see John Guillory, "The Father's House: *Samson Agonistes* in its Historical Moment" in *Re-Membering Milton: Essays on the Texts and Traditions*, ed. Mary Nyquist and Margaret Ferguson (New York: Methuen, 1987), 148–76.
4. Winn proposes that *The State of Innocence* was never performed because the leadership of the King's Company decided against staging it, probably for financial reasons, in *DHW*, 262. In his edition of Dryden's works, Scott speculates that Adam and Eve's nudity would have made performance problematic, but, as Dearing notes, Adam and Eve had been appearing on stage since medieval times (XI: 322).
5. Often retold is John Aubrey's anecdote in his "Life of Milton" in which Dryden pays a visit to Milton to ask his permission to "tag his verses." For example, see Watson, *of Dramatic Poesy*, I: 195.
6. Dryden, *Works*, vol. III, ed. Earl Miner, 253.
7. The adaptability of Shakespeare during the Restoration can be partially explained by the ways in which his non-authorized texts were open for collaboration and appropriation. Included under the patents that established the reopening of the theatres in 1660, Shakespeare's plays were thus marked as available for posthumous collaboration. These reasons, however, emphatically do not apply to the rewriting of Milton.
8. Abbe Blum, "The Author's Authority: *Areopagitica* and the Labour of Licensing," in *Re-Membering Milton*, ed. Nyquist and Ferguson, 81.
9. On Milton's career, see William Kerrigan, *The Sacred Complex: on the Psychogenesis of Paradise Lost* (Cambridge, Mass.: Harvard University Press, 1983), 40; Richard Helgerson, *Self-Crowned Laureates: Spenser, Jonson, Milton and the Literary System* (Berkeley: University of California Press, 1983). On Jonson's authority, see Murray, *Theatrical Legitimation*, 39–94. On Milton's extension

of his voice through a text, see Jonathan Goldberg, *Voice Terminal Echo: Postmodernism and English Renaissance Texts* (New York: Methuen, 1986), 126.
10. See Christopher Kendrick, *Milton: A Study in Ideology and Form* (New York: Methuen, 1986), 30–35, and Stanley Fish, "Driving from the Letter: Truth and Indeterminacy in Milton's *Areopagitica*" in *Re-Membering Milton*, ed. Nyquist and Ferguson, 234–55.
11. On the courtly context for operas, semi-operas and other musical entertainments written for Charles II, see Winn, "*When Beauty Fires the Blood*," chs. 4 and 5. See also Curtis Price, *Henry Purcell and the London Stage* (New York: Cambridge University Press, 1984).
12. For example, Dustin Griffin queries, "In the context of Dryden's own successful career as a man of letters, especially in the 1670s, we may wonder why he attempted a project that must – in our eyes – have been doomed from the start" (*Regaining Paradise*, 144).
13. See Winn, *DHW*, 262–65. In "*When Beauty Fires the Blood*," Winn elaborates Dryden's relation to Milton by suggesting that the libretto of *The State of Innocence* reveals Dryden's ambivalence towards opera as a genre (227).
14. Steven N. Zwicker, "Milton, Dryden and the Politics of Literary Controversy" in *Culture and Society in the Stuart Restoration: Literature, Drama, History*, ed. Gerald MacLean (New York: Cambridge University Press, 1995), 137–58.
15. John Milton, *Samson Agonistes* in *Complete Poems and Major Prose of John Milton*, ed. Merritt Y. Hughes (Indianapolis: Bobbs Merril, 1957), 549–50. Hughes's introduction to *Paradise Lost* in the same volume summarizes the plans for a drama on the fall of man in the Trinity manuscript (175–76). Subsequent references to Hughes's edition of *Paradise Lost* (*PL*) are given by book and line number in the body of the text.
16. Anne D. Ferry, *Milton and the Miltonic Dryden* (Cambridge, Mass.: Harvard University Press, 1968), 21.
17. Lee's poem is reproduced in Scott and Saintsbury's edition of *The Works of John Dryden* (Edinburgh: Archibald Constable and Co., 1821), V: 11. Subsequent references to this edition are given by book and line number in the body of the text.
18. Cf. "Defense of the Epilogue" in Dryden, *Works*, XI: 211–12. Grafting, which Dryden calls "graffing," is yet another way to improve language that Dryden mentions in "Defense of the Epilogue" (XI: 212).
19. Andrew Marvell, "On Mr. Milton's 'Paradise Lost'" in *Andrew Marvell: A Critical Edition of the Major Works*, ed. Frank Kermode and Keith Walker (New York: Oxford University Press, 1990), 119–20.
20. Joseph A. Wittreich, "Perplexing the Explanation: Marvell's 'On Mr. Milton's *Paradise Lost*'" in *Approaches to Marvell: The York Centenary Lectures*, ed. C. A. Patrides (Boston: Routledge and Kegan Paul, 1978), 280–305.
21. "The Readie and Easie Way" in *The Complete Prose Works of John Milton*, vol. VI, ed. Robert W. Ayers (New Haven: Yale University Press, 1980), 387.
22. For another self-conscious use of "The Good Old Cause" as nostalgic, but also as compatible with royalism, see Andrew Marvell, who states "The

Cause was too good to have been fought for" in *The Rehearsal Transpros'd and The Rehearsal Transpros'd the Second Part*, ed. D. I. B. Smith (Oxford: Clarendon Press, 1971), 135.
23. See Winn, *DHW*, 264, and Christopher Hill, *Milton and the English Revolution* (New York: Penguin, 1979), 483. Jonathan Goldberg and Stephen Orgel propose that Milton's Note may well be a response to Dryden's treatment of rhyme in the dedication to his play *The Rival Ladies* (1664) and elsewhere. See their introduction to a selection of Milton's works, *John Milton* (London: Oxford University Press, 1990), x. Zwicker argues more positively that Milton's repudiation of rhyme in the Note exhibits a combativeness essential to the redefinition of heroic action he offers as against Dryden's ("Milton, Dryden and the Politics of Literary Controversy," 140–41).
24. Kendrick, *Milton*, 82–83.
25. Richard Kroll, *The Material Word: Literate Culture in the Restoration and Early Eighteenth Century* (Baltimore: Johns Hopkins University Press, 1991), 324.
26. Antony Easthope, "Towards the Autonomous Subject in Poetry: Milton 'on His Blindness'" in *1642: Literature and Power in the Seventeenth Century: Proceedings of the Essex Conference on the History of Sociology*, ed. Francis Barker *et al.* (Essex, 1980), 301–14. Jonathan Goldberg notices that although Easthope demystifies the traditional historicist reading of the poem, his reading still depends on it in "Dating Milton" in *Soliciting Interpretation*, ed. Elizabeth Harvey and Katharine Maus, 202–7. Other critics who emphasize Milton's dependence on the voice include Kendrick, *Milton*, 72, and Kerrigan, *The Sacred Complex*, 53–54.
27. In *Poetic Authority: Spenser, Milton and Literary History* (New York: Columbia University Press, 1983), John Guillory discusses Milton's use of invocation in *Paradise Lost* from this perspective. See esp. p. 145.
28. David Marshall argues that Hume's strategies for creating a "standard of taste" depend on the transitional status of "taste" between literal and figurative registers in "Arguing By Analogy."
29. Regarding the Latin phrase *convenire in aliquo tertio*, Dearing notes, "A stock phrase signifying to find some means of agreement, in a third term, between two opposites" (XII: 353).
30. Dryden refers to Wycherley as follows: "Many of our present writers are eminent in both [comedy and satire]; and particularly the author of the *Plain Dealer*, whom I am proud to call my friend" (XII: 89). Winn points out that *The Country Wife* had its premier in January, 1675, in *DHW*, 271.
31. Sedgwick, *Between Men*, 73.
32. John Dennis, "The Impartial Critic" in *The Critical Works of John Dennis*, ed. Edward Niles Hooker (Baltimore: Johns Hopkins University Press, 1939), 1: 16. For Dennis's reference to "hypercritics," see p. 24.
33. When Dryden paraphrases "not any Man of so false a judgment who would choose rather to have been Apollonius or Theocritus, than Homer," his

syntax is confusing – significantly so. T. S. Dorsch translates the same phrase, "Yet would you not choose to be Homer than Apollonius?" in *Classical Literary Criticism* (New York: Penguin, 1965), 144, and W. R. Roberts renders it, "Yet would you not, for all that, choose to be Homer rather than Apollonius?" in *Critical Theory Since Plato*, ed. Hazard Adams (New York: Harcourt, Brace, Jovanovich Inc., 1971), 96. Dryden's addition, the negative characterization, "not any man," makes more oblique the man of true judgment's wish to identify with the poet he criticizes.

34. David Bywaters, *Dryden in Revolutionary England* (Berkeley: University of California Press, 1991). See especially the last chapter which treats the critical essays Dryden wrote in the 1690s.
35. For an argument consonant with my own, see Michael McKeon's reading of the contributions Dryden makes to the articulation of a secularized aesthetic sphere in his most overtly political poem, *Absalom and Achitphel*, in "Politics of Discourses and the Rise of the Aesthetic in Seventeenth-Century England" in *Politics of Discourse: The Literature and History of Seventeenth-Century England*, ed. Kevin Sharpe and Steven Zwicker (Berkeley: University of California Press, 1987), 35–51.
36. For a comparison between Dryden's and Addison's understanding of the role of the critic as social arbiter, see Peter Stallybrass and Allon White, *The Politics and Poetics of Transgression* (Ithaca: Cornell University Press, 1986), 80–100.
37. John Dryden, "The Discourse Concerning Satire" in *Of Dramatic Poesy*, vol. II, ed. Watson, 85.
38. Dryden "grows weary of his long-lov'd Mistris, Rhyme" in the prologue to *Aureng Zebe* (1676) in Dryden, *Works*, vol. XII, ed. Vinton A. Dearing, 159.
39. Whether or not Dryden knew it, Milton had intentionally backdated some of the poems in the 1645 edition. See Kerrigan, *The Sacred Complex*, 306.

3. IMITATING SHAKESPEARE: GENDER AND CRITICISM

1. Johnson, *Lives of the Poets*, I: 412.
2. Gary Taylor, *Reinventing Shakespeare: A Cultural History from the Restoration to the Present* (New York: Weidenfeld and Nicolson, 1989), 44–45.
3. Laura Runge, *Gender and Language in British Literary Criticism: 1660–1790* (New York: Cambridge University Press, 1997).
4. Laqueur, *Making Sex*.
5. Straub, *Sexual Suspects*. For descriptions of the uneven application of the term "perverse" to male and female reversibility, see Valerie Traub, "The Perversion of 'Lesbian' Desire," *History Workshop Journal* 41 (1996), 23–49; Bray, *Homosexuality in Renaissance England*; and Randolph Trumbach, "The Birth of the Queen: Sodomy and the Emergence of Gender Equality in

Modern Culture, 1660–1750" in *Hidden From History*, ed. Martin Duberman, Martha Vicinius and George Chauncey (New York: New American Library, 1989), 129–40.
6. Goldberg, *Desiring Women Writing*, 46.
7. McKeon, "Historicizing Patriarchy," 300.
8. John Guillory, "From the Superfluous to the Supernumerary: Reading Gender into *Paradise Lost*" in *Soliciting Interpretation*, ed. Harvey and Maus, 68–88.
9. The work of Denise Riley suggests that gender comes to be increasingly embodied by women. In *"Am I That Name?"*: Riley specifies the late seventeenth-century debate over whether or not women can or should be educated as a turning point in the history in which women come to be increasingly saturated by their sex.
10. On the gender dynamics of this Renaissance stage practice, see Stephen Orgel, " 'Nobody's Perfect': Or Why Did the English Stage Take Boys for Women?" *South Atlantic Quarterly* 88, 1 (1989), 7–30, and Katharine Eisaman Maus, "Playhouse Flesh and Blood: Sexual Ideology and the Restoration Actress," *ELH* 46 (1979), 595–617.
11. John Dryden, prologue to *The Tempest* (lines 1–8) in Dryden, *Works*, vol. x, ed. Maximillian E. Novak, 6. Further citations from this edition are given in the body of the text by volume and page number.
12. *Of Dramatic Poesy*, ed. Watson, 1: 133.
13. Johnson, *Lives of the Poets*, 1: 410.
14. Moody E. Prior claims that "Dryden's *All for Love or the World Well Lost* is generally acknowledged as his best play, and without much question it is the best tragedy of its age" ("Tragedy and the Heroic Play" in *Dryden: A Collection of Critical Essays*, ed. Bernard Schelling (New Jersey: Prentice Hall, 1963), 93). See also *All for Love*, ed. N. J. Andrew (London: A. and C. Black Ltd., 1986), xxviii; and Dryden, *Works*, vol. XIII, ed. Maximillian Novak, XIII: 363. Further citations from Novak's edition of the play are given by act, scene and line numbers in the body of the text.
15. See, for examples, almost all the essays in Bruce King, ed., *Twentieth-Century Interpretations of "All for Love": A Collection of Critical Essays* (New Jersey: Prentice Hall, 1968).
16. David Bruce Kramer makes a compelling case for seeing Dryden's claim to be imitating Shakespeare in *All for Love* as a distraction from the real source of his inspiration in Racine, in *The Imperial Dryden*, 45–62. His account, particularly since he sees Dryden writing in silent opposition to Shakespeare's style rather than in imitation of it, is consonant with my own desire to extract from *All for Love* Dryden's critical relation to Shakespeare.
17. Laura Brown, *English Dramatic Form, 1660–1760* (New Haven: Yale University Press, 1981), 69.
18. The contrast between Shakespeare's and Dryden's Cleopatras is also central to Eugene Waith's discussion of *All for Love* in *Ideas of Greatness: Heroic Drama*

in England (New York: Barnes and Noble, 1971), 231–35. It should be noted that, although in Shakespeare's play Cleopatra claims her wifely title in death, saying "Husband I come" (v.ii: 287), in Dryden's play she aspires to wifehood throughout.

19. Samuel Johnson, *Preface to Shakespeare* in *Works of Samuel Johnson*, vol. VII: *Johnson on Shakespeare*, ed. Arthur Sherbo (New Haven: Yale University Press, 1968), 74.
20. Bloom, *A Map of Misreading*.
21. James Winn reads Dryden's Ulysses analogy "straight": he sees Dryden casting himself as Telemachus, playing son to a literary father, in *DHW*, 331. This observation makes the classical analogy into another example of Dryden's self-presentation as weaker than his literary forefathers. Like Gary Taylor, Winn oedipalizes Dryden's relation to Shakespeare. Although it could be argued that Dryden does portray himself that way (among others), the oedipal readings give no sense of how Dryden manipulates being a weak son to his own, i.e. critical, advantage.
22. Winn describes the conflict in terms of status in *ibid.*, 248–55, 302–11.
23. *The Complete Poems of John Wilmot, Earl of Rochester*, ed. David M. Vieth (New Haven: Yale University Press, 1968), lines 120–26.
24. Sedley's *Antony and Cleopatra* was licensed and performed in 1677; it can be read in *The Poetical and Dramatic Works of Sir Charles Sedley*, ed. V. de Sola Pinto (London: Constable and Co., Ltd., 1928).
25. V. de Sola Pinto, *Sir Charles Sedley 1639–1701: A Study in the Life and Literature of the Restoration* (London: Constable and Co., Ltd., 1927), 61–63.
26. *Ibid.*, 111–12. In *Homosexuality in Renaissance England*, Alan Bray claims that homosexual culture *per se* only came into visibility in the later part of the seventeenth century with the systematic raids on the Molly Houses beginning in 1699. In *Sexual Suspects*, Kristina Straub demonstrates that the actor is a crucial figure in the emergence of regulatory definitions of gender and sexuality. I would propose that Sedley and Kynaston's interaction be seen as an early example of the transition to visibility and the definitional struggles that Bray and Straub describe.
27. David Vieth characterizes the relationship between Antony and Dolabella as explicitly homosexual in the introduction to his edition of *All for Love* (Lincoln: University of Nebraska Press, 1973), xxiv–xxv.
28. The fight between Dryden's women has a more violent counterpart in *The Rival Queens*, a contemporary play by Dryden's sometime collaborator Nathaniel Lee. Because it stages direct and physical conflict between the titular rivals, and more explicitly homoerotic scenes between Alexander and Hephestion, *The Rival Queens* clarifies the relation between representations of female rivalry and male homoeroticism in *All for Love*. P. F. Vernon discusses the fact that, to a large extent, *The Rival Queens* and *All for Love* also shared a cast. See Nathaniel Lee, *The Rival Queens*, ed. P. F. Vernon, The Regents Restoration Drama Series (Lincoln: University of Nebraska Press, 1970), xiv–xvi.

29. Jay Caplan argues that a link between castration and tears underwrites the sentimental in *Framed Narratives: Diderot's Genealogy of the Beholder* (Minneapolis: University of Minnesota Press, 1985), 19.
30. Novak points out that "the last age" would be heard/read as Shakespeare's especially in the aftermath of Rymer's publication of *Tragedies of the Last Age* in August 1677 (Dryden, *Works*, XIII: 440 n. 25).
31. On this point, see Novak's commentary (*Works*, XIII: 501).
32. For a similar reversal, see Nathaniel Lee's *Lucius Junius Brutus* (1679), in which Titus, Brutus' loyal son, performs a similar function to that of Dryden's Troilus: he is feminized and then killed in order to consolidate Brutus' republican legacy. On Titus' feminization, see Turner, "The Libertine Sublime." I discuss the strange inheritance paradigm of *Lucius Junius Brutus* in comparison to Dryden and Lee's *Oedipus* in Chapter 1.
33. Dryden's representation of brotherhood as the stabilizing ground of value may also express his wish to ward off the threat posed to the status of royal siblinghood. In 1679, the brotherhood of Charles and James Stuart did not guarantee the transmission of power from one to the other. In the translation from the problem of inheriting a throne to the problem of inheriting a literary tradition, Dryden introduces brotherhood to underwrite a modern masculinity as a way of bolstering genealogical continuity.
34. Robert Markley, *Two-Edg'd Weapons: Style and Ideology in the Comedies of Etheredge, Wycherley and Congreve* (Oxford: Clarendon Press, 1988), 58–59. Markley argues that Dryden consolidates the cavaliers' nostalgic misrepresentation of Fletcher's courtly absolutism, 78–99.
35. Jeff Masten, "My Two Dads: Collaboration and the Reproduction of Beaumont and Fletcher" in *Queering the Renaissance*, ed. Jonathan Goldberg (Durham: Duke University Press, 1994), 280–309.
36. See McKeon's *Origins of the English Novel, 1600–1740* (Baltimore: Johns Hopkins University Press, 1987) for an elaboration of aristocratic and progressive ideologies.
37. In "Historicizing Patriarchy," McKeon argues that aristocrats and sodomites are linked by their "anomalous positions in the respective emergent systems of sexuality and class" (312); he discusses the "surprisingly positive (if temporary) contribution" effeminacy makes to early modern masculinity (313).

4. THE FEMALE PLAYWRIGHT AND THE CITY LADY

1. Anonymous, *A Comparison Between the Two Stages* (London: 1702).
2. Paula Backscheider, *Spectacular Politics: Theatrical Power and Mass Culture in Early Modern England* (Baltimore: Johns Hopkins University Press, 1993), 70–71. In *Thomas Betterton and the Management of Lincoln's Inn Fields, 1695–1708* (Carbondale: Southern Illinois University Press, 1979), Judith Milhous suggests that the market for new plays, which spawned the offerings of hitherto

unknown writers, including women, expanded in the season of 1695/96 with the competition created by the advent of the new theatre company at Lincoln's Inn Fields.
3. Winn, "*When Beauty Fires the Blood*," 7.
4. John Dryden, "Preface to Ovid's Epistles" in *Of Dramatic Poesy*, ed. Watson, 1: 273. Janet Todd points out that Dryden compliments Behn in terms that suggest he did not know her very well, in *The Secret Life of Aphra Behn* (New York: Pandora, 2000), 256.
5. *The Nine Muses* (London, 1700). Roger Lonsdale, editor of *Eighteenth-Century Women Poets: An Oxford Anthology* (New York: Oxford, 1989), proposes that Mrs. Manley edited *The Nine Muses* (26), an attribution accepted by Paula Backscheider, *Spectacular Politics*, 73. *The Nine Muses* indicates that women writers were also marketed as such, as Kathryn Shevelow notes in *Women and Print Culture: The Construction of Femininity in the Early Periodical* (New York: Routledge, 1989), 34.
6. Despite a veritable explosion of feminist work on women writers of the late seventeenth and early eighteenth centuries, little attention has been paid to critical writing by women. In the preface to Janet Todd (ed.), *Dictionary of British and American Women Writers, 1660–1800* (London: Methuen, 1987), critical writing by women is not even mentioned.
7. Finke, "Aphra Behn," 17, 25. Although in her introductory remarks, Finke takes pains to emphasize that she is "not suggesting that Behn's critical statements somehow magically remain free from any hegemonic contamination, providing us with some privileged access to true critical practice" (20), she nevertheless goes on to argue that Behn's position as a writer "is (ambiguously) nonhegemonic" (25).
8. *Women Critics*, xiii.
9. As Marta Straznicky argues, however, in "Restoration Women Playwrights and the Limits of Professionalism," *ELH* 64 (Fall 1997), 712, the association of female playwrights with female actresses was only made in the misogynist attacks on women writers.
10. Milhous, *Thomas Betterton*, 200.
11. Catherine Gallagher, "Who Was That Masked Woman? The Prostitute and the Playwright in the Comedies of Aphra Behn" in *Rereading Aphra Behn*, ed. Hutner, 73.
12. Catherine Gallagher, *Nobody's Story: The Vanishing Acts of Women Writers in the Marketplace 1670–1820* (Berkeley: University of California Press, 1994).
13. Agnew, *Worlds Apart*, ix–xiv.
14. See McKeon's *Origins of the English Novel* for an argument which traces the process through which the novel comes to represent the autonomy of literature from the socio-political contexts out of which it emerges. McKeon's treatment of the novel brings out the strange dehistoricizing implications of Gallagher's choice of the term "fiction," over the generic category.

15. See Eleanor Boswell, *The Restoration Court Stage: 1660–1702* (1932; New York: Benjamin Blom, 1965), part II, for a detailed account of Crowne's *Calisto*. *Calisto* can be read in *The Dramatic Works of John Crowne* (New York: Benjamin Blom, 1967), 1.
16. R. O. Bucholz, *The Augustan Court: Queen Anne and the Decline of Court Culture* (Palo Alto: Stanford University Press, 1993), 12–35. Robert D. Hume, *The Development of English Drama in the Late Seventeenth Century* (Oxford: Clarendon Press, 1976), 487–88.
17. According to Langbaine, Princess Anne acted the part of Semandra in a court production of *Mithridates*, and Dibden reports that she took the same role again in a presentation at Holyrood House on November 15, 1681. See the introduction to Lee's *Mithridates* in *The Works of Nathaniel Lee*, vol. 1, ed. Thomas Stroup and Arthur Cooke (New Jersey: Scarecrow Reprint Corporation, 1968), 287.
18. Finke, "Aphra Behn," which proceeds from the assumption that Behn can offer a perspective on the contingencies of Restoration culture which is for some reason unavailable through the examination of her male contemporaries (32–39), and Munns, "'Good, Sweet, Honey, Sugar-Candied Reader,'" which argues that Dryden genders the preface as male.
19. Preface to *The Dutch Lover* in *The Works of Aphra Behn*, ed. Janet Todd (London: William Pickering, 1996), V: 162.
20. Preface to *The Lucky Chance* in *Works*, VII: 215.
21. David Roberts, *The Ladies: Female Patronage of Restoration Drama 1660–1700* (Oxford: Clarendon Press, 1989), 32.
22. See Jonathan Goldberg's discussion of gender in Aphra Behn's writing for an acute treatment of this problem in *Desiring Women Writing*, 42–72.
23. Backscheider, *Spectacular Politics*, 71–104.
24. "To the Excellent Orinda" is included in *Kissing the Rod: An Anthology of Seventeenth-Century Women's Verse*, ed. Germaine Greer, Susan Hastings, Jeslyn Medoff, Melinda Sansone (New York: Farrar Strauss, 1988), 204–9. The poem was included among the eulogies in the 1667 edition of Philips's works.
25. They also bespeak the competition between the two models of gender difference which Thomas Laqueur identifies as the older, hierarchical model in which women are inferior versions of men and the newer, incommensurate model in which men and women belong to opposite sexes (*Making Sex*).
26. Addison and Steele set out the program of the *Spectator* "to bring learning out of the closets and universities and into the Coffee houses" (*Spectator* 10); they frequently issue statements of intent "to establish among us a taste of polite writing" (*Spectator* 58). See Habermas, *Structural Transformation of the Public Sphere*, on the public sphere's relation to the market, but see also Paula McDowell's *The Women of Grub Street: Press, Politics and Gender in the London Literary Marketplace 1678–1730* (Oxford: Clarendon Press, 1998) for an account of how women writers and printers contributed to the shape of the

public sphere, and Alexandra Halascz, *The Marketplace of Print* (New York: Cambridge University Press, 1998), which establishes the roles the sixteenth-century English book trade, the pamphlet, and the print commodity play in the development of the public sphere.
27. Both poems in Edna Steeves (ed.), *The Plays of Mary Pix and Catharine Trotter*, vol. II (New York: Garland Publishing, 1982), n.p.
28. *Ibid.*, II: 15.
29. Wycherley's prologue to *Agnes de Castro* in *ibid.*, II: n.p.
30. McKeon, "Historicizing Patriarchy," 312–13.
31. Trotter's prologue to *Love at a Loss* in Steeves (ed.), *The Plays of Mary Pix and Catharine Trotter*, II: n.p.
32. In her introduction to *Love at a Loss*, which she includes in *Love and Thunder: Plays by Women in the Age of Queen Anne* (London: Methuen, 1988), 64–65, Kendall quotes from Piers's and Trotter's letters, noting that the nature of their relationship was more troubling than a "romantic friendship."
33. Valerie Traub has argued that Crowne's rewriting of the Calisto story constitutes an important contribution to what she calls "the perversion of 'lesbian' desire." See "The Perversion of 'Lesbian' Desire." In this context, Anne's childhood letters to Frances Apsley record in a striking manner the influence of theatrical performance on her self-presentation: they are addressed to "Semandra," and signed "Zephares." Beatrice Curtis Brown, editor of Anne's letters, explains that Frances, Anne and her sister Mary had all participated in a performance of Lee's *Mithridates*: "Anne had acted Semandra then, but as Mary [who was primarily Frances's friend], addresses Frances as 'Husband,' Frances may have arranged to change about and play at 'Wife' with Anne." See *The Letters of Queen Anne*, (London: Cassell and Company, 1968), 4.
34. Trotter's prologue to *The Revolution of Sweden* in Steeves (ed.), *The Plays of Mary Pix and Catherine Trotter*, II: n.p.
35. Milhous discusses Trotter's progressivist interests in reform and morality in the prologues to *Love at a Loss* and *The Unhappy Penitent*, drawing an important contrast between Trotter, who believes in reforming the stage, and other advocates for the reformation of manners and morals who have a special animosity towards the stage that is explicitly conflated with misogyny, in *Thomas Betterton*, 125. For an example of the latter sort of reform, see Arthur Bedford, the Vicar of Bristol, *The Evil and Danger of Stage-Plays Showing their Natural Tendency to Destroy Religion and Introduce a General Corruption of Manners* (London, 1706).
36. Mary Astell, *A Serious Proposal to the Ladies for the Advancement of their True Interest by a Lover of her Sex* (1694) cited in *The "Other" Eighteenth Century: English Women of Letters 1660–1800*, ed. Robert Uphaus and Gretchen Foster (East Lansing: Colleagues Press, 1991), 5. For a provocative discussion of Astell's tracts, see Ellen Pollak, *The Poetics of Sexual Myth: Gender and Ideology in the Verse of Swift and Pope* (University of Chicago Press, 1985), 47.

37. Habermas, *The Structural Transformation of the Public Sphere*, 27–31. In his elaboration of the relations between the intimate, the private and the public spheres as the latter consolidates itself as the domain of rational debate about politics, Habermas makes two related assumptions that careful historical attention to the emergence of literary criticism in England calls into question: that debates about literature are not also debates about politics (at least initially), and that they are about the formation of bourgeois subjectivity. The full interpenetration of residual aristocratic codes and emergent bourgeois ones in Dryden's critical practice, evident in his mode of often violent engagement with the aristocratic circle of wits at Charles II's court, in, for example, the highly politicized debates over rhyme, reveals that it is only possible retrospectively to separate literary from political questions. This suggests that Habermas's terms are not useful for describing the processes through which literature (and aesthetics more generally) come to seem autonomous from politics, since they are already separated in his account. Moreover, it is misleading to present, as Habermas does, debates about literary questions as a dry-run for debates about politics – as if literature provided a sort of "safe" space that is primarily psychological.

38. *The Works of Mrs. Catharine Cockburn (Trotter): Theological, Moral, Dramatic, Poetic with an Account of the life of the Author*, vol. 1, ed. Thomas Birch (London, 1751), 11.

39. Trotter's dedicatory letter for *The Unhappy Penitent* in Steeves (ed.), *The Plays of Mary Pix and Catharine Trotter*, 11: A2r.

40. For the critiques of William's court, see Dennis Rubini, "Sexuality and Augustan England: Sodomy, Politics, Elite Circles and Society" in *The Pursuit of Sodomy: Male Homosexuality in Renaissance and Enlightenment Europe*, ed. Kent Gerard and Gert Hekma (New York: The Hawthorne Press, 1989), 349–82.

41. George Savile, Lord Halifax, *The Lady's New-Year's Gift*, an advice book to women dedicated to his daughter in 1700, outlines how nature compensates women's smaller share of reason: "Nature is so far from being unjust to you, that she is partial on your side. She hath made such large Amends by other Advantages, for the seeming Injustice of the first distribution [of reason], that the Right of Complaining is come over to our Sex." Women's superior natural beauties balance their inferior reason, and, according to Halifax's paradigmatic logic, justify male self-pity. *The Lady's New-Year's Gift* (Stamford, Conn.: The Overbrook Press, 1934), 16.

42. Ballaster *et al.*, *Women's Worlds*, 39–40. Kristina Straub contends that the central place given to "objectivity" in literary criticism has inhibiting consequences for feminist criticism in "Women, Gender and Criticism." The complicated gender dynamics in play in the history of criticism, however, problematize Straub's reliance on the Lacanian paradigm that would gender the objective gaze male.

43. Fidelis Morgan (ed.), *The Female Wits: Women Playwrights of the Restoration* (London: Virago, 1981), 24.

5. SCANDALS OF A FEMALE NATURE

1. Fidelis Morgan, *A Woman of No Character: An Autobiography of Mrs. Manley* (London: Faber, 1986). See also Dolores Diane Clarke Duff, "Materials toward a Biography of Mary Delariviere Manley" (diss., University of Indiana, 1965).
2. Manley wrote a number of political pamphlets between 1711 and 1714, including "A true Narrative of what pass'd at the examination of the Marquis de Guiscard," "The Duke of M–h's Vindication," "A True Relation ... of the Intended Riot and Tumult on Queen Eizabeth's Birth-Day" and others. See Rosalind Ballaster's introduction to her edition of *The New Atalantis* for a complete account of Manley's political writing (*The New Atalantis*, ed. Ballaster (New York: Penguin, 1992), xvii). Further citations of this edition will be given in the body of the text. For a wonderful account of Manley as a political writer, see McDowell, *The Women of Grub Street*, 217–301.
3. See R. Ballaster, *Seductive Forms: Women's Amatory Fiction from 1684–1700* (Oxford: Clarendon Press, 1992), for an account of the influence of the French sources on Manley.
4. Ballaster notes that Manley's purpose is the making and breaking of political careers in "Manl(e)y Forms: Sex and the Female Satirist" in *Women, Texts and Histories 1575–1760*, ed. Clare Brant and Dianne Purkiss (New York: Routledge, 1992), 233.
5. The correspondence between Sarah, Duchess of Marlborough, and Arthur Maynwaring suggests the extent to which *The New Atalantis* was perceived as politically threatening, as Ballaster notes in her introduction to *The New Atalantis* (p. v).
6. Fidelis Morgan gives biographical motivation for Manley's disavowal of Trotter which Manley provides in her fictionalized autobiography *The Adventures of Rivella* (1714), ed. Katherine Zelinsky (Ontario: Broadview Literary Texts, 1999), in *The Female Wits: Women Playwrights of the Restoration* (London: Virago, 1981), 39–40.
7. Delarivier Manley, *The Lost Lover* (London, 1696), A4r.
8. Paula McDowell observes – correctly, in my view – that Manley inscribes both debt and critique in her response to Behn as a literary model, especially when she poses the Lady Intelligence rather than Astrea as an authorial persona in *The New Atalantis*. See *The Women of Grub Street*, 226–41. I differ from McDowell, however, who argues that Manley affiliates herself only with the narratorial position of Intelligence, and not also with Mrs. Nightwork.
9. Jonathan Kramnick, "Pre-publicity," unpublished conference paper delivered at the Group for Early Modern Cultural Studies, New Orleans, Nov. 19, 2000.
10. Gallagher, *Nobody's Story*, 118–19.
11. Catharine Trotter, *Olinda's Adventures: Or the Amours of a Young Lady*, ed. Robert Adams Day (Los Angeles: University of California Press, 1969).

12. According to Edna Steeves, Trotter first appeared in print in a poem addressed to Bevil Higgons in 1693, the same year as *Olinda's Adventures* was published. Steeves suggests that, publishing at fourteen, Trotter was something of a child prodigy, pointing out that she also taught herself Latin and French (*The Plays of Mary Pix and Catharine Trotter*), II: ix.
13. *The Novels of Mary Delariviere Manley*, 2 vols., ed. Patricia Köster (Gainesville: Scholars' Facsimiles and Reprints, 1971), xxii.
14. Anonymous, *The Female Wits*, ed. Lucyle Hook (Los Angeles: University of California Press, 1967). Hook speculates that the play was written by Joe Haines in collaboration with the other actors at Drury Lane.
15. *Ibid.*, iv.
16. Edna Steeves points out that Trotter's plays all amalgamate heroic codes with those of the pathetic she-tragedies in her introductory remarks to *The Plays of Mary Pix and Catharine Trotter*, II: xiv–xxv.
17. On the love–duty conflict as generic marker of the heroic play, see Waith, *Ideas of Greatness*.
18. McFadden, *Dryden the Public Writer: 1660–1685*.
19. *The Royal Mischief* is reprinted in Morgan (ed.), *The Female Wits: Women Playwrights of the Restoration*, 202–62. However, this edition does not reproduce Manley's preface, which I cite from *The Royal Mischief* (London, 1696), [A]3v.
20. Manley, *The Lost Lover*, A4r; *The Royal Mischief*, [A]3v.
21. See Judith Butler on performativity in *Gender Trouble*, 24–25, 137ff.
22. Delarivier Manley, *The Secret History of Queen Zarah and the Zarazians*, ed. Michael F. Shugrue (New York: Garland, 1972).
23. John L. Sutton Jr., "The Source of Mrs. Manley's Preface to Queen Zarah," *Modern Philology* 82 (1984), 167–72.
24. Addison and Steele also contribute to this transition. The *Spectator*'s efforts to discipline the audience at plays, reforming their unruliness into more uniform and polite responses, is often effected through a contrast between playgoing and reading. See the *Spectator* 208, 240 and, especially, 502, for examples. On later seventeenth- and early eighteenth-century efforts to discipline the audience, see also Stallybrass and White in *The Politics and Poetics of Transgression*, 80–124.
25. John Dryden, "A Discourse Concerning the Original and Progress of Satire" (1693) in *Of Dramatic Poesy*, ed. Watson, II: 116.
26. Ballaster points out that although Manley claims in her autobiographical *The Adventures of Rivella* (1714) that she received instruction in Latin, French, Spanish and Italian, there is evidence in Manley's writing only of fluency in French. She suggests that this claim is meant as a playful substantiation of the trope of translation that introduces all of Manley's scandal fictions in *The New Atalantis*, vii. For a more elaborated discussion of the role of translation in Manley's satire, see Ballaster's "Manl(e)y Forms," 234–35.
27. In her account of Manley's debt to Marie Catherine La Motte, Baronne d'Aulnoy, Ballaster notes the attractions of the scandal chronicle for the woman writer, whose gender provides her with special access to scandal.

See "Manl(e)y Forms," and "Seizing the Means of Seduction: Fiction and Feminine Identity in Aphra Behn and Delarivier Manley," in *Women, Writing, History 1640–1740*, ed. Isobel Grundy and Susan Wiseman (London: Batsford, 1992), 93–108.

28. John Dryden, "Discourse Concerning Satire," in *Of Dramatic Poesy*, ed. Watson, II: 130.

29. Catherine Gallagher, "Political Crimes and Fictional Alibis: the Case of Delarivier Manley," *Eighteenth-Century Studies* 23 (1990), 502–21, reprinted with changes in *Nobody's Story*, 88–144.

30. Both Gallagher and Ballaster remark on Manley's scenes of sapphism, though neither sees them as marks of her femininity. As we have seen, however, Manley herself resists such unproblematic associations of gender with genre.

31. In *The Augustan Court*, R. O. Bucholz treats Anne's rhetoric of being her nation's "nursing mother," present in her Coronation speech and also in other ceremonies throughout her reign, as an expression of the maternal, but he also emphasizes her affiliation with Elizabeth I, England's Virgin Queen, in her ceremonial style, which complicates this aspect of her self-presentation (202–22).

32. Ballaster points out that even if the role of Anne's female favorites was exaggerated, "a government in which both a female ruler and her female favorites took an active part in public life (Sarah Churchill even campaigned at St. Albans in the 1705 general election despite the fact that as a women she had no personal franchise) was unprecedented," in "Manl(e)y Forms," 220. Although neither the terms "homosexuality" and "lesbianism," nor the sexual identities they designate, existed in the period, nevertheless, representations of female–female homoeroticism and same-sex sexual involvement are prevalent, particularly in the satires aimed at Queen Anne's court. Another example would be John Dunton's *King Abigail: or the Secret reign of the She-Favorite Detected and Applied In a Sermon Upon these Words, "And Women rule over them" Isa. 3.12* (London, 1715), a satire on Masham. See also Rubini, "Sexuality and Augustan England," on the use of homosexuality in court satire during the reigns of William and Anne. See Emma Donoghue, *Passions Between Women: British Lesbian Culture 1668–1801* (New York: Harper Collins, 1993), for a discussion of Manley's "New Cabal" (232–43), and on the "partnership" of Queen Anne and Sarah Churchill (158–63).

33. See, for example, John Richetti, *Popular Novels Before Richardson: Narrative Patterns 1700–1739* (Oxford: Clarendon Press, 1969), 119–67.

34. Paula McDowell's work on Manley as a political writer in *The Women of Grub Street* is exemplary in its treatment of Manley alongside her contemporaries of both sexes. Moreover, her research on their contributions to the shape of early public opinion helps to explain the difficulty of distinguishing in their texts political from literary-critical writing.

35. Richetti depicts Manley's use of pathos in similar terms, though he condemns her prose as pornographic (*Popular Novels Before Richardson*, 122–25).

36. See Straub, *Sexual Suspects*, 69–88, and Pollak, *The Poetics of Sexual Myth*.
37. In "Historicizing Patriarchy," 312–13, McKeon observes that aristocratic masculinity comes increasingly to be identified with effeminacy as bourgeois masculinity emerged. Pope's purer and more ancient aristocracy of taste should thus be understood as a proto-bourgeois phenomenon, as is confirmed by his status as the first author to make a living from subscriptions to his translations of Homer.
38. See Erin Mackie's *Market à la Mode: Fashion, Commodity and Gender in "The Tatler" and "The Spectator"* (Baltimore: Johns Hopkins University Press, 1997), chapters 4 and 5, for a fascinating account of the roles of gender and fashion in Addison and Steele's construction of literary taste.
39. Phiddian argues that Swift's satire is better understood as parody because this term draws attention to its pre-texts (Robert Phiddian, *Swift's Parody* (New York: Cambridge University Press, 1995), 24–43).
40. See Pollak, *The Poetics of Sexual Myth*, and Laura Brown, *Ends of Empire: Women and Ideology in Early Eighteenth-Century Literature* (Ithaca: Cornell University Press, 1993), chs. 4 and 6.
41. Chris Baldick, *The Social Mission of English Criticism: 1848–1932* (Oxford: Clarendon Press, 1983).

Bibliography

Agnew, Jean-Christophe. *Worlds Apart: The Market and the Theater in Anglo-American Thought, 1550–1750*. New York: Cambridge University Press, 1986.
Anderson, Benedict. *Imagined Communities: Reflections on the Origin and Spread of Nationalism*. Revised edn. London: Verso, 1991.
Anne, Queen. *The Letters of Queen Anne*. Ed. Beatrice Curtis Brown. London: Cassell and Company, 1968.
Anonymous. *A Comparison between the Two Stages*. London, 1702.
   The Female Wits. Ed. Lucyle Hook. Los Angeles: University of California Press, 1967.
Astell, Mary. *A Serious Proposal to the Ladies for the Advancement of Their True Interest by a Lover of her Sex* (1694). In *The "Other" Eighteenth Century: English Women of Letters 1660–1800*, ed. Robert Uphaus and Gretchen Foster. East Lansing: Colleagues Press, 1991.
Auerbach, Erich. "La Cour Et La Ville." In *Scenes from the Drama of European Literature*. University of Manchester Press, 1984, 133–82.
Austin, J. L. *How to Do Things with Words*. Ed. J. O. Urmson and Marina Sbisa. Cambridge, Mass.: Harvard University Press, 1975.
Backsheider, Paula. *Spectacular Politics: Theatrical Power and Mass Culture in Early Modern England*. Baltimore: Johns Hopkins University Press, 1993.
Baldick, Chris. *The Social Mission of English Criticism: 1848–1932*. Oxford: Clarendon Press, 1983.
Ballaster, R. "Manl(e)y Forms: Sex and the Female Satirist." In *Women, Texts and Histories 1575–1760*. Ed. Clare Brant and Dianne Purkiss. New York: Routledge, 1992, 217–41.
   Seductive Forms: Women's Amatory Fiction from 1684–1700. Oxford: Clarendon Press, 1992.
   "Seizing the Means of Seduction: Fiction and Feminine Identity in Aphra Behn and Delarivier Manley." In *Women, Writing, History 1640–1740*. Ed. Isobel Grundy and Susan Wiseman. London: Batsford, 1992, 93–108.
Ballaster, R. Margaret Beetham, Elizabeth Frazer and Sandra Hebron. *Women's Worlds: Ideology, Femininity and the Woman's Magazine*. London: Macmillan, 1991.

Barish, Jonas. *The Antitheatrical Prejudice*. Berkeley: University of California Press, 1981.
Bedford, Arthur. *The Evil and Danger of Stage-Plays Showing their Natural Tendency to Destroy Religion and Introduce a General Corruption of Manners*. London, 1706.
Behn, Aphra. *The Works of Aphra Behn*. 8 vols. Ed. Janet Todd. London: William Pickering, 1996.
Bloom, Harold. *The Anxiety of Influence: A Theory of Poetry*. New York: Oxford University Press, 1973.
    A Map of Misreading. New York: Oxford University Press, 1975.
Blum, Abbe. "The Author's Authority: *Areopagitica* and the Labour of Licensing." In *Re-Membering Milton*. Ed. Nyquist and Ferguson, 74–96.
Boswell, Eleanor. *The Restoration Court Stage: 1660–1702*. 1932; New York: Benjamin Blom, 1965.
Bourdieu, Pierre. *Distinction: A Social Critique of the Judgement of Taste*. Trans. Richard Nice. Cambridge, Mass.: Harvard University Press, 1984.
Brady, Jennifer. "Dryden and Negotiations of Literary Succession and Precession." In *Literary Transmission and Authority: Dryden and Other Writers*, ed. Earl Miner and Jennifer Brady. New York: Cambridge University Press, 1993, 27–54.
Bray, Alan. *Homosexuality in Renaissance England*. London: Gay Men's Press, 1982.
Brown, Laura. *Ends of Empire: Women and Ideology in Early Eighteenth-Century Literature*. Ithaca: Cornell University Press, 1993.
    English Dramatic Form, 1660–1760. New Haven: Yale University Press, 1981.
Bucholz, R. O. *The Augustan Court: Queen Anne and the Decline of Court Culture*. Palo Alto: Stanford University Press, 1993.
Butler, Judith. *Gender Trouble: Feminism and the Subversion of Identity*. New York: Routledge, 1990.
Bywaters, David. *Dryden in Revolutionary England*. Berkeley: University of California Press, 1991.
Caplan, Jay. *Framed Narratives: Diderot's Genealogy of the Beholder*. Minneapolis: University of Minnesota Press, 1985.
Clive, Catherine. *The Rehearsal, or Bayes in Petticoats*. London, 1753.
Cohen, Ralph, Alan Fisher and Phillip Harth. *New Homage to John Dryden*. Los Angeles: William Andrews Clark Memorial Library, 1983.
Crowne, John. *The Dramatic Works of John Crowne*. Reprint of 1874 edn. 4 vols. Vol. 1. New York: Benjamin Blom, 1967.
Dennis, John. *The Critical Works of John Dennis*. 2 vols. Ed. Edward Niles Hooker. Baltimore: Johns Hopkins University Press, 1939.
Donaldson, Ian. "Fathers and Sons: Jonson, Dryden and 'Macflecknoe.'" *Southern Review* 18 (1985): 314–37.
Donoghue, Emma. *Passions Between Women: British Lesbian Culture 1668–1801*. New York: Harper Collins, 1993.
Dryden, John. *All for Love*. Ed. David M. Vieth. Lincoln: University of Nebraska Press, 1973.

All for Love. Ed. N. J. Andrew. London: A. and C. Black Ltd., 1986.
Of Dramatic Poesy and Other Critical Essays by John Dryden. Ed. George Watson. 2 vols. London: J. M. Dent, 1962.
The Poems and Fables of John Dryden. Ed. James Kinsley. Oxford University Press, 1980.
The Works of John Dryden. Ed. H. T. Swedenberg. Berkeley: University of California Press, 1956– .
The Works of John Dryden. Vol. v, ed. George Saintsbury and Walter Scott Edinburgh: Archibald Constable and Co., 1821.
Duff, Dolores Diane Clarke. "Materials toward a Biography of Mary Delariviere Manley." Dissertation, University of Indiana, 1965.
Durfey, Thomas. *The Two Queens of Brentford: Or Bayes No Poetaster*. London, 1721.
Eagleton, Terry. *The Function of Criticism: From the Spectator to Post-Structuralism*. London: Verso, 1984.
Easthope, Anthony. "Towards the Autonomous Subject in Poetry: Milton 'On His Blindness.'" In *1642: Literature and Power in the Seventeenth Century*, ed. Francis Barker. Colchester: Department of Literature, Essex, 1980, 301–14.
Elledge, Scott, ed. *Eighteenth-century Critical Essays*. 2 vols. Ithaca: Cornell University Press, 1961.
Ezell, Margaret. *Writing Women's Literary History*. Baltimore: Johns Hopkins University Press, 1993.
Ferry, Anne D. *Milton and the Miltonic Dryden*. Cambridge, Mass.: Harvard University Press, 1968.
Finke, Laurie. "Aphra Behn and the Ideological Construction of Restoration Literary Theory." In *Rereading Aphra Behn*. Ed. Hutner, 17–43.
Fried, Michael. *Absorption and Theatricality: Painting and the Beholder in the Age of Diderot*. Berkeley: University of California Press, 1980.
Gallagher, Catherine. *Nobody's Story: The Vanishing Acts of Women Writers in the Marketplace 1670–1820*. Berkeley: University of California Press, 1994.
"Who Was That Masked Woman? The Prostitute and the Playwright in the Comedies of Aphra Behn." In *Rereading Aphra Behn*, ed. Hutner, 65–85.
Gerard, Kent, and Gert Hekma, eds. *The Pursuit of Sodomy: Male Homosexuality in Renaissance and Enlightenment Europe*. New York: The Hawthorne Press, 1989, 349–82.
Gilbert, Sandra, and Susan Gubar. *The Madwoman in the Attic: The Woman Writer and the Nineteenth-Century Literary Imagination*. 2nd edn. New Haven: Yale University Press, 2000.
Goldberg, Jonathan. "Dating Milton." In *Soliciting Interpretation*, ed. Harvey and Maus, 199–220.
Desiring Women Writing: English Renaissance Examples. Palo Alto: Stanford University Press, 1997.
Sodometries: Renaissance Texts, Modern Sexualities. Palo Alto: Stanford University Press, 1992.

Voice Terminal Echo: Postmodernism and English Renaissance Texts. New York: Methuen, 1986.

Goldberg, Jonathan, and Stephen Orgel, eds. *John Milton.* London: Oxford University Press, 1990.

Goux, Jean-Joseph. *Oedipus, Philosopher.* Trans. Catherine Porter. Palo Alto: Stanford University Press, 1993.

Greenberg, Mitchell. *Subjectivity and Subjugation in Seventeenth-Century Drama and Prose: The Family Romance of French Classicism.* New York: Cambridge University Press, 1992.

Griffin, Dustin. *Regaining Paradise: Milton and the Eighteenth Century.* New York: Cambridge University Press, 1986.

Guibbory, Achsa. *The Map of Time: Seventeenth-Century English Literature and the Idea of History.* Urbana: University of Illinois Press, 1986.

Guillory, John. "The Father's House: *Samson Agonistes* in Its Historical Moment." In *Re-Membering Milton,* ed. Nyquist and Ferguson, 148–76.

"From the Superfluous to the Supernumerary: Reading Gender into *Paradise Lost.*" In *Soliciting Interpretation,* ed. Harvey and Maus, 68–88.

Poetic Authority: Spenser, Milton and Literary History. New York: Columbia University Press, 1983.

Habermas, Jürgen. *The Structural Transformation of the Public Sphere: An Inquiry into a Category of Bourgeois Society.* Trans. Thomas Burger. Cambridge, Mass.: MIT Press, 1991.

Halascz, Alexandra. *The Marketplace of Print.* New York: Cambridge University Press, 1998.

Haley, David. *Dryden and the Problem of Freedom: The Republican Aftermath 1649–1680.* New Haven: Yale University Press, 1997.

Harvey, Elizabeth and Katharine Maus, eds. *Soliciting Interpretation: Literary Theory and Seventeenth-Century English Poetry.* University of Chicago Press, 1990.

Helgerson, Richard. *Forms of Nationhood: The Elizabethan Writing of England.* University of Chicago Press, 1992.

Self-Crowned Laureates: Spenser, Jonson, Milton and the Literary System. Berkeley: University of California Press, 1983.

Hill, Christopher. *The Century of Revolution: 1603–1714.* New York: Norton, 1961.

Milton and the English Revolution. New York: Penguin, 1979.

Hume, Robert. *The Development of English Drama in the Late Seventeenth Century.* Oxford: Clarendon Press, 1976.

Dryden's Criticism. Ithaca: Cornell University Press, 1970.

Hutner, Heidi, ed. *Rereading Aphra Behn: History, Theory and Criticism.* Charlottesville: University Press of Virginia, 1993.

Johnson, Samuel. "Life of Dryden." In *Lives of the Poets.* Ed. George Birbeck Hill. 1905; New York: Octagon Books, 1967, 331–480.

Works of Samuel Johnson. Vol. VII: *Johnson on Shakespeare.* Ed. Arthur Sherbo. New Haven: Yale University Press, 1968.

Jones, J. R. *Country and Court: England 1658–1714.* Cambridge, Mass.: Harvard University Press, 1978.

Jonson, Ben. *Ben Jonson's Works*. Vol. I, ed. C. H. Herford and P. Simpson. Oxford: Clarendon Press, 1925.
Kendall, ed. *Love and Thunder: Plays by Women in the Age of Queen Anne*. London: Methuen, 1988.
Kendrick, Christopher. *Milton: A Study in Ideology and Form*. New York: Methuen, 1986.
Kenyon, John. *The History Men: The Historical Profession in England since the Renaissance*. 2nd edn. London: Weidenfeld and Nicolson, 1993.
Kerrigan, William. *The Sacred Complex: On the Psychogenesis of Paradise Lost*. Cambridge, Mass.: Harvard University Press, 1983.
King, Bruce, ed. *Twentieth-Century Interpretations of "All for Love": A Collection of Critical Essays*. New Jersey: Prentice Hall, 1968.
Kramer, David Bruce. *The Imperial Dryden: The Poetics of Appropriation in Seventeenth-Century England*. Athens: University of Georgia Press, 1994.
Kramnick, Jonathan Brody. "The Making of the English Canon." *PMLA* 112 (1997): 1087–101.
  Making the English Canon: Print-Capitalism and the Cultural Past 1700–1770. Cambridge University Press, 1998.
  "Origins of the Present Crisis." *Profession* (1997): 84–92.
  "Pre-publicity." Paper presented to the Group for Early Modern Cultural Studies, New Orleans, 2000.
Kroll, Richard. *The Material Word: Literate Culture in the Restoration and Early Eighteenth Century*. Baltimore: Johns Hopkins University Press, 1991.
Langbaine, Gerard. *An Account of the English Dramatick Poets*. Vol. I, 1691. Los Angeles: William Andrews Clark Memorial Library, 1971.
Laqueur, Thomas. *Making Sex: Body and Gender from the Greeks to Freud*. Cambridge, Mass.: Harvard University Press, 1990.
Lee, Nathaniel. *Lucius Junius Brutus: Father of his Country*. 1681. Ed. John Loftis. Lincoln: University of Nebraska Press, 1967.
  Mithridates. In *The Works of Nathaniel Lee*. Vol. III, ed. Thomas Stroup and Arthur Cooke. New Jersey: Scarecrow Reprint Corporation, 1968.
  The Rival Queens. Ed. P. F. Vernon. The Regents Restoration Drama Series. Lincoln: University of Nebraska Press, 1970.
Levine, Joseph M. *The Battle of the Books: History and Literature in the Augustan Age*. Ithaca: Cornell University Press, 1991.
Longinus. "On the Sublime." In *Classical Literary Criticism*, ed. T. S. Dorsch. New York: Penguin, 1965, 97–158.
  "On the Sublime." In *Critical Theory since Plato*, ed. Hazard Adams. New York: Harcourt, Brace, Joranovich Inc., 1971, 76–102.
Lonsdale, Roger, ed. *Eighteenth-Century Women Poets: An Oxford Anthology*. New York: Oxford University Press, 1989.
Mackie, Erin Skye. *Market à La Mode: Fashion, Commodity and Gender in the "Tatler" and the "Spectator."* Baltimore: Johns Hopkins University Press, 1998.
Mallin, Eric S. "Emulous Factions and the Collapse of Chivalry: *Troilus and Cressida*." *Representations* 29 (1990): 145–79.

Manley, Delarivier. *The Adventures of Rivella*. Ed. Katherine Zelinsky. Peterborough: Broadview, 1999.
The Lost Lover. London, 1696.
The New Atalantis. Ed. Rosalind Ballaster. New York: Penguin, 1992.
The Novels of Mary Delariviere Manley. 2 vols. Ed. Patricia Köster. Gainesville: Scholars' Facsimiles and Reprints, 1971.
The Royal Mischief. London, 1696.
The Secret History of Queen Zarah and the Zarazians. Ed. Michael F. Shugrue. New York: Garland, 1972.
Manley, Delarivier, ed. *The Nine Muses*. London, 1700.
Markley, Robert. *Two-Edg'd Weapons: Style and Ideology in the Comedies of Etheredge, Wycherley and Congreve*. Oxford: Clarendon Press, 1988.
Marshall, David. "Arguing by Analogy: Hume's Standard of Taste." *Eighteenth-Century Studies* 28 (1995): 323–43.
The Figure of the Theater: Shaftesbury, Defoe, Adam Smith, and George Eliot. New York: Columbia University Press, 1986.
Marvell, Andrew. *Andrew Marvell: A Critical Edition of the Major Works*. Ed. Frank Kermode and Keith Walker. The Oxford Authors. New York: Oxford University Press, 1990.
The Rehearsal Transpros'd and the Rehearsal Transpros'd the Second Part. Ed. D. I. B. Smith. Oxford: Clarendon Press, 1971.
Masten, Jeff. "My Two Dads: Collaboration and the Reproduction of Beaumont and Fletcher." In *Queering the Renaissance*, ed. Jonathan Goldberg. Durham: Duke University Press, 1994, 280–309.
Maus, Katharine Eisaman. "Playhouse Flesh and Blood: Sexual Ideology and the Restoration Actress." *ELH* 46 (1979): 595–617.
McDowell, Paula. *The Women of Grub Street: Press, Politics, and Gender in the London Literary Marketplace 1678–1730*. Oxford: Clarendon Press, 1998.
McFadden, George. *Dryden, the Public Writer: 1660–1685*. Princeton University Press, 1978.
McKeon, Michael. "Historicizing Patriarchy: The Emergence of Gender Difference in England, 1660–1760." *Eighteenth-Century Studies* 28 (1995): 295–322.
Origins of the English Novel, 1600–1740. Baltimore: Johns Hopkins University Press, 1987.
"Politics of Discourses and the Rise of the Aesthetic in Seventeenth-Century England." In *Politics of Discourse: The Literature and History of Seventeenth-Century England*. Ed. Kevin Sharpe and Steven Zwicker. Berkeley: University of California Press, 1987, 35–51.
Milhous, Judith. *Thomas Betterton and the Management of Lincoln's Inn Fields, 1695–1708*. Carbondale: Southern Illinois University Press, 1979.
Milton, John. *The Complete Prose Works of John Milton*. Vol. VI, ed. Robert W. Ayers. New Haven: Yale University Press, 1980.
Paradise Lost. In *Complete Poems and Major Prose of John Milton*, ed. Merritt Y. Hughes. Indianapolis: Bobbs Merril, 1957.

Miner, Earl. "The Poetics of the Critical Act: Dryden's Dealings with Rivals and Predecessors." In *Critical Essays on John Dryden*. Ed. James Winn. New York: Simon and Schuster Macmillan, 1997, 33–47.

Morgan, Fidelis. *A Woman of No Character: An Autobiography of Mrs. Manley*. London: Faber, 1986.

Morgan, Fidelis, ed. *The Female Wits: Women Playwrights of the Restoration*. London: Virago, 1981.

Munns, Jessica. "'Good, Sweet, Honey, Sugar-Candied Reader': Aphra Behn's Foreplay in Forewords." In *Rereading Aphra Behn*, ed. Hutner, 44–64.

Murray, Timothy. *Theatrical Legitimation: Allegories of Genius in Seventeenth-Century England and France*. Oxford University Press, 1987.

Nettleton, George, and Arthur Case, eds. *British Dramatists from Dryden to Sheridan*. 2nd edn. Rev. edn. George Winchester Stone, Jr. Carbondale: Southern Illinois University Press, 1969.

Nyquist, Mary and Margaret Ferguson. *Re-Membering Milton: Essays on the Texts and Traditions*. New York: Methuen, 1987.

Orgel, Stephen. "'Nobody's Perfect': Or Why Did the English Stage Take Boys for Women?" *South Atlantic Quarterly* 88, 1 (1989): 7–30.

Parker, William Riley. *Milton: A Biography*. 2 vols. Oxford: Clarendon Press, 1968.

Patey, Douglas Lane. "The Eighteenth Century Invents the Canon." *Modern Language Studies* 18 (1988): 17–37.

Pechter, Edward. *Dryden's Classical Theory of Literature*. London: Cambridge University Press, 1975.

Phiddian, Robert. *Swift's Parody*. New York: Cambridge University Press, 1995.

Philo-philippa. "To the Excellent *Orinda*." In *Kissing the Rod: An Anthology of Seventeenth-Century Women's Verse*. Ed. Germaine, Greer, Susan Hastings, Jeslyn Medoff, Melinda Sansone. New York: Farrar Strauss, 1988, 204–13.

Pinto, V. de Sola. *Sir Charles Sedley 1639–1701: A Study in the Life and Literature of the Restoration*. London: Constable and Co. Ltd., 1927.

Pollak, Ellen. *The Poetics of Sexual Myth: Gender and Ideology in the Verse of Swift and Pope*. University of Chicago Press, 1985.

Price, Curtis. *Henry Purcell and the London Stage*. New York: Cambridge University Press, 1984.

Prior, Moody E. "Tragedy and the Heroic Play." In *Dryden: A Collection of Critical Essays*, ed. Bernard Schelling. New Jersey: Prentice Hall, 1963, 95–114.

Ragussis, Michael. "Jews and Other 'Outlandish Englishmen': Ethnic Performance and the Invention of British Identity under the Georges." *Critical Inquiry* 26 (2000): 776–77.

Reverand, Cedric D., III. "Dryden's 'Essay of Dramatic Poesie': The Poet and the World of Affairs." *Studies in English Literature* 22 (1982): 375–93.

Richetti, John. *Popular Novels before Richardson: Narrative Patterns 1700–1739*. Oxford: Clarendon Press, 1969.

Riley, Denise. *"Am I That Name?": Feminism and the Category of "Women" in History*. New York: Macmillan, 1988.

Roberts, David. *The Ladies: Female Patronage of Restoration Drama 1660–1700.* Oxford: Clarendon Press, 1989.

Ross, Trevor. "The Emergence of 'Literature': Making and Reading the English Canon in the Eighteenth Century." *ELH* 63 (1996): 397–442.

The Making of the English Literary Canon: From the Middle Ages to the Late Eighteenth Century. Montreal: McGill-Queen's University Press, 1998.

Rubini, Dennis. "Sexuality and Augustan England: Sodomy, Politics, Elite Circles and Society." In *The Pursuit of Sodomy,* ed. Gerard and Hekma, 349–82.

Ruffhead, Owen. "Life of Alexander Pope." In *John Donne: The Critical Heritage,* ed. A. J. Smith. Boston: Routledge and Kegan Paul, 1975, 181–82.

Runge, Laura. *Gender and Language in British Literary Criticism: 1660–1790.* New York: Cambridge University Press, 1997.

"'The Softness of Expression and the Smoothness of Measure': A Model of Gendered Decorum from Dryden's Criticism." *Essays in Literature* 20 (1993): 177–212.

Savile, George, Lord Halifax. *The Lady's New-Year's Gift.* 1700; Stamford: The Overbrook Press, 1934.

Scott, Joan W. "Experience." In *Feminists Theorize the Political,* ed. Judith Butler and Joan W. Scott. New York: Routledge, 1992, 22–40.

Sedgwick, Eve Kosofsky *Between Men: English Literature and Male Homosocial Desire.* New York: Columbia University Press, 1985.

Epistemology of the Closet. Berkeley: University of California Press, 1990.

"Queer Performativity: Henry James's *The Art of the Novel.*" *GLQ* 1 (1993): 1–16.

Sedley, Charles. *The Poetical and Dramatic Works of Sir Charles Sedley.* Ed. V. de Sola Pinto. London: Constable and Co. Ltd., 1928.

Shakespeare, William. *Antony and Cleopatra.* In *The Riverside Shakespeare.* Ed. Harry Levin. Boston: Houghton Mifflin Company, 1974.

Shapin, Steven. *A Social History of Truth: Civility and Science in Seventeenth-Century England.* University of Chicago Press, 1994.

Sheridan, Richard Brinsley. "The Critic, or a Tragedy Rehearsed." In *British Dramatists from Dryden to Sheridan,* ed. Nettleton and Case, 877–901.

Shevelow, Kathryn. *Women and Print Culture: The Construction of Femininity in the Early Periodical.* New York: Routledge, 1989.

Spencer, Christopher, ed. *Five Restoration Adaptations of Shakespeare.* Urbana: University of Illinois Press, 1965.

Spender, Dale. *Mothers of the Novel: 100 Good Women Writers before Jane Austen.* New York: Routledge and Kegan Paul, 1986.

Spingarn, J., ed. *Critical Essays of the Seventeenth Century.* 3 vols. New York: Oxford University Press, 1957.

Stallybrass, Peter and Allon White. *The Politics and Poetics of Transgression.* Ithaca: Cornell University Press, 1986.

Steeves, Edna, ed. *The Plays of Mary Pix and Catharine Trotter.* 2 vols. New York: Garland, 1982.

Straub, Kristina. *Sexual Suspects: Eighteenth-Century Players and Sexual Ideology*. Princeton University Press, 1992.

"Women, Gender and Criticism." In *Literary Criticism and Theory: The Greeks to the Present*, ed. Laurie Finke and Robert Con Davis. New York: Longman, 1989, 855–76.

Straznicky, Marta. "Restoration Women Playwrights and the Limits of Professionalism." *ELH* 64 (1997): 703–26.

Stroup, Thomas and Arthur Cooke, eds. *The Works of Nathaniel Lee*. Vol. 1. New Jersey: Scarecrow Reprint Corporation, 1968.

Suckling, Norman. "Dryden in Egypt: Reflections on *All for Love*." In *Twentieth-Century Interpretations of All for Love: A Collection of Critical Essays*. Ed. Bruce King. New Jersey: Prentice Hall, 1968, 46–54.

Sutton, John L., Jr. "The Source of Mrs. Manley's Preface to Queen Zarah." *Modern Philology* 82 (1984): 167–72.

Taylor, Gary. *Reinventing Shakespeare: A Cultural History from the Restoration to the Present*. New York: Weidenfeld and Nicolson, 1989.

Todd, Janet. *The Secret Life of Aphra Behn*. New York: Pandora, 2000.

Todd, Janet, ed. *Dictionary of British and American Women Writers, 1660–1800*. London: Methuen, 1987.

Traub, Valerie. "The Perversion of 'Lesbian' Desire." *History Workshop Journal* 41 (1996): 23–49.

Trotter, Catharine. *Olinda's Adventures: Or the Amours of a Young Lady*. Ed. Robert Adams Day. Los Angeles: William Andrews Clark Memorial Library, 1969.

The Works of Mrs. Catharine Cockburn (Trotter): Theological, Moral, Dramatic, Poetic with an Account of the life of the Author. Vol. 1. Ed. Thomas Birch. London, 1751.

Trumbach, Randolph. "Are Modern Lesbian Women and Gay Men a Third Gender?" In *A Queer World: The Center for Lesbian and Gay Studies Reader*. Ed. Martin Duberman. New York University Press, 1997, 87–99.

"The Birth of the Queen: Sodomy and the Emergence of Gender Equality in Modern Culture, 1660–1750." In *Hidden from History: Reclaiming the Gay and Lesbian Past*. Ed. Martin Duberman, Martha Vicinius and George Chauncey. New York: New American Library, 1989, 129–40.

Turner, James Grantham. "The Libertine Sublime: Love and Death in Restoration England." *Studies in Eighteenth-Century Culture* 19 (1989): 99–115.

Waith, Eugene. *Ideas of Greatness: Heroic Drama in England*. London: Routledge and Kegan Paul, 1971.

Weinbrot, Howard. *Britannia's Issue: The Rise of British Literature from Dryden to Ossian*. New York: Cambridge University Press, 1993.

Wellek, René. *The Rise of English Literary History*. Chapel Hill: University of North Carolina Press, 1941.

Wilmot, John. *The Complete Poems of John Wilmot, Earl of Rochester*. Ed. David M. Vieth. New Haven: Yale University Press, 1968.

Winn, James. *Dryden and His World*. New Haven: Yale University Press, 1987.

"*When Beauty Fires the Blood*": *Love and the Arts in the Age of Dryden*. Ann Arbor: University of Michigan Press, 1992.

Wittreich, Joseph A. "Perplexing the Explanation: Marvell's 'On Mr. Milton's *Paradise Lost.*'" In *Approaches to Marvell: The York Centenary Lectures*. Ed. C. A. Patrides. Boston: Routledge and Kegan Paul, 1978, 280–305.

Women Critics 1660–1820: An Anthology. Ed. Folger Collective on Early Women Critics. Bloomington: Indiana University Press, 1995.

Zwicker, Steven N. "Milton, Dryden and the Politics of Literary Controversy." In *Culture and Society in the Stuart Restoration: Literature, Drama, History*. Ed. Gerald MacLean. New York: Cambridge University Press, 1995, 137–58.

Index

A Comparison Between the Two Stages, 91–93
A Lady's New-Years Gift, 112
Addison, Joseph, 1, 6, 10–12, 18, 60, 89, 96, 102, 113, 137
   and Trotter, 114
Agnew, Jean-Christophe, 5, 14, 95, 140
Anderson, Benedict, 17
Ariadne
   She Ventures, and He Wins, 91
Astell, Mary, 108
Auerbach, Erich, 23, 97
authorship, female, 3, 10, 91–92, 100, 134–135, 136

Backscheider, Paula, 91, 100–101
Baldick, Chris, 137–138
Ballaster, Ros, 12, 113, 117, 129–131
Barry, Elizabeth, 121, 124–125
Behn, Aphra, 1–2, 4, 11, 12, 18, 105
   and Dryden, 92, 96–98
   criticism by, 93, 96–100
   Agnes de Castro, 104
   Oroonoko, 91
   preface to *The Dutch Lover*, 96–98
   preface to *The Lucky Chance*, 96–100
   The Younger Brother, 91
Bloom, Harold, 10, 76
Blum, Abbe, 45
Boswell, Eleanor, 95
Bourdieu, Pierre, 6
Brown, Laura, 73–74, 82, 122
Bucholz, R.O., 95–96
Butler, Judith, 14, 140, 143
Bywaters, David, 59

canon, the, 2, 6, 7, 10, 16, 28, 138
Centlivre, Susannah, 92
Clive, Catherine, 3
Cohen, Ralph, 15–16
Congreve, William, 10, 94
Corneille, Pierre, 36, 38, 100

criticism, 3, 4, 7, 134–135
   female genealogy of, 10, 93
   genealogy of, 11, 137–138
   historical orientation of, 1, 3, 4, 8, 21–22
   impartiality of, 12–13, 14, 16, 64, 81–83, 95, 111, 113, 131, 134
   self-consciousness of, 112–114
   theatrical orientation of, 1, 2, 3, 4, 5, 11, 27–32, 43, 102, 125–127
Crowne, John, 94–96, 157
   Calisto, 94–96

Davenant, Sir William, 4, 68
Dennis, John, 58
drama, 1, 3, 91
   affective tragedy, 73–74
   comedies of manners, 55, 61
   French vs. English, 19, 28–30, 38–39
   heroic play, 4, 73, 121–123
   masque, 95 *See also* Crowne, John *Calisto*
   modern vs. ancient, 19, 30–31
   rehearsal play, 2–3
      The Critic, or A Tragedy Rehearsed, 3
      The Rehearsal, 2–3, 121
      The Rehearsal, or Bayes in Petticoats, 3
      The Two Queens of Brentford, 3
Dryden, John, 1–4, 6, 121
   and historicism, 1, 8, 10, 15, 20–27
   as the father of criticism in English, 7, 10, 18, 72
   as translator, 92
   influence on women writers, 121
   neo-classicism of, 15–16, 17, 41
   All for Love, 12–12, 36, 64, 72–84, 109, 121
      Epilogue to, 83–84
      Preface to, 74, 75–83, 131
   Astrea Redux, 22, 32
   Aureng Zebe, 121
   "The Author's Apology", 9, 42–43, 55–63
   The Conquest of Granada, 26, 121, 122

Index

Dryden, John (*cont.*)
"Defense of the Epilogue", 8, 20, 23–27, 39, 50, 127
Epilogue to, 7, 20–23, 122
Preface to, 122, 127
"Dedication of the Aeneid", 62
"The Discourse Concerning Satire", 60, 128, 129–130
Essay of Dramatick Poesy, 18, 19, 27–32, 34–35, 40, 64, 97, 102
"The Grounds of Criticism in Tragedy", 12, 34–35, 38, 64, 86–88, 111–112
Oedipus, 20, 32, 35–38, 98
"Preface to the Fables", 16
"Preface to Ovid's *Epistles*", 92
"Preface to *The Sylvae*", 61
"Remarks on *The Empress of Morocco*", 8
The Secular Masque, 15, 18, 22, 95
The State of Innocence, 4, 9
preface to, See "The Author's Apology" *above*
The Tempest, or the Enchanted Island
prologue to, 37l, 68–72
Troilus and Cressida, 12, 16, 64, 84–86
preface to See "The Grounds of Criticism in Tragedy" *above*
prologue to, 18, 20, 32–35, 36, 40, 84
To Congreve, 10
Durfey, Thomas, 3

Fashion, 50–51, 58
The Female Wits, 121
Ferry, Anne, 48
Finke, Laurie, 93, 97, 155
Fletcher, John, 32, 65, 86–87, 88
Fried, Michael, 5, 140

Gallagher, Catherine, 94, 119, 130–131
gender, 2–4, 11, 12, 13–14, 55, 66–68, 110, 134, 136
and authorship, 93–94, 99, 100–102, 104, 114, 137
See also authorship, female
and genre, 11, 13, 123, 130
and sexuality, 131, 138
Gilbert, Sandra, and Susan Gubar, 10
Goldberg, Jonathan, 66, 87
Guillory, John, 67

Habermas, Jürgen, 5, 96, 157–158
and bourgeois public sphere, 5–6, 6, 8, 11, 94, 96, 102, 108, 115
Hume, Robert, 15, 95, 122

Johnson, Samuel, 7, 8–12, 64
"Life of Dryden", 8, 18, 64
Preface to Shakespeare, 76

Jonson, Ben, 16, 18–20, 23–27, 41, 45–46
Cynthia's Revels, 31
The Silent Woman, 32, 97

Kendrick, Christopher, 53
Köster, Patricia, 120
Kramer, David Bruce, 17, 144, 146, 152
Kramnick, Jonathan Brody, 6, 14, 118, 140, 141
Kroll, Richard, 53–54
Kynaston, Edward, 80

Langbaine, Gerard, 26, 111, 156
Laqueur, Thomas, 13, 66–67, 86, 105, 143
Lee, Nathaniel, 4, 35, 40, 109
Lucius Junius Brutus, 40, 154
Mithridates, 96
prefatory poem to *The State of Innocence*, 49–50
The Rival Queens, 109, 122, 153
See also and Dryden, *Oedipus*
Levine, Joseph, 19

Manley, Delarivier, 1, 2, 4, 11, 12, 18, 116–139
and Behn, 117, 123–124
and Dryden, 125, 127
and Trotter, 117, 118, 131
Letters Written on a Stage Coach, 116
The Lost Lover, 91, 116, 121, 123
The New Atalantis, 4, 116–117, 127–137
The Nine Muses, 92, 117
The Royal Mischief, 4, 91, 116, 121–122, 123–125
The Secret History of Queen Zarah, 125–127
"To the Author of *Agnes de Castro*", 103, 107
Markley, Robert, 88
Marshall, David, 5, 140
Marvell, Andrew, 50–51, 149
Masten, Jeff, 88
McDowell, Paula, 135, 156, 159
McKeon, Michael, 11, 40, 66–67, 89, 106–107, 110
Milhous, Judith, 122
Milton, John, 4, 9, 17, 67
as classic, 43–43, 45–46
Areopagitica, 45, 54
Paradise Lost, 4, 9, 16, 42–49, 53–54, 62
Paradise Regained, 47
The Readie and Easie Way, 51–52
Samson Agonistes, 47
Miner, Earl, 15–16
monarchical succession, 3, 10, 14, 16, 26, 27, 122
Munns, Jessica, 98

Index

national literary tradition, 15–18, 27, 91, 92, 104
   as patrimony, 7, 8, 123
   as product of criticism, 1, 17
   domestic organization of, 2, 65–66
novel, the, 3, 74, 94–95, 126

opera, 46, 149
Otway, Thomas, 109
   Venice Preserv'd, 109, 121

paraphrase, 5
Patey, Douglas Lane, 6
Pechter, Edward, 15
performativity, 2, 13, 14, 65, 100, 115, 124–125, 139
periodicals, 1, 3, 96
   the *Spectator* and the *Tatler*, 12, 137, 160
Phiddian, Robert
Philips, Katherine, 100
   Philo-philippa, 101–102
Piers, Lady Sarah, 92, 103, 107
Pix, Mary, 91, 92
   Ibrahim, 91
   The Spanish Wives, 91
Pope, Alexander, 10, 11, 18, 136–137

rhyme, 27, 50–54, 60
Roberts, David, 99
Rochester, Earl of, *See* Wilmot, John
Ross, Trevor, 6, 141
Runge, Laura, 13, 143
Rymer, Thomas, 58

satire, 3, 116, 118, 128, 133–135, 136, 137
Sedgwick, Eve Kosofsky, 14, 58, 140, 143, 145
   homosocial desire, 55, 57, 58–59, 61–62
Sedley, Sir Charles, 79
sexuality, 2, 11, 12–13, 137
   female, 128, 131
   homoeroticism, 13, 82, 130
   lesbian, 157
   sapphism, 128, 130, 131–134
   sodomy, 110, 133
Shakespeare, William, 4, 10, 12, 16, 18, 20, 44–46
   the character, Henry IV, 39
   Dryden's love of, 32

   Dryden's ventriloquizing of, 32–35
   universality of, 40, 64–65, 84–88, 90, 92
   Antony and Cleopatra, 4, 40, 72
   The Tempest, 4
   Troilus and Cressida, 4, 32, 40, 85
Sheridan, Richard Brinsley, 3
Sophocles, 4, 35, 36–37
   Oedipus Rex, 4, 32, 35
Spender, Dale, 10
Steele, Richard, 1, 11, 12, 18, 89, 96, 102, 113, 137
   Manley's critique of, 135
   uses of effeminacy, 106
Sutton, John L., 126
Swift, Jonathan, 18, 116, 137

talent, 43, 60, 61
taste, 43, 55–57, 61
Taylor, Gary, 64–65
theatre, 2, 3, 6, 43, 47, 124
   theatricality, 5, 14, 138
   and gender, 68–72, 96
   of *Paradise Lost*, 48
Trotter, Catharine, 1, 2, 4, 11, 13, 18, 91, 102–115
   and Behn, 112
   and Dryden, 108–113, 111
   and Shakespeare, 113
   Agnes de Castro, 4, 91, 104–105, 121
   The Fatal Friendship, 121
   Love at a Loss, 107
   Olinda's Adventures, 4, 119
   The Revolution of Sweden, 107–108, 114, 121
   The Unhappy Penitent, 108–114, 121

Weinbrot, Howard, 19
Wellek, René, 18–19
Wilmot, John, 78, 110, 117
Winn, James, 13, 46, 92, 143, 144, 148
wit, 24–26, 43, 55–58, 61, 98
Women Critics 1660–1820: An Anthology, 11, 93–94, 99
Wycherley, William
   The Country Wife, 58
   prefatory poem to *Agnes de Castro*, 105–106, 129

Zwicker, Steven, 47

9 780521 818100